The Sportsman's Wilderness

The Sportsman's Wilderness

A Ridge Press / Pound Book

Editor-in-Chief: Jerry Mason
Editor: Adolph Suehsdorf
Executive Art Director: Albert Squillace
Art Director: Harry Brocke
Managing Editor: Moira Duggan
Associate Editor: Barbara Hoffbeck
Associate Editor: Mimi Gold
Art Associate: David Namias
Art Associate: Nancy Louie
Art Production: Doris Mullane

Contents

Introduction

For several years a quiet revolution has been taking shape in writing about hunting, fishing, wilderness camping, packing-in by foot or horse, canoeing, and allied outdoor activities. Experts in these pursuits have been turning away from simplistic "how-to" articles on baiting hooks or leading ducks, and conducting far more instructive, incisive explorations of the wild world in which sportsmen and their quarry exist.

This book is by leaders of the wilderness revolution in writing, the new journalism of the outdoors. The stories they tell are of the total wilderness experience. Without overlooking such infinitesimal and yet crucial components as estimating range or handling terminal tackle, they put the technical details in proper perspective.

They convey the almost mystical exhilaration that can be experienced in the wilderness, an emotion well and fully understood by mountain men and Indians who gazed into the mist hovering above white water. It is an emotion akin to the Indians' spiritual visions, and one forgotten by, or unknown to, people caught up in getting and spending, or in bracing themselves against urban tensions.

Such writers are true woodsmen and therefore true environmentalists. They know that the moment they set foot in the woods they are as much a part of the habitat as their quarry. They are no longer mere spectators but active participants—predators in a strange, dramatic world of pursuers and pursued, the eaters and the eaten. How peculiar that this world of harsh dynamism is also a world of unequaled peace. In these surroundings, while a man learns the methods of taking his fish or game, he prepares himself for the fullest appreciation of the climactic moment: the catch or the kill. It is at such moments of initiation that he realizes the wilderness is as much his as it is the cougar's. The writers in this book sharply evoke this realization: the wilderness experience that alters a sportsman's view of life.

A theory prevails among some of us who collect sporting literature that the Second World War inaugurated a Dark Age in outdoor reportage. Men of letters no longer took holidays from the writing of serious fiction to record in outdoor magazines their impressions of favorite bass lakes, grouse coverts, and sheep mountains. Writers departed to record the harsher and more momentous activities on the battlefields. Those who survived the war did not, for the most part, return to the chronicling of sport.

Editors of sporting journals soon adopted new policies regarding story content, based on the assumption that their readers wanted shallow stories. Some of the stories were adventures combining overwrought narrations of charges by ferocious beasts with the formula of the "trophy climax"—the fantastic success at the last moment in a not-very-surprising surprise ending. Others—countless others—were compendiums of tips "guaranteed" to bestow equally fantastic success on the reader.

The reader never was so dull-witted and crass as editors supposed. Far more typical than the imagined buffoon, demanding spurious thrills from the charge of the kit fox, or a false gospel guaranteed to get him meat every time, was and is the businessman who sheds his tensions in the cool quiet of a trout stream. He does not need to be told that live bait may awaken hunger in a torpid trout, but he would like to know more about the entomology and the game-sustaining ecology of a healthy river. Typical, too, is the executive, artist, factory worker, farmer or rancher or salesmen who delights in learning all he can about the behavior and habitat of game and fish.

Recently I received a letter from a friend, Joe Martin, a retired rural mail carrier in Texas. When he was younger he worked as a part-time hunting and fishing guide. Now he spends many hours reading the new journalism of the outdoors, stories like the ones in this book, because, in Joe's words, "they make me feel as if I am there." A while ago, he read a story by a big-game hunter about a trip to remote high country. The author evoked for him the essence of that wilderness, and Joe wrote to me of his reaction: "I have been to the top of the world with that man. I can't guide any more. In fact, I can no longer follow my pointers. But I can sit in a bass boat, and I can match wits with the coyote, the sly little prairie wolf, and I can read some stories twice. Here was a writer who found his Mecca on top of the world for a moment, just as I find mine on the plains of Texas every day."

This book is for outdoorsmen who understand and share that response to an authentic wilderness portrait.

The twenty selections are from *The American Sportsman*, which I had the joy of editing during much of its existence. It was a publication, according to some commentators, that heralded this revolution in the literature of the rod, the gun, and the campfire.

It may, in fact, have been slightly ahead of its time. Yet I wonder if I can be right in calling a regard for quality and truth revolutionary. What we have been witnessing is more like an impatiently awaited revival. There was, after all, a high-quality periodical called *The American Sportsman* in the 1870's—a century ago—and shortly afterward *The Canadian Sportsman and Naturalist* appeared. Both are memorialized in the Boone and Crockett Club's 1930 *Bibliography of American Sporting Books* as having been devoted to hunting, fishing, and natural history, a triumvirate that cannot logically be pruned of its life-giving third segment.

In the opening feature of the present collection, "The World of the Whitetail Deer," Angus Cameron is concerned not with the casual or game-greedy shooter but with the genuine connoisseur of hunting, the "hunter-naturalist." His revival of the term reminds me that in 1851 Charles Wilkins Webber published a deservedly popular volume of sporting anecdotes and lore entitled *The Hunter-Naturalist*. Today's hunting or fishing naturalist has, in addition to far superior equipment, far greater sophistication regarding the ways of wild creatures. No longer do writers give credence, as Webber did, to reports that "thirty or forty" or (God help us!) "hundreds" of huge wolves will chase a wilderness traveler for mile after mile, ravenously snapping their jaws with a "sound like the ring of a steel trap," or surround him, "turning up their fiery eyes to his, and howling at him with red hot open mouths and lolling tongues."

Scientific naturalists, from Adolph Murie in Alaska in 1939 to L. David Mech in Minnesota today, have virtually lived among wolves, chronicling their wild dignity, family affection, hunting intelligence, and role in the balance of nature. And sportsmen like Angus Cameron and Bob Hagel, penetrating wilderness regions that Webber never saw, have observed the real behavior of such animals. In another of this book's selections, "Denizen of the Crags," Hagel notes that "wolves may kill a goat when they find one away from the cliffs, but that isn't often." A firsthand observer like Hagel—a veteran hunter, guide, wildlife lecturer, and nature writer—knows from experience that goats, fantastically sure-footed though they are, occasionally fall to their deaths from high cliffs and that "perhaps snowslides and rockslides account for the most deaths." For those of us who have ventured into America's wilds there is the keen pleasure of recognition in reading such observations. In British Columbia I recall finding suspiciously copious tufts of white hair in a wolf's scat, and then discovering upon investigation that the wolf had retrieved a goat from a small avalanche in which it had perished.

I must say a little more about Angus Cameron's profile of deer and deer woods, for it sets the tone and flavor of this volume. That keen sense of recognition—the urge to exclaim, "Precisely!"—is downright reflexive upon reading his description of a raven's scruffy neck feathers as giving it the "look of a Dickens character," or his instant sketch of "the blunt-headed great horned owl" flying away "on mothlike wings." Of course, one expects a perfect delineation of owls from Angus, whose book *The Nightwatchers* has won the accolades of naturalists. In the aromatic mast of such fine outdoor writing a hunter also expects (and finds) woods lore that will certainly help to get him meat if he emulates the author's alertness: the browse and cover a whitetail seeks, the elements that mark a good deer stand, the time to be at that stand.

A far different kind of feature is "The Course of a River," Steven C. Wilson's pic-torial essay. Yet here, too, are insights denied to the city-bound or even to the less than observant, less than thoughtful outdoorsman. It is a revelation to think about the ice of a winter river as water in hibernation and to realize that energy from a star ninety-three million miles away forms and releases the river drop by drop and brings it alive. The photographs are both recordings of fact and works of art.

There is more traditional but equally stimulating art in Paul A. Rossi's exhibit of the golden age of western hunting, "When the Game Outnumbered the Hunters." Former curator of the western collection at The Gilcrease Institute of American History and Art in Tulsa, Rossi was able to present here some of the most exciting paintings ever to portray the hunting of buffalo, bear, elk, bighorn sheep, and pronghorn antelope.

The pronghorn, incidentally, is an exclusively American life form, sole survivor of an ancient mammalian group, and one of this continent's most peculiar, most intriguing, most exciting, least understood game species. I have an old friend named Bert Popowski, who has lived since the Great Depression in a log cabin he built in South Dakota's Custer State Park, who is author of the classic *Hunting Pronghorn Antelope*, and who is generally conceded to be the ranking authority on the subject. Bert is a rarity among plains hunters; with his superbly accurate handloads in his rifle he can make clean kills at exceedingly long range, but he is also one of the few men I know who can, with fair regularity, stalk really close to a nervous pronghorn buck. "Swift, Wild and Elusive," his contribution to this volume, combines the veteran hunter's expertise with the naturalist's curiosity. The Great Plains and plains game may be seen both in their present state and in historical context after reading this selection, the Rossi feature on western hunting art, and the 1832 journal entries by Washington Irving, "A Tour on the Prairies" (illustrated with watercolor masterpieces by Alfred Jacob Miller).

There are two southern gentlemen who ought to be singled out in this introduction, as several westerners have been, because they bring to the collection special regional knowledge. Most of us tend to think of the most bountiful, remote, and forest-bound fishing streams as northern—in the Adirondacks, perhaps, or in Quebec or Michigan or Washington or the Yukon, but somewhere in the North. When, in "Fishing the Solitude

Streams," Charley Dickey writes of trout in brooks isolated by dense, difficult forest, he thinks primarily of waters like Tennessee's Bald River Gorge. Anyone who has not quite mastered the techniques of the short rod might have difficulty accompanying him except in print. Here, however, he presents both the beauty of the constricted, isolated streams and the tackle and methods they require. The other southern gentleman is Frederick C. Baldwin, who writes of "Quail, Old Plantation Style." Fred, like most of us, has hunted upland birds in less aristocratic settings than the ante- or barely post-bellum estates of Georgia and northern Florida, and he has interesting things to say about bobwhite quail, their needs, their management, their ability to frustrate dog and gun.

I have spoken so far of fishing and hunting, the primary but not exclusive obsessions of the outdoorsman. I must not end without commenting on several other topics, and particularly on the late Paul L. Errington's "Winter on the Trapline." One of this nation's foremost biological investigators and teachers, Errington might never have become a professional naturalist if he had not endured a lonely, austere, intermittently dangerous winter in Minnesota's Big Bog in the early 1920's, when he was a very young man. He earned hardly more than expenses as a trapper, but he learned things about survival in the wilderness and about the ways of wildlife that are not found in biological texts. In this reminiscence he shares experiences that helped him to become one of this century's finest woodsmen and ecologists.

I have not yet introduced them all. Dr. Roman Vishniac has been acclaimed for his pioneering stream studies and microphotography of aquatic life; Charles F. Waterman and Lee Wulff are two of this country's most renowned hunting and fishing authorities; Jack Denton Scott is familiar to anyone who reads periodicals devoted to natural history and exploration; John Gardner, a scholar associated with Mystic Seaport, Connecticut, may well know more about the history of canoes than any other writer; Nelson Bryant, who conducts the "Wood, Field and Stream" department of *The New York Times*, has been called dean of New England anglers and hunters; Euell Gibbons is, of course, an international celebrity as a result of his encyclopedic knowledge of edible wild plants; Robert Frisch is an erudite young Latvian-born naturalist who has forsaken civilization for the voyageur's life in the wilderness

of Canada, his adopted land; Erwin A. Bauer, who has lately been conducting a very informative column on recreational vehicles in the pages of *Outdoor Life* (but who concentrates in this book on the horseman's delights provided by a Montana pack trip), is famous for stories and photographs covering every kind of wilderness adventure; and Wyatt Blassingame, an effective defender of the Everglades against the encroachments of innumerable despoilers, has become a friend and adviser in print to many thousands of hunting and fishing enthusiasts visiting or living in Florida.

I must resist the temptation to comment at greater length on each author and feature. The space can be better employed to present the stories themselves, and they will stand on their merits. Readers will find here neither screaming reels nor world-record fish allegedly caught on a gossamer line of incredibly light test weight, nor any wild-eyed, teeth-gnashing, charging foxes. They will find something far more valuable for being genuine: the sportsman's wilderness, the way it really is.

Robert Elman
Cabot, Vermont
1974

The whitetail deer lives in fascinating country and he is surrounded by most engaging neighbors. For the observant, *interested* hunter, an intimate knowledge of those woods and animals is almost as rewarding as the stalk itself. He sees and feels himself to be not simply a deadly interloper, but an integral part of the life of the forest. His own role in the vital balance of nature becomes clearer to him.

Deer woods often seem untenanted, especially in the fall when their bird life is scanty and their mammals are mostly nocturnal. Yet there is always much for the careful hunter to see. If he hunts as he should, spending more time watching than traveling, he'll not only see more deer, but more of everything else. Squirrels, chipmunks, mice, and voles are most visible, but once the hunter attunes himself to watch for the little private dramas in the rodents' lives, he'll see uncommon creatures, too. If he hunts in a true wilderness, or if he canoes the stream-lake chains to get to his hunting areas, he may occasionally see exotic animals as well as common ones.

Whether the late John Alden Knight's "Solunar" theory accounts for the phenomenon or not, there is some factor that periodically controls or, at least, strongly influences the activity of birds and mammals. Observant hunters often have encountered "dead woods"—that curious autumnal period when all seems lifeless. Nothing moves. The leafless trees stand mute. No bird calls. Even the squirrels are silent. The hunter feels utterly isolated. His very animate, sentient nature seems out of place. If ever the deer hunter should feel encouraged to move around, rather than stand or sit, this is the time, for the deer seem as scarce in these dead periods as their fellow creatures.

These spells of inactivity may come at any time of the day. Often the morning hours are the silent ones. On other days the afternoon is blank and still. Eventually the mood changes, and when it does it is exciting to observe, for the woods come to life suddenly. Perhaps one hears a jay or nuthatch; then a red squirrel may be seen scurrying along a log. The woods seem to stir, to release their hidden potential motion. Downy woodpeckers dart from tree to tree; the nervous siskin begins his seedy search. The hunter senses a change even in himself; his presence will be dis-

14

by Angus Cameron

photography by Leonard Lee Rue

whitetail deer

covered by a keen-eyed squirrel that churrs and barks at the unwelcome intrusion.

Now is the time for the hunter-naturalist to make hay. Now the creatures of the woods fill him with expectation, for when they show signs of activity, hope is justified that whitetail may be present, too.

A deer hunter's day should begin before sunup. He should be on his way to watch a likely runway in the first light, while the hunting owls are still awing. If he's lucky he may see the blunt-headed, great horned owl fly away on mothlike wings, silent as a shadow. Sometimes he will flush one of these night hunters watching his own runway in a snow-shrouded alder bottom. He may even hear the clatter of wings against dry twigs and see the snow flurry from the dis-

turbed branches as the dark figure accents itself against the white-gray monochrome of morning light. The curious hunter should mark that perch and later examine the ground beneath it for one of the pellets owls disgorge to rid themselves of the fur, feathers, and bones of their victims. These tightly packed, feltlike pellets give clues to the owl's diet and his success as a hunter: the skulls of mice, birds, and shrews; the bones and feathers of grouse, jays, and other birds; the fur and bones of the snowshoe rabbit; and sometimes the black, shiny fur of the skunk. Once in the wintry, dark green gloom of an Ontario spruce swamp I saw where an owl had killed and eaten a skunk on the snow. The skunk, whose only defense does not daunt the great horned owl, had been seized just a few feet from where his shred-

ded remains were found. The sweep of the owl's wing primaries could be traced in the soft snow, revealing how the silent hunter had mantled his victim, propping and bracing himself with his five-foot wingspread while he tightened his grip and drove his talons into the victim's chest cavity. The skunk had thrown his scent, but to no avail. He had waddled a few feet in a half circle of desperation, carrying his nemesis, and had soon succumbed.

The chipmunk is one of the more diverting of all the woodsy creatures. When the beechnuts are in plenty, this little fellow becomes a tireless worker, scurrying from his neat and smoothly rounded burrow entrance to the sources of supply. The observer who singles out individual animals to watch will soon discover that the chipmunk's foraging

area is surprisingly small, as little as ten yards square. Once I watched the activity on an open beech hillside for an hour and a half. On occasions there were as many as two dozen foragers in view at the same time. One, which had a den near the base of a white pine quite close to my own position, collected beechnuts assiduously for forty minutes, his contours changing with each busy trip. When he returned to the smooth-edged hole his cheek pouches swelled with nuts; when he reemerged he had lost his mumpsy look. Once he perched on a nearby stump to preen himself. Then, to my surprise, he wiggled his nose and produced a beechnut he had held out from storage and ate it daintily, extracting the meat with tiny, practiced nips of his chisel-edged incisors.

On one occasion as I watched a gleaming chipmunk forage for fallen beechnuts, I noticed that the tree under which he gathered was a beech whose top had died. While the chipmunk filled his pouches on the ground, a blue jay scurried back and forth on a branch, picking the nuts that had not exploded

16

*Freshly torn or
shredded shrubs and bushes
are welcome signs to
deer hunters, for
they mark the range of
rutting buck, like animal
at left venting
his sexual aggression by
slashing the brush.
Earlier in season, in less
bumptious mood, he
scrubs "velvet" off antlers
in same manner.*

*Twig ends of red
maple (above left)
are whitetail's
favorite food. Tricorned
beechnut (left) is another
staple of diet.
"Caribou moss" (above),
a lichen, is
sometimes nibbled, too.*

from their burrs and caching them with hammerlike strokes in the niche where the branch grew from the tree. That same tree showed black, three-lined scars where in some past autumn the black bear had left his claw marks as he climbed to feed on the fat and abundant nuts. The trunk's upper surface, the dead area, was pocked with the huge, oval holes made by a great pileated woodpecker that had found in the beech's deadened pith a source of delectable ants.

The most charming companion of the November woods is surely the chickadee. When he and his fellows first announce themselves, they seem to be deployed as skirmishers, making their way by infiltration, and "dee-deeing" in animated conversation. When the lively company has passed on, it leaves the woods a little lonely. Sometimes kinglets join these bands, and occasionally the nuthatch. But the chickadee is most welcome at the noon tea fire. A gleaner of crumbs, he comes close with nervous courage, sometimes venturing onto one's sleeve or shoulder if one remains motion-

Whitetail doe browses
in snow. Deer will feed on bark,
twigs, lichen in regular
order, stretching neck to get
tender bark or
trampling snow to find
underlying moss or
lichen-covered rocks.

Gracefully handsome
poplar (aspen to Westerners)
is the tree beavers cut
first, for the bark is their
favorite food. Also enjoyed
by whitetails, its
leaves (close-up) turn
deep red in autumn.

Maples supply food for
many animals. Deer and
moose nibble sugar (top) and
red varieties for twigs,
leaves, and bark. Squirrels,
foxes, and birds feed
heavily on seed. Porcupines
like inner bark.

less, with just the right feeling of approachability. One can almost will a friendliness to which the little bird invariably responds.

Noon tea provides one of the hunter's finest moments. That quick, hot little fire is a prime refresher. Produced from kindling of fat pine, split and then resplit from stumpy remnants of an old burn, it cheerfully divides a hard day into two easier parts. A green poplar pole is cut and trimmed, the heavy end shoved into the dirt, and propped and weighted with two stones, so the blackened tea bucket will hang nicely just over the flames. A scoop of fresh water from lake, spring, or brook, and the hunter settles down on the windward side to escape the smoke and to nudge fresh sticks in and around the pail's bottom to keep the fire hot and hasten the boiling. A sandwich or two and a tin cup with its handle wrapped in string to reduce the heat on his fingers are set out handy to a plastic container holding the tea leaves. While the water comes to a boil, he takes a jackknife and cuts an alder branch, leaving a small snag untrimmed at the butt end. When the water bubbles this tea stick catches the tea pail's bail and lifts it off to receive the brown leaves. Then, ceremoniously, he holds the pail over the flames to toll it a second or two. Then a dash of cold water reserved in a tin cup to settle the leaves and the tea is ready. Plenty of tea should go into that pail to give it strength and color, lest the guide should say, "Hell, a man could see to

*Snowshoe rabbit, white
in winter, gray-brown in
summer, is often called
"bread of the woods."
Most carnivores and birds
of prey get large part
of protein requirement
from this big hare.*

*Slow waddle of
woodchuck (top), sometimes
seen in open pastures
and clearings on edge of
woods, contrasts with
quick-as-a-wink motion of
chipmunk (above) hunting
nuts on a beech ridge.*

*Squirrel holes in trees
(top) may house red or gray
varieties (middle and above).
To red squirrel, everyone
and everything is an intruder.
His soft, churring sound can
turn to a tail-jerking bark.
Gray squirrel, who dens less
commonly in deep woods, is
noisy in dry leaves. His
rustling is sometimes
mistaken by hopeful hunters
for approaching deer.*

spear eels in thirty feet of that!"

Unlike the chickadee, who always seems a guest at these noon repasts, the Canada jay, or whisky-jack, as he is somehow properly nicknamed, comes not as a guest but as a panhandler. One always feels conned by these well-tailored gray and black birds, but few can resist tossing out a piece of sandwich meat or a crust of surplus bread. Often the jay will perch in a dead spruce stub high overhead and cock his head this way and that for signs of prov-

ender. Nothing escapes his black beady eye, and once he has spotted a morsel he sets his wings and glides to the food in an accurate and purposeful motion, seizes his portion and flies away, as often as not to cache the offering and return for another.

The evening grosbeak and the rose-breasted grosbeak add a touch of color to the chilly grayness of the deer hunter's woods, but the raven accents their somber quality. This great bird, whose call is more often a silvery, bell-

A peck of wood chips
is occasionally found on
the ground beneath
trees in which the hungry
pileated woodpecker has
dug huge, oval-shaped holes.
It is a lucky deer
hunter who sees one of
these fine crow-sized,
red-headed birds.
Tree below has been
attacked several times for
insects and grubs.

The trout fisherman
may see the grouse hen
on her nest (above),
in the spring;
the autumnal deer hunter is
sometimes startled by
the sudden wild whirr of
a whole covey of
grouse rising near him as
he stalks the whitetail.

The noisy blue jay
(top) has strident cry.
Together with the
bright yellow evening grosbeak,
he brings flashes of color to
the late fall woods. The
screech owl (middle) is small
for an owl, but a mighty
hunter. The chickadee (above),
often a cheerful noon tea
companion, is little more than
a fluff of feathers on a
thimble-sized body.

The common loon
has cry familiar to many
hunters: a loud call
resembling a yodel, that
can shatter the
silence of the woods.
A large bird, the loon
is an expert diver
and fisher, but must
kick along the water as
it takes off in flight.
Northern forest lakes are
home of the loon.

Next to the beaver,
the porcupine (bottom) is
our largest rodent.
Here, quills on back have
been raised defensively.
Girdled tree (below)
is mark the porcupine
leaves in the
forest. He is not too
choosy in his preferences:
The barks of the maple,
beech, pine, hemlock, birch,
spruce, and fir are eaten.

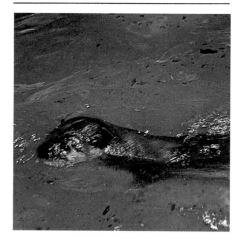

A man canoeing in
the lake chains will see
the large, graceful
otter surprisingly often.
Three otters,
diving, rolling, and
surfacing, will seem like
six. Their droppings
on rocky shores and jutting
boulders show by the
chitinous shells how much
these fishermen like
to feed on crawfish.

Beaver (above) is
animal known for his
works. He is seldom
seen, but sometimes heard
when he slaps his wide tail on
the water in alarm. His
cuttings, dams, and
his isolated lodges on lonely
ponds give a hunter an
eerie sense of the meaning
of the phrase: "My
home is my castle." Chewed
log (top) is characteristic sign.

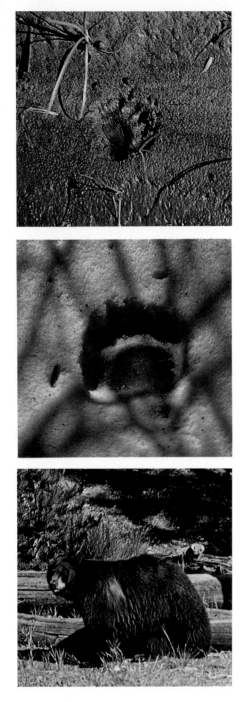

Ontario, Quebec, and New Brunswick deer hunters are most apt to see the majestic and elusive moose (above). His coughing grunt from a fog-shrouded lake shore is a sound once heard, never forgotten. The incisors of the moose's lower jaw make neat, parallel streaks in the trunks of young maples (top), whose bark he prefers.

Deer hunters who have visited woods every fall for years may have thrilled to bear tracks in the mud or snow, but never laid eyes on the beast itself. The black bear (above) is a wary animal whose presence makes a deer hunter's woods seem even more wild than usual and thus more appealing.

Deer tracks are the hunter's favorite sign. In snow (top), even a novice hunter can recognize fresh tracks and the experienced hunter can often get a shot by careful trailing. In winter, during deep snow (middle and above), the deer "yards": He beats down trails in a feeding area and exhausts the browse to the limit of his reach.

over-water sound than the croak so often associated with it, appears to me as a kind of gloomy deacon. His great size and ragtag scruffy neck feathers give him the wonderful down-at-the-heels look of a Dickens character. His black hat and his tattered scarf make him seem dressed for the winter that will follow. "Tuloo-ak," he says, in a kind of falsetto register, a single comment with a pessimistic tone that belies its curiously musical quality. It's a lucky deer watcher who sees and hears the raven.

The deer hunter's woods can seem quite depressing at first, but it is a passing emotion, for one knows that, in spite of the coming cold, the frost-covered leaves soon to be mantled in deep snow, the winter woods house creatures who successfully make their livings despite the desolation. The dark reaches of hemlock and spruce, the unrelieved grays and blacks of the leafless hardwoods and shrubs, the wet deadness of the leaves—these things are skin-deep only. Every rotting blow-down, the leafy mold, the musty earth itself shelter a myriad of creatures from the mouse to the hibernating insect. The fall woods of the deer hunter are throbbing habitats; only the surface seems lifeless

The bewildering variety of trees, shrubs, grasses, and flowering plants that presses in upon the hunter is a world of its own, but it is also the deer's world, indeed his very livelihood. A man ought to have some respect for these things—for their own sake and because knowing about them can make a man a better hunter. It is an indignity offered to living things if one can't name them. But there is a practical reason for the hunter to know plants, for his success can depend on his ability to see what deer are feeding on. Scuffed leaves, dark and wet on the underside turned up by a pawing deer, can often show feeding areas in beech woods. The clipped twig ends of the red or striped maple, always a favorite food, can also show the observant hunter a feeding area—if he can identify his maples. The bracken fern, like everything else in the deer's habitat, relates to both deer and hunter. In woods covered with early snow a casual observer can see torn fronds greenly decorating the patches churned by the deer's searching hooves. It is good for the soul—and for the chase—to know these revealing things.

A small Bausch & Lomb engraver's glass is a fine item for the deer hunter's shirt pocket. With it he can extend his appreciation of his sport enormously. If he is a traveler, he may use the glass seldom, but if he sits as much as he walks (as he should), he can explore the miniature, as well as the larger, natural world around him. I remember once becoming restive with curiosity about a nuthatch's pertinacious exploration of a maple trunk a few feet from a deer stand I was watching. I feared to move, for my hunting partner was still hunting a ridge toward my runway and my position was a likely one. The nuthatch, in that crazy upside-down style of his, busily probed the bark, adding to my growing tension. Finally, when my friend's head showed above the ridgetop and I thought he had moved away, I hunkered down to examine with my glass the crevices under the bark's corrugation and found the tiny pear-shaped eggs of the insect that had provided the nuthatch with his protein. The nuthatch, always a deer hunter's neighbor, also finds hibernating adult insects in his tireless search. Considering the millions of these tiny, animate bits of fat that lie dormant in the winter woods, it is no wonder the nuthatch need not migrate. The nuthatch is fascinating to watch, but sometimes he has another function for the deer hunter. Hugh Fosburgh, the novelist-naturalist, says he trusts the *rapid* "yank-yank" alarm call of this bird far more than he does the noisy shrieks of the blue jay or the nervous churr and bark of the red squirrel as an indicator of the presence of some other creature in the area. The slow, tin-horn call of the nuthatch means nothing, but the rapid nervous yanking often indicates a deer in the vicinity.

The pocket glass also will reveal the beautiful abstraction of a birch bud's cross section, or the design of the vagrant snowflake, marvelous before it melts on the sleeve of your stag shirt. And it will transform a jay's feather, enabling you to see clearly the barbs of the shaft and to note how the barbules hook on to each other to hold the interlocking strands against the rushing air in flight. The little glass is an educational companion for the deer hunter; its extension of the hunter's world is limited only by the hunter's degree of imagination and industry.

The observant deer hunter will see a surprising variety of animals during a hunting career. For the fun of it, my wife and I made up lists of frequencies. My list included, in order, squirrel, chipmunk, mouse, rabbit, porcupine, muskrat, weasel, fox, otter, mink, beaver, skunk, raccoon, bear, shrew, bobcat, fisher. My wife, not surprisingly, listed the same animals, with slightly different frequencies of appearance.

Not only the forest but the campsite itself can provide a setting for nature's small dramas. Here, too, an observant hunter will see the life cycle of the forest in full chase.

Roy Smith's one-room camp, a reasonably roomy, peeled-cedar cabin, overlooked a gracefully descending, low and smooth rock slope to the water of the west bay of a lake called Horseshoe. It was surrounded by a few spruce and hemlock, firs and birches, and squatted comfortably with a low seemliness, as if a Frank Lloyd Wright had designed and planted it on the one spot where it belonged. Its low peaked roof had an overhang at the front to shield a man who might have to get into the breadbox nailed on the front wall or take down a tool on a mean, rainy day. The roof was made of corrugated metal, canoed and portaged in in awkward sheets, but worth the trouble because it would be far better than tar paper in the long run. And, besides, it was bear-proof.

One night the Coleman gas lantern had

finally blinked out its last diminishing light, but had given a respite of illumination between the turning off and the actual blackout. (That time is so brief it must be planned for. It is a tiny contest to wriggle quickly into one's sleeping bag and be settled in time to watch the extinction of the light.)

Silence came with the loss of light, broken only by the slow fizz of the dying fire in the wood range. In a matter of seconds, the darkness would bring out the white-footed mice that had gratefully moved in when we did to share our grub with us. Welcome though these little, large-eared beauties were as companions, they were troublesome, too (as when they left their tracks in the carelessly uncovered butter). We reduced their numbers with backbreaker traps baited with butter and oatmeal, and were careful to set our mink traps at a distance from the cabin, so as not to catch the camp weasel who invariably showed up after a day or two to take advantage of the fine mouse supply. In the dying light of evening, I often watched his camera-shutter movements as he raced in and out of the spaces of the woodpile. Sometimes we'd hear his hunts in the cabin after dark. A wild, noisy, scrambling race and a high, abruptly stopped squeak of the little victim invariably told the tale. There would be silence again, then more tiny furry scurryings of the rummaging mice, and soon, when the weasel had cached his first mouse somewhere outside the camp, he'd return and take another. The camp weasel was better as a mouse hunter than we were as mice trappers.

Night sounds came from outside the cabin as well, and one cold, wet November we had a barred owl for a neighbor. We'd hear his muffled hoots, and though an owl's hoots have a curious quality that makes them hard to locate, we could tell from the volume that he was close. Finally one evening in the weak gray light, I flushed the round-headed bird as I hurried toward the warm cabin from the chilly discomfort of the log outhouse. All I saw was the level, flat trajectory of the gliding owl as he picked his way through the hemlock stand.

So, the influx of mice in our camp had beckoned a second mouser. Sad to say, once the owl took up residence near us, we lost the services of the camp weasel. Though the white-foot supply seemed inexhaustible, the weasel's visits ceased and I concluded that probably the slim, swift, four-footed mouser had been picked up by the winged one.

In the evenings, after we had returned from the trap line or from the day's hunt, I began to search out this owl's feeding roosts and from a lucky discovery of his pellets I located one perch, at least, in a big hemlock a hundred yards back in the bush from the cabin. I spotted him fairly regularly during that three weeks' period, usually perched on a limb halfway up and quite close to the bole of the hemlock, but often I found him tucked away on a spruce limb where he suffered me to observe him. This owl appeared a most mild-mannered bird when perched, seemingly little disturbed by my pokings about and persistent observations. When sometimes he flushed, he displayed a light buoyant flight. He slipped his way among the trunks and saplings with a delicacy that was most pleasing for such a big bird, for the barred owl is fully crow-sized.

One night as I lay on the top bunk in the silent, pitch-dark camp I heard a dull thump on the corrugated roof directly above my head and not three feet away. The creature was undoubtedly a flying squirrel that had glided to a noisy landing on the roof from some higher limb that had served him as a launching pad. I listened a moment to the scratchy bumpings and scurryings of the squirrel. Suddenly there was only silence, and as suddenly a soft brush of wings on the metal surface. Instantly there was a loud, anguished squeal from the squirrel. I held

Winter hunters of 1850's are shown shooting whitetails in northern New York State.

my breath and listened for further evidence of the little tragedy out there in the dark, but the owl had evidently plucked the flat-bodied squirrel from the roof and made off without a formal landing. I lay there scarcely daring to breathe, for the closeness of the drama had raised my own hackles. As I dozed off, I visualized "my" barred owl perched on a limb of his feeding station be-heading the hapless flying squirrel. The owl was a hunter, too.

Hunting is a way of understanding the natural world we live in by participating in that world. In the hunt one becomes a part of the life process that the hunter and the hunted daily and nightly reenact. There are psychic relationships involved here that arise out of these natural processes, and a hunter senses them by participation in the chase. It is said by some that this participation

brutalizes, but of that I am very doubtful. As my then-eight-year-old daughter once said from the half-darkness of her bunk in Roy Smith's Ontario trapping shack: "You know, even though Roy kills animals and traps them, he is still the best animal-lover I ever knew." The little girl had sensed the same thing that had caused my wife and me to return there fall after fall to live the hunting and trapping life with a man whose relationship to the wilds was surpassingly simple and at the same time infinitely complicated.

When Roy spoke of otters he used a kind of folk terminology. He always referred to "The Otter" or "The Mink" and no matter how often the stories ended in the tragedy of death by some predator or accident, the creature lived on, timeless and inextinguishable. Roy Smith took a crop off the wilderness every fall, but the species, himself included, persisted and reenacted their dramatic ways, generation after generation.

"Why is it," asked my fifteen-year-old son the year we introduced our children to Roy and his world, "that game you yourself have shot, skinned, packed in, butchered, cooked in crude utensils, and eaten on a plank table covered with scratched oilcloth tastes so much better?" One can say that the reason lies in the extra hunger one feels from hard exertion, or that this feeling shared by most hunters is a sentimental rationalization. One can say that, but it will not be true. Living the hunting life, absorbed in the world of the hunter and the hunted, is a special kind of experience. Hunting is a natural pursuit; it is deeply ingrained in men (and women), but it is hidden only skin-deep. What hunter has not seen most unlikely men who have gone on a first hunting trip, for business reasons, perhaps, suddenly respond to the profound urge to hunt, in a manner that surprises themselves most of all?

The "other rewards" of hunting, the communion with and participation in nature, to put it blandly, are not at all unconnected with the pursuit and killing and eating of game. They are not static pleasures of nature observation; rather they are integral to the hunting act itself, a not-unnatural need of the psyche of man.

The relationship between nature, game, and hunting man has nowhere been more penetratingly analyzed than by Paul Shepard, Jr., a professor of biology at Smith College. In a paper read before the twenty-fourth North American Wildlife Conference in 1959, Shepard observed: "If the real value of hunting is to get a hearing, its spokesmen must insist on greater perspective by all concerned. The essential point must clearly be understood to turn on a broader philosophy of man in nature. Opposition to hunting for sport has its accusing finger in the morality of the act of killing. The answer is not a matter of forming the admission that we are all human, bipedal, carnivorous mammals, damned to kill, but consists in showing through anthropology, history, and the arts that the superb human mind operates in subtle ways in the search for an equilibrium between the polarities of nature and God. To share in life is to participate in a traffic of energy and materials, the ultimate origin of which is a mystery, but which has its immediate source in the bodies of plants and other animals. As a society, we may be in danger of losing sight of this. It is kept most vividly before us in hunting."

The reason why my young daughter recognized the trapper, Roy Smith, as an animal-lover, and why my son found the eating of game a special delight, and why a closely observing relationship with the deer woods is important is found in the last two paragraphs of Shepard's paper. "It follows," he wrote, "that hunting is not, as even hunters sometimes claim, just an excuse to get out-of-doors, to which killing is incidental. Killing and eating the prey are the most important things that hunters do. The successful hunt is a solemn event, and yet it is done in a spirit of joy. It puts modern man for a moment in vital rapport with the universe from which civilization tends to separate him in an illusion of superiority and independence. The natural environment will always be mysterious, evoking an awe to be shared among all men who take the trouble to see it....

"Regardless of technological advance, man remains part of and dependent on nature. The necessity of signifying and recognizing this relationship remains. The hunter is our agent of awareness. He is not only an observer, but a participant and receiver. He knows that man is a member of the natural community and that the processes of nature will never become so well understood that faith will cease to be important." ◉

Man and His Environment

The Course of a River

From the time of its beginning
in high mountains until it loses itself
in the sea, the stream enriches
each environment
through which it flows.

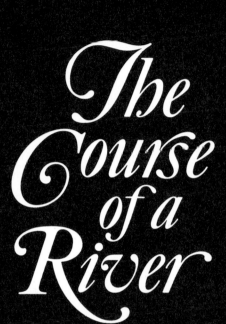

Text and photography by
Steven C. Wilson

I have traveled much with rivers, have cooperated with the dignity of water, with free-flowing rivers in the western forests, with the silent strength of deep waters descending deeper gorges. I have savored the frolicsome spirit of a swift-falling snow-melt brook that greens across an alpine meadow. I have tampered with the frailties of young water; have dammed and diverted; have struggled from the sea through the turmoil of a west-flowing river meeting the east-pounding waves of the Pacific, when the outcome of a safe homecoming was decided by a river's sand bar. Yet I still know no river—not in the same sense that I know my woman or my boys, a consuming, intense way.

Amid snow packed into ice, the warmth from that ninety-three-million-mile-distant star releases, drop by drop, the rivers. Percolating, battering amid rocks, gamboling out onto short-season meadows of primrose and paintbrush, among marmots and conies, beneath hawks and jays, the water inexorably descends, pulled by gravity as a man is pulled by fear and curiosity. A river must find the sea. The tiniest rill, the raging flood, each restlessly pushes, pulses, gathers, and then rests, its load of silted rock in the sea.

Wily as a snake, strong and endless as time, with infinite persistence, the river is the leveler of the land. It would strip away every mountain till all was flat plain, were it not for the earth's unsteady crust, lifting here, sinking there. Rivers contour the world. Countless gullies and canyons, flood plains and valleys flow across the earth's surface.

From the placid, unhurried world of Huckleberry Finn to the mountain music of pebble-strewn streams where fish spawn, the cooperations of water temper the tensions of growth. Where the gradient is steep the velocity is great, cutting quickly to bedrock, pausing only to fill a basin or lose itself in a pond choked with green-growing things and teeming life, splashing, rustling, swishing, almost too quickly to be seen.

Preceding pages: Snake River cuts between Oregon (left) and Idaho at Hell's Canyon. Left: Mendenhall Glacier, Alaska. Right: Falls at Rainier National Park, Washington.

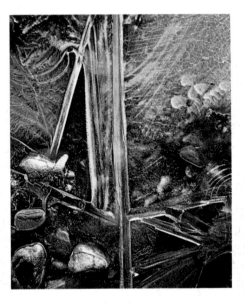

Young water is noisy water. It has its start in high mountain country at freezing levels where live things—and the water itself —hibernate much of the year. Winter water is locked in lacy ice crystals and compacted snow; animals lie dormant beneath. In spring, both bestir themselves. But fast water seldom runs deep. *Right: Logged reservoir area on Oregon's Santian River. Above, top, and top right: Waters of Washington State—Upper Hoh River ice crystals, beginning of early spring run on Dosewallips River, and eroded ice at headwaters of White River atop Mount Rainier.*

Time and the delicate strength of water etch into bedrock: They find weaknesses, corrode rock, erode earth, leaving only space, time, and the delicate strength of water. Out of the space comes the lushness of flora and fauna; from time comes time and more time; implicit in the delicate strength are struggle, destruction, the force of change—constituent elements of poetry. *Below: Gold Creek, Washington, frog. Right: Cool shade of awesome Oneta Gorge, Oregon. Far right: Tumble of waters at Gold Creek, whitetail doe and young clambering up bank of Donner und Blitzen River, Oregon.*

In the river environment, life's profusion and diversity are accommodated and encouraged. Every dimension of the water is utilized: Living things exist on its surface, send root and stem to the oozy bottom, release eggs to its current, retrieve them to eat. Those not of the river live in harmony with it, visiting its banks to feed and drink, and so to mate, reproduce, and prosper. *Opposite: Firehole River marsh flats in Yellowstone National Park, Wyoming. Left: Elk across Niobrara River, Nebraska, also is seen among lily pads. Below: Duck near Tumwater, Washington.*

Rivers grow quiet with distance and time. They work hard while young, smoothing pathways with turbulence, carving deep, wide, gently curving beds. Later on, the staccato diminishes, overborne by broadened streams with heavy currents. Backwaters are quiet homes. A river grows old with grace, serenity, and silt. *Movement on the Donner und Blitzen River: Lone trumpeter cygnet, reeds and canoe-men, ducks and widgeon in twilight's glow.*

Quail, Old Plantation Style

To hunt bobwhite on shooting estates of the Old South is to move back in time to classic gunning traditions.

Text and photography by
Frederick C. Baldwin

The bobwhite quail must be the most pampered little bundle of game bird in the world. A great deal of research has been undertaken and enormous amounts of money have been spent to find out what makes the bobwhite happy and healthy. Hundreds of thousands of acres of southern farmland are kept free of modern commercial agriculture because the bobwhite prefers it this way. Plantation owners spurn the encroachments of industry, housing projects, and what in general has come to be known as "progress." Quail don't like progress. There is a current trend toward dual-purpose farming, and a great deal of land throughout the nation is now being carefully cultivated to bestow two kinds of harvest—game birds as well as conventional agricultural produce. But in parts of the Deep South, where I have hunted, vast plantations give hardly a nod to high-yield modern farming, for such pedestrian matters as crops are secondary where the bobwhite reigns.

Plantations with superb quail shooting range from North and South Carolina west to Alabama, but the biggest concentration of shooting plantations lies in the rolling clay country of the Thomasville-Tallahassee region of south Georgia and north Florida—about a hundred square miles of these plantations, butted one next to the other. Some of the names go back to antebellum days when the region was a prosperous agricul-

*Far left:
Mule-drawn Georgia
quail wagon
carries two hunters
plus pointers and
retrievers.
Top: Shooter
breaks open
gun and reloads
after covey
has flushed and
scattered.
Above: Hunters
ride through fields,
dismount when
dogs are seen on
point. Left:
Cock quail "holds
tight" in tall
concealing grasses.*

tural center, with beautiful plantation houses and feudal magnificence: El Destino and Horseshoe, Pebble Hill, Melrose, Susina, and Greenwood. A few still stand, and a few names go back still further, to the wars with the Creek and Apalachee Indians, bloody battles during the War of 1812. One such is Welaunee Plantation, bought from the Indians by my great-great-grandfather, Colonel Robert Gamble.

By the end of the Civil War, the area was ruined. Cotton moved to Texas and the planters were finished. The fields grew up to brown sage, and the second growth began to attract bobwhite quail. By 1880 the Thomasville-Tallahassee area was invaded by society from Cleveland, Philadelphia, and New York. Some of these people came for the pleasant winter climate, others for the fine shooting. A number of hotels were built, and gradually sportsmen began to buy some of the broken-down plantations for the excellent dove, turkey, and quail shooting. The purchases became, curiously enough, rather ingrown, tribal affairs. Clevelanders, all of whom seem to have been relatives or business associates, tended to buy north from Tallahassee; New Yorkers and Philadelphians worked south from Thomasville, Georgia, in the same manner. By 1910, one hundred and fifty thousand acres of shooting preserves had been pur-

chased, establishing a tribal pattern and a way of life which incredibly exists today. Again the wealthy plantation owners, this time Yankees, have stopped the clock. Quail hunting is enjoyed in many parts of the nation, but nowhere is it done with more grace, more attention to the esthetics of the sport, than on these plantations where the owners and their guests regard bobwhite hunting as a delicate, mannered art.

The Georgia shooting wagon is perhaps the most splendidly archaic and traditionally important fixture of classic plantation quail shooting. This vehicle is a perfect embodiment of the philosophy of correct quail shooting, and as such was appropriately invented during an age which few of us can remember, in about 1880. The purpose of the wagon is to transport up to ten dogs and a couple of hunters. The dogs are kept in cages under an open seat, rather Victorian in design. Drawn by mules or sometimes horses, the wagon is equipped with gun racks or gun boxes. It also carries all the supporting hardware, water for the dogs, ammunition, soft drinks, and snacks. The front seat, situated lower than the rear passenger seat, is for the driver and a couple of retrievers that are not penned. The rig is open, having no roof or top. The fittings are polished brass; red plumes and tassels waving from the mules give the whole rig a

special elegance with its black body and red trim, reminiscent of a fine Sicilian hearse.

The inventor of the Georgia shooting wagon has unfortunately not been remembered, but some of the first models were made by the Studebaker Company in the late nineteenth century. The wagons I've ridden on were equipped with balloon rubber tires, a scientific breakthrough which occurred around 1938 and which makes this form of transportation remarkably pleasant, even in relatively rough terrain. You sway around at high altitude on a private throne well padded on the bottom, enjoying a commanding view and a feeling of splendid detachment.

A few plantation and commercial pre-serve owners have forsaken the past, replacing the old wagon with Jeeps or other four-wheel-drive vehicles that can accommodate passengers, gun racks, and carrying cages for the dogs. But there remains a hard core of traditionalists to whom the wagon and its accouterments are an indispensable part of the bobwhite scene.

The traditional southern quail hunt involves a great deal of gentle conversation before and after the actual shooting. The quail shooter has plenty to talk about. There are enough variables to keep him guessing for years. There is the weather. When it is too hot or too dry, the dogs can't pick up the scent. Or a low-pressure front may make the birds behave queerly. Some-

Left: Pointer suddenly freezes as he scents covey in brush. Above: Flushed bird heads toward trees as shooter smoothly swings gun ahead of swift target. Far left: After the shot, Labrador finds fallen bird and fetches it. Some plantation owners allow pointing dogs to double as retrievers.

times, too, there are rattlesnakes to watch for. Then there is the quality and temperament of the bird dog, the characteristics and suitability of pointers, setters, Brittany spaniels. For quail talk is also talk about dogs, their training, breeding, and style and performance. There is the question as to whether a pointing dog should retrieve, and the inevitable comparison between field dogs and trial dogs.

Almost every shooter has his favorite breed of bird dog, one that impresses him as being far superior to any other. On the large, open-field plantations of the South, English pointers and English setters are the favorites, for they are fast and wide-ranging; they show hunting initiative and eagerness and stamina; and they hunt and carry themselves with true style. There is no denying, however, that some other breeds such as the Brittany spaniel and Gordon setter do a commendable job. On many commercial preserves, German shorthaired pointers and a few other breeds have also become popular, because they are relatively slow, close-working dogs that are easily directed by a handler. Finding and pointing birds is only part of the job, the retrieve of game being the obvious third component of good dog work. Some plantations maintain retrievers—often yellow or black Labradors—for the sole purpose of fetching birds, while the actual hunting is done by setters or pointers.

It soon becomes apparent to the uninitiated that there is very much more to quail shooting than shooting quail. Sustained contact leads the intelligent hunter gradually and invariably to so wide a range of related interests that the shooter can sometimes find himself becoming an ecologist rather than a bagger of game.

The southern, or Florida, bobwhite quail (*Colinus virginianus floridanus*) is a plump and delicately beautiful little bird, slightly smaller and darker than its northern and western relatives. There are several subspecies of bobwhite, ranging throughout most of eastern North America. An average southern bobwhite weighs five to six ounces, is eight to ten inches long, and has a wingspread of about fourteen inches. In coloration, the bird is mottled, gray, brown, rufous, and whitish, with darker stripes across the top and side of the head. On the male, these stripes are black and they alternate with off-white which also shows up as a light throat patch. On the female, the stripes are less distinct and the lighter color is cream or tan rather than off-white. There is nothing flamboyant about the appearance of the bobwhite—just a quiet, handsome elegance.

It is not appearance alone—or even the delicious flavor of well-prepared quail—that makes this bird such a darling of the discriminating sportsman. The mature quail is also a very fast, elusive target. These birds reach speeds of forty miles per hour, though their endurance is not great. The average covey rise is about two hundred yards and several covey rises in close succession will leave the birds exhausted. The characteristic whirring, the explosion of birds and noise that is so familiar to the hunter at the rise, is a defensive tactic and is absent when a bobwhite is in no danger.

Quail feed and rest in groups—coveys of anywhere from several birds to more than twenty, though twelve to sixteen can be considered average. The birds usually roost on the ground in a circular formation with heads out, tails together. During cold weather the birds in a covey huddle so close that their tails are pushed straight upward.

When quail are resting, their wings are tightly compressed against their bodies and they give off little scent. When they are nesting, on the other hand, with their feathers fluffed out, their odor can be distinctive even to the relatively insensitive human nose, particularly after hatching.

The vast assortment of odors which a dog encounters changes from day to day and hour by hour, due to heat, wind, humidity, and atmospheric pressure, but the quail's scent is governed by the same laws of nature as the scent of other animals. As the bird moves about, preening and shaking itself, a trail of odor is dispersed. When the bird flies, the scent is emitted like the smoke trail of a jet plane. It is only when the quail freezes, tightly compressing his feathers, that this scent does not escape. This is done during times of emergency, but as soon as the quail relaxes, the characteristic odor once more is emitted.

The traditional van shooting as practiced on the great quail plantations of the Thomasville-Tallahassee area is still largely built around the Georgia quail wagon. Of the eight or so hunters in the party, a couple may ride the wagon, the others are on horseback. There are an equal number of attendants, dressed in traditional white or red coats, a mule driver, dog handlers, the trainer, and outriders.

The ten dogs loaded into the high-sided cages of the wagon are released in pairs as the hunting starts and they work for about half an hour at a clip. They cover eight to ten miles during this time, after which they are put back in the wagon and replaced with two fresh dogs. The style and performance of each dog is different. A good pointer must have the intelligence to know the likely places where quail hide, and must cover these spots, rather than waste time in unproductive areas. His speed must take him over a maximum amount of ground without exhausting him. The dog must remain on a preselected course determined by his handler, and must not range out of control of whistle or hand signals or voice. The pointer's nose must quickly locate birds;

the dog must not approach so close that the covey flushes prematurely. He must hold the point—remain stock still—at the report of the gun, until ordered to move again.

When a distant dog is spotted on point, the cry goes up: "Point!" Then the whole entourage takes on the semblance of a cavalry charge.

After the confusion and dust have settled, two hunters dismount with the white-coated dog handler and proceed to the dog on point. Here, presumably, lies a covey of perhaps a dozen birds. They suddenly rise and then, if the two gunners are good shots, down go two quail, maybe three. The retrievers are called from the wagon and they sniff around until they recover the downed birds, which are returned to the wagon.

It is sometimes tempting simply to shoot quail, rather than savor the esthetics of dog handling, and this has its effect on a dog. A bird dog is a highly charged animal whose instincts are at constant war with his training. Every instinct tells him to get his mouth on the quail, but he must not. A very particular hunter, deeply involved in the mystique of the sport, will not allow himself to shoot unless the dog is behaving correctly at the time of the covey rise. The dead bird is the dog's reward, and this kind of excruciating discipline is a kind of ultimate refinement which is difficult to achieve.

Another important element in quail hunting is the choice of guns. Quality double-barreled guns are usually favored, not because they have any shooting edge over pumps and autoloaders, but because they have such good looks, good balance, reliability, style. And also because they are simply traditional.

If conversation during the hunt does not turn on dogs or guns, it may dwell on bobwhite habits. Coveys like to roost in brier patches, tangled grass, or brush. At dawn, they move into the fields to feed on grain, soybeans, peas, weed seeds, and berries. In these fields, the birds fan out, covering an area of sixty feet or more. Feeding continues through most of the morning, and is followed by a resting period; in midafternoon, the birds take up feeding again until the evening calls them back to roost. A single covey's range rarely extends more than about half a mile.

It is often said that a covey rise is like an explosion, with birds whirring off in all directions. But the fact is that at least some of the quail will invariably head toward the nearest heavy cover when flushed. An experienced hunter can take advantage of this trait, placing himself in position for a good shot. However, the covey rise is so abrupt and startling that novice gunners become unstrung; they tend to fire into the middle of the covey, almost blindly, rather than picking and concentrating on individual birds. If a gunner remains calm, he usually has time for two quickly but carefully placed shots.

When a covey flushes, the survivors scatter in thick cover. Obviously, it is important to mark down where the singles alight so that the dogs can be cast off in the proper direction to find and point them. After landing, these singles generally run only a few feet before hiding in the camouflaging foliage. Singles will hold well for a dog, just as coveys do, and it is important not to rush a shot too much when the flush comes. The bird should be allowed to fly twenty-five or thirty yards before the shot is made; otherwise, a well-placed pattern of pellets may leave little edible meat.

The Thomasville-Tallahassee shooting plantations are fiefs, many of which have been in the same families since the turn of the century. Their sole purpose is hunting, as modern agriculture disrupts the delicate relationship between the quail's need for food and adjacent cover. The quail needs a lot of land; you can roughly figure one quail per acre. The land is worth from three hundred to five hundred dollars per acre and the tracts run from three thousand to ten thousand acres in size. The cost of running such plantations is high, as little or no income accrues from the land. Kennels, handlers, dog trainers, horses, mules, and domestic as well as plantation maintainance all run up a bill which may reach five hundred thousand dollars per annum. All of this to shoot a couple of hundred birds a year. If the cost of plantation-raised wild birds was calculated as the cost of cattle is, the total bill would run from seventy-five to one hundred dollars per bird. Only a fraction of the quail are shot, while seventy or eighty percent fall prey to various predators during their average two-year life span. It is clear that in order to maintain a shooting plantation it is necessary to be very rich. To roll back the clock to 1910 is a very expensive undertaking.

It is axiomatic that hunting pressure will cause succeeding generations of birds to become wilder and wilder, harder and harder to hunt. The old professional dog handlers, some of whom have been in the quail fields for the last forty years, all seem to tell the same story: "In the old days when you hunted a cornfield, a good dog would find covey after covey. The coveys would rise and spread out into cover after about a hundred yards' flight. The guns would usually get three or four singles from the split-up covey, and you wouldn't have to go too far to do it. Today it's hard to predict what's going to happen when a covey flushes. The birds are very spooky. They fly far and fast, changing direction as soon as they're out of sight. One covey rise may trigger several others nearby. This used to happen much less often thirty years ago. Birds behave queerly. Singles and coveys rise from under the shooting wagon or under the horses. They're full of surprises, and they go in all directions."

After World War II, Mexican quail were introduced to replenish the shooting plantations, and today some of the tricks of the Florida bobwhite quail are credited to breeding with the Mexican quail. For example, there are now more runners—quail which take off on foot when pointed, rather than freezing and waiting to be flushed. The interbreeding theory is unlikely because the Mexican quail, pen-raised birds, probably didn't survive two seasons.

Some commercial shooting plantations regularly stock quail because of the necessity of providing more than one bird per acre, or about ten acres per covey. Hunters are paying from one hundred and fifty dollars per day to shoot, to thirty-five hundred dollars per week to rent a whole plantation. These hunters must have birds, so the quail are raised in flight pens and then released at strategic points around the plantation just prior to the shoot. The hunter thus can be assured a full bag; the surviving birds are retrapped in cages which are baited with feed and the birds are used over again. Stocking increases the quail population only temporarily. Pen-raised quail do not survive predation.

The most effective way to support wild quail is to provide them with plenty of cover. The bobwhite thrives on old-fashioned patch-row farming—a field of corn here and there, widely isolated; no dairy cattle, livestock, or poultry; plenty of beggarweed and bull grass. If the hedge and fence rows are cleared, the quail is exposed to attack by its natural enemies. Plantation agriculture, therefore, must be tailored to the needs of the quail.

The farming pressures of the twentieth century notwithstanding, plantation owners hold to tradition: Only three birds are shot out of each covey; no more than two guns are allowed in a field; ritual unloading is observed when hunters return to the horses; and gunners maintain a preference for the double. These and most of the other field rules have survived for fifty years.

As with the observation of fine dogs, there is an esthetic quality to the study of the birds themselves. The period between pairing and nesting lasts from fifteen to twenty days, depending on the weather, and the paired couple is inseparable. The cock is very devoted, generally following the hen as she hunts for food.

The cock is brave as well as dedicated to his nesting duties. He not only shares the incubation chore with his mate, but will take over and hatch the chicks should the female be killed by a predator. The cock will also fight for the nest, even at great risk to himself. The hen is more timid, but to lead an enemy away from the nest, either a cock or a hen will feign the fluttering and dragging of wings of a badly injured bird. The impulse to chase the apparent cripple is irresistible to many predators, and often the nest is saved by this stratagem.

The simpler defense tactic of a covey of mature birds is perhaps even more effective and certainly just as intriguing. When they explode into the air with a whirr and swiftly scatter in all directions—some of them seeming to dart straight at the attacker—the effect is startling to say the least. Whether the predator is a fox, or a dog, or a man with a gun, the result may be momentary but total confusion, during which the bobwhites streak for safety. If a tradition-minded southern sportsman misses in a situation like that, he will mark down the singles, but he will also smile and wish the birds well. For in the esthetics of classic southern quail hunting, a gentlemanly attitude counts for as much as luxury or good dog work, swift reflexes, or the colorful regalia of the finest Georgia quail wagon. ◉

Life in the stream

the vital
chain of nature
from
microörganism
to trout

text and photography by

Dr. Roman Vishniac

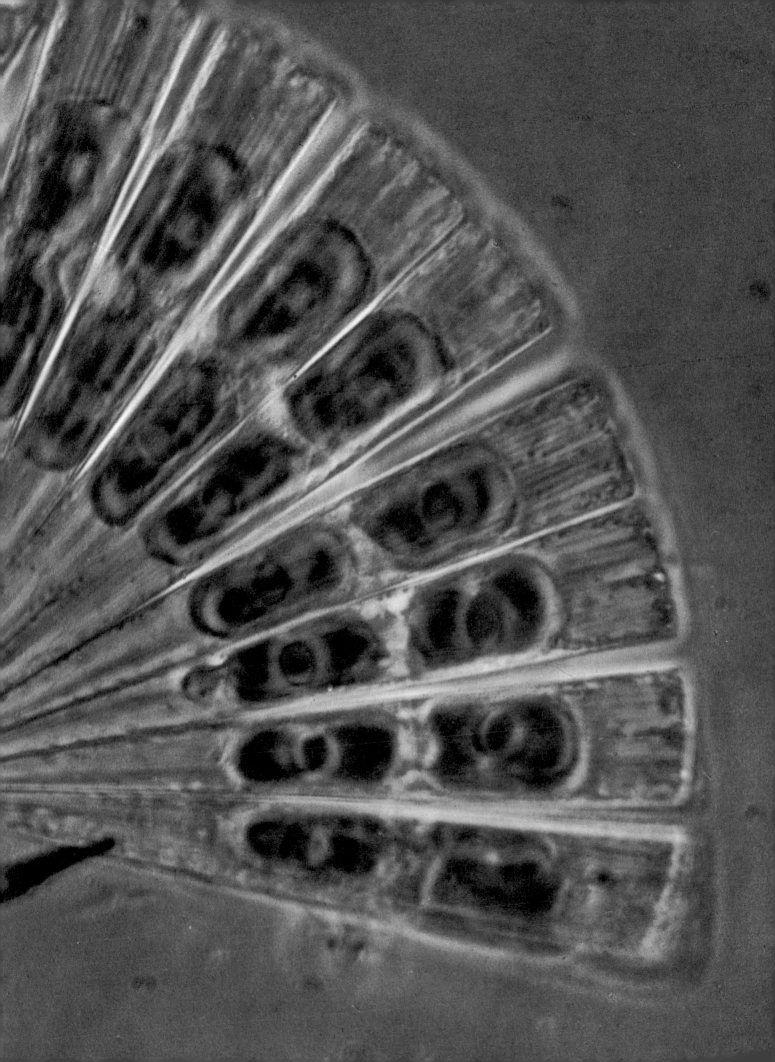

The angler is innately a student of natural history. Thus, when naturalist Stephen Forbes said in 1887 that "the lake or river is a microcosm" he was speaking as much to the serious fisherman as to his fellow scientists. Forbes meant that the plants and animals of a lake or stream are integrated with each other and adjusted to their environment in such a way that they form an ecological system, or ecosystem.

The man who comes to the lake or stream to fish becomes a part of that ecosystem. He can have a profound effect on the life of the stream, especially if —through ignorance of the living network—he destroys the balance that exists among the elements present: the fish that lurk in the pools, the aquatic plants rooted close to the shore, the drifting microscopic algae, the tiny crustaceans, the little worms on the bottom, and the other seen or unseen inhabitants of the environment.

But if the angler is, as he should be, a naturalist too, he will respect the environment, taking care not to pollute it, and leaving the balance of life intact. He will become a knowing participant with the rest of its elements in the fascinating cycle of life and survival.

Life in the stream or lake is not by any means a completely sub-surface matter, as the angler, by habit of thought, might suppose. This microcosm, and indeed the whole living world,

obtains the energy for its basic existence, its activities, and its maintenance from the energy of the sun functioning through the photosynthetic process. Through photosynthesis the sun's energy is transformed into food—into microalgae in the stream or pond, into grasses in the field. These organisms are in turn the producers of nutrition for themselves as well as for us. As food energy is transferred through a succession of different animals eating and being eaten, we have what is called the food chain. Man's place in the life of the stream is at the uppermost position on the food chain. He eats the fish that eats the nymph that eats the plant that produces nourishment through the sun's radiant energy.

Feeding is a constant activity in the animal world. Only those animals that are dormant can maintain life without food. But if animals are expending energy in any way, they require food to sustain and increase their living structures. Fish, unlike land animals, do not have solid support for their bodies and so cannot lie idle without effort or exertion. This problem is solved by a built-in system of bladders that enables fish to float and balance in the water. The more wide-ranging and active the fish, the larger the bladders. In quiet waters fishes would have little work to do to keep themselves motionless. But in all natural waters there are streaming, flowing currents. Every water-

Preceding pages: Life in stream begins with basic, unicellular organisms like Diatom Licmophora, here seen through microscope.

Raft of Culex eggs floats on surface.

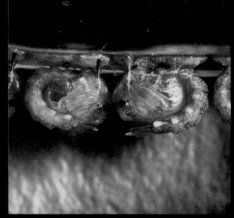

Hatching pupae hang from surface.

End result of above development is adult

Larva breathes with siphon-like tube.

Emerging adult drys on floating shell.
Culex mosquito with transparent wings.

course, whether creek or river, evokes resistance, work, expenditure of energy. So, to meet the energy demand, fish feed, and their food is turned into energy by the physical process of metabolism.

Animals of several groups or phyla are found in fresh water, but most of them are not suitable for fishes to eat because of their size (Rotifera, Protozoa), consistency (sponges), poisonous organs (Coelenterates), hidden parasitic characters (intestinal flatworms), or protective shells (Mollusca). No animal is actually designed by nature to serve as food, but the brutality of the struggle for existence condemns the weaker to be the prey of the stronger.

An understanding of the working of the ecosystem might best begin with the surface itself. The surface is actually a kind of "water skin" which is highly elastic. It is the result of the physical laws of cohesion, by which water molecules attract each other from all directions. At the surface there is no upward attraction to counterbalance the downward attraction and thus a film of molecules, each one fifty-five millionths of an inch in diameter, is formed. This feature is important to the life functions of the dwellers in that habitat, especially in the cycle of reproduction. It provides an anchorage for eggs and pupae. Again, at the stage when the adult is emerging, a pupa or nymph rises to the surface where molecular tension holds the splitting skin in position and prevents it from sinking while the insect is emerging.

Or consider the phenomenon of the mayfly spinner as she descends into the water to deposit eggs. She crawls beneath the water film but remains surrounded by a thin film of air. Creeping down a blade of vegetation, she lays her eggs and then releases her hold on the grass. The buoyant thrust of the surrounding air shoots her above the surface, as dry as if she had never submerged.

Another surface phenomenon is readily observable: According to the principle of adhesion, water molecules are attracted to a substance or organism; but if the body of an insect is covered with an infinitesimally thin layer of oil, it repels the molecules of the water film and the animal is thus enabled to walk or stand on the water's surface.

If pollutants or water scum are present on the surface, nature's wise protection of the animal world is endangered. When a nymph rises through a surface film that is polluted, debris clings to its thorax reducing its water-repelling property. When the adult emerges from the skin, debris wets its legs. After drying its newly-emerged wings, the insect is ready to fly away, but with water repellancy lost, it is unable to do so and perishes. (Dry-fly anglers know that a greased line sinks when the water surface is covered with scum.)

However, in unpolluted waters the life cycle goes on undisturbed and many of its activities are easily observed by the angler. As he learns and as he sharpens his naturalist's eye, the life network of the environment becomes more and more apparent to him. But he must turn to the scientist for many explanations, for example, about the microscopic beginnings of the food chain. What is eaten first?

The first link of the predatory chain is self-nourishing or autotrophic green plants. These range from microscopic algae, such as the unicellular diatoms and desmids, to grasses and trees. Microscopic doses of carbohydrates and fats accumulate inside microplants, turning them into pastures for microconsumers, such as the protozoans and microcrustaceans.

Next in the food chain of the angler's aquatic environment are the more complex plant-eaters. These include mosquito larvae and mayfly nymphs. They also include minute crustaceans like the planktonic copepods, feeders on microscopic vegetation. These are of enormous importance, for now the micronutrition is becoming sizable and can be consumed by many small animals. Newly born fishes swallow the small crustaceans; other animals consume them by suspension feeding, straining them out of the water in the breathing process.

Beyond the level of the herbivores are the smaller carnivores,

Hellgrammite

Dobsonfly adult

Stonefly nymph

Stonefly imago

Fish of the stream, such as Rocky Mountain Brook Trout below, feed on a variety of

Damselfly nymph

Caddisfly adult

Mayfly dun

Mayfly spinner

insect forms. Those above, in wide range of shapes, are prime sources of food.

which offer themselves in turn to the larger carnivores. Thus, directly or indirectly, the whole animal kingdom, from protozoa to fishes to man, feeds upon the plant world.

One particular link in the food chain—the relationship between the trout and its food—is of keenest importance to the fisherman, for, as any man who ever tied a lure knows well, angling success depends on getting the fish to bite. What follows is a scientist's description of the life phases of some important fish-food insects.

One of the most dramatic episodes in this feeding relationship happens in the spring of the year, with the hatching of the sub-adult mayflies, or duns. The angler sees a small break in the surface of the pool, with ripples forming around it. There is more agitation of the surface and the rings widen as a trout takes something from the surface and submerges again. A floating dun appears and in a short while the water's surface is sprinkled with duns, some violently fluttering, others standing motionless as the current takes them downstream. Trout are rising to snatch them from beneath and swifts are taking the glistening insects on the wing. The duns that complete their labored flight to the surrounding protective vegetation will survive, most of them, to attain the final, brief stage of life, during which they copulate, lay their eggs and die. When the trout are taking these mayfly duns, an angler will choose a fly similar in shape and color to the dun.

The abundant mayflies are only one source of food for trout. They belong to the very large group of joint-legged invertebrate animals called arthropods, of which large numbers of species have evolved every million years or so. This order, which includes the insect class, is dominant in the animal kingdom by reason of the number of species that belong to it and their distribution on all continents, in all bodies of fresh water, and in the seven seas. The insects are the most successful, diversified group of animals.

Trout feed on various aquatic arthropods: larval forms of many orders or groups, small crustaceans, and aquatic insects in full maturity. The aquatic insects show tremendous diversity in structure, habit, and adaptation to different environments. Whatever and wherever the habitat, there are insects to enrich it. Among those important to our fishing streams are the nymphs of the mayfly and stonefly, and the larvae of the dobsonfly, midge, and mosquito.

The often spectacular hatching and swarming of the mayflies is a visible manifestation of the life of the stream. This single phase is an illustration of the beauty of the ecosystem, its complexity and harmony, the working out of the harsh but provident laws of survival. It has attracted the interest of anglers and naturalists for centuries and, thanks to their investigations, we now know much of the life of the mayfly, whose likeness, fashioned of delicate feathers and wire, lies among the lures in every freshwater angler's tackle box.

The mayfly dun, which hatches from the nymph, is a stage of development apparently unique with the mayfly. It precedes the fully developed adult stage, though resembling it in many ways. The dun, like the adult, has two pairs of wings, the front pair much larger than the hind pair. It has a hard skin, however, and molts on becoming an adult, when it is called an imago or spinner.

Why the mayfly alone should have this special hard-shell, pre-adult stage is an interesting question. I believe it is a reminder of the gray beginnings, a relic of the far past. The Ephemeroptera, the order of short-lived insects to which the mayflies belong, evolved almost two hundred and fifty million years ago, during the Carboniferous period. It was a time of luxurious plant life and huge trees. There were giant dragonflies (twenty-five inch wingspread) and thousands of enormous insects—cockroaches, scorpions, centipedes, and spiders. Around the edges of water bodies colossal horsetails and primitive conifers with hard needles stood silently. An unfriendly, harsh environment for the slender tails and fragile bodies of the ephemeral insects! Delicate imagines that emerged directly from the nymphal stage perished easily in these conditions and only the pubescent forms protected by subimaginal cuticle survived.

However, in today's modified environment, the dun—the first winged stage of the mayfly—is a useless vestige. The hard cuticle is no longer functional. The stage lasts for a few days at most, in some species for only a few minutes. It is a time of relative inactivity during which the legs and tail filaments of the sub-adult grow to full length and the reproductive organs mature.

When the moment for shedding its skin arrives, the dun, on its leaf high in the sunny treetops, spreads its long forewings sideways. A split appears in the hard cuticle on the dorsal side of the thorax, extending forward to the head. Through this opening emerges the shiny spinner. Head first, it arches itself backward, pulling out of the shell, until only the tip of the abdomen remains in the case. Then it straightens out and with its long legs pulls itself entirely free, leaving the gauze-like exuvia adhering to the leaf. Now the mayfly has become a truly aerial insect.

With dusk approaching, the nuptial flight of the imagines begins. The delicate airborne males gather in swarms near the body of water where the inseminated females will lay their eggs. The pattern of this flight is most striking. Each spinner beats upward on his flashing wings, his long forelegs extended. Reaching the peak of his ascent, he floats down gently on open wings, swaying from side to side on the wind currents. The swarm is in perpetual motion, some spinners ascending, others descending.

Soon females appear flying in the swarm of males. A female chooses her mate by flying above him in the swarm. The male then approaches her from below and grasps her with his two elongate forelegs as he bends the end of his abdomen upward. Insemination takes place, the copulating pair float toward the ground. Before reaching either land or water, they separate.

The male is polygamous and returns to the swarm to continue the ritual dance. The gravid female flies to the water and zig-zags back and forth looking for a suitable place to lay her eggs. This she does in the manner proper to her species. She may submerge the end of her abdomen in the water and attach the eggs to a reed, a stone, or a rock. A spinner of the Grey Drake *Ephemera danica* presses the tip of her abdomen to the water and releases the egg batch. The British Sherry spinner, recently observed in Maine, merely touches the water surface in flight and drops the eggs which sink to the bottom.

With this act of producing her offspring, the female's life is exhausted. She joins the dead or dying spinners floating on the water, and the trout, as anglers know, rise quickly to this natural lure.

The eggs, however, have already begun their period of embryonic development. In some species they have intricate attachment organs: for example, a thread-like tail terminating in an adhesive knob, or an adhesive cap on the egg pole that anchors it securely to a rock.

As the eggs hatch, the prolonged nymphal stage begins. This can last two years or more, during which the nymph develops abdominal gills, compound eyes, and wing cases. The nymphs are herbivores that graze on algae such as diatoms and desmids. As they grow, they go through many successive moltings necessitated by the fact that the skin of the nymph hardens on exposure to air and water; growth goes on under this cuticle, eventually causing it to split. After casting off the old skin, the nymph emerges colorless and transparent, but with exposure the skin will harden and darken again. The stages between moltings of the nymph are called instars and, according to the species, they vary in number from eleven to twenty-three before the dun stage is finally reached. Such is the life of the mayfly nymph in its two or three years underwater.

When the moment for the hatching of the dun approaches, the nymph swims to the surface of the water. Here molecular tension of the surface film steadies the splitting thorax and prevents it from sinking. The dun struggles to free itself and soon a shining winged creature, long-legged and fragile, is fluttering on the water. Instinctively it takes to toilsome flight, making for the vegetation on the bank, where shortly the final stage of metamorphosis will take place.

Throughout this transformation from nymph to airborne dun, the insect is prey first to trout, then to birds. But it is one of the countless number of its kind and, whether it lives to reproduce itself or is eaten before its natural term, it carries out the harmony of the ecosystem. For no single link in the food chain stands alone. The trout and the insects they eat are not an independent relationship of predator to prey, but rather integrated parts of a great whole. They are influenced by the conditions of their environment, but they also create and change their circumstances and surroundings, affecting both the other living organisms and the nonliving elements present.

The river offers an endless variety of ecological habitats. In the quick flowing water of the rapids, in the still water of the reed beds are hundreds of niches providing food and shelter. And in all these places dwell other organisms that are important sources of food for fish.

Fish flies, a common term for insects that have aquatic larvae, include the large dobsonfly, whose imagines are seen making awkward flights along the margins of streams. Dobsonfly larvae, or hellgrammites, as they are called, are important trout food.

A very common inhabitant of all kinds of water places are mosquito larvae. Known as "wrigglers," they are a staple item in the diet of trout and other fishes. The main hatch of mosquitoes takes place between morning and mid-day. The pupae ascend to the surface and hang there suspended while the mosquitoes emerge from their skins. During this phase they are fed upon avidly by trout swimming near the surface.

Anglers are exposed to mosquito bites because of the aquatic life of the larvae of the subfamily Culicinae, the "true" mosquitoes. The chief groups are the tribes Culicini and Anophelini, and there are important differences between these biters. The larvae of Culicines hang head downward from the water surface while those of Anophelines lie parallel just below the surface. The Culicines larvae respire by sucking air through a siphon-like tube. Mosquito eggs deposited on the surface assume characteristic patterns. Culex eggs are laid on the water in raft-like masses. The egg of an Anopheline resembles a boat, whose stability is increased by a pair of lateral floats centrally located.

The angler can easily distinguish these species. When standing or sucking blood, the Culicine female holds her body parallel to the surface and her beak points downward from her head. The Anopheline female points her head and proboscis in a straight line toward the surface with her abdomen pointing away from it.

Chironomidae midges, like mosquitoes, are widely distributed in all fresh waters and serve as food for the young trout. Their larvae live in tubes attached to stones. Some species are red owing to the presence of hemoglobin dissolved in the blood plasma, and thus their name "blood worms." To feed, mosquito and midge larvae sweep tiny plants and plant-animals, protozoa, desmids and diatoms into their mouths. Despite the huge number and minute size of the insect larvae on which trout feed, we should not forget that they are living animals, complexly built with well developed nervous systems.

These basic facts of the ecosystem sometimes come as a revelation to the angler. As close as he is to the life of the stream, the fisherman who is not also a naturalist can live his entire life without an insight into the facts and mysteries of aquatic life. Thus the pleasure of fishing remains but a fraction of what it might be. It is for the angler-naturalist to enjoy fishing in the way described by Sir Henry Wotton, a seventeenth-century poet and diplomat, who said, "Fishing is to the angler a rest to his mind, a cheerer of his spirit, a diverter of sadness, a moderator of passions and a calmer of unquiet thoughts." The angler sees the sky reflected in the water, the trees along the river, birds, fishes, heaven and earth. If this is his world to enjoy and to understand, his also is the battle to save our great heritage and to preserve the living waters. ◉

Secret Life of the Southwest

In an adaptation from his extraordinary and successful
book, The Hunter's World, the author reveals
the many dimensions of a harsh yet bountiful environment.

by Charles F. Waterman / photography by Bill Browning

Nothing moves but a black speck of a vulture and the writhing heat waves. The vulture is high over the immense Sonoran Desert, and the heat waves distort the entire shimmering sweep of sand and cactus as if the whole scene were burning from below. At midday the distant saguaro cactus plants, some of them almost fifty feet high, appear to be involved in a wriggling dance, their upthrust arms adding to the rippling delusion of the mirage.

It is cooler up where the buzzard makes drowsy turns and it is cooler in the shade of conifer forests visible on distant mountains, but the desert floor is frying hot—so hot that many of its thousands of residents would die in minutes if they left their shady nooks and burrows. The desert's nighttime legions are silent at midday, and even the day shift pauses at this hottest of all times. Among the desert's countless unseen residents are more reptiles than in the rest of the United States combined—including about a hundred and seventy kinds of snakes. The game is varied, often plentiful, but nearly always hard-earned, ranging from mule and whitetail deer in the brushy arroyos to desert bighorns in the broken heaps of dry mountains. There are four kinds of quail, three species in huntable numbers. There is the javelina, or collared peccary, and there are doves, both

*Near right: Cholla, bristling
with thorns, abounds in some areas
where scaled quail are hunted.
Spiny plants are hazardous obstacles
for man or dog, but provide
roosts and food for many birds. Far
right, from top: roadrunner
hunting lizards; saguaro fruit, eaten
by most herbivorous birds and
animals in arid country; scaled quail,
also called blue quail or "cottontop";
and close view of scaled quail
breast plumage, which explains name.*

mourning and white-winged, that twist through the passes on softly whistling wings. But few of these things are likely to be seen or heard when the desert is hottest.

Much of the Sonoran Desert is in Mexico and it forms a border for the Gulf of California. It comprises much of Arizona, a little of Nevada, and part of California. To the west is the Mojave —similar but with a different plant and animal population. To the east is the Chihuahuan Desert, taking in eastern Arizona and much of New Mexico. All are part of the American Southwest, a region barricaded from rain-bearing ocean winds by the high coastal ranges. These arid and semiarid lands appear harsh, and they are harsh, yet they teem with a secret life, and for the hunter who is familiar with their ecology they hold an incredible bounty.

The Sonoran Desert contains one hundred and twenty thousand square miles within a ragged outline, invaded on the edges by higher land where the ecology changes abruptly and where there are islands of irrigation or forested mountains. "Desert" has varying meanings; the game biologist thinks in terms of vegetation, others consider total annual rainfall. There are deserts of empty sands and deserts of lush vegetation. There are oases and water holes in the desert that bring together resi-

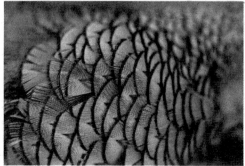

Right: Author's Brittany points Gambel's quail concealed in typical cover. This brushy area produced large coveys of both Gambel's and blue quail. Below, from left: Gambel's cock, his jaunty topknot quivering, chooses to run rather than fly from intrusion; four Gambel's quail hide under low vegetation; desert tortoise crawls slowly over sand; and great horned owl watches for prey.

dents of the dehydrated land—predator and prey—in a cautious truce.

The true desert has specialized vegetation. Annual flowers are short-lived opportunists that flash in brilliant colors after the winter rains and then fade immediately to shriveled monotones. Ocotillo plants, some of them two hundred years old, look like dead, thorny sticks in dry periods, then quickly grow tiny leaves when rain comes. The cacti have pleats, folds, and knobs to hold moisture, and can expand when rain does come.

At dawn the birds move freely, even in hot weather. A Gambel's quail covey, wearing military plumes, spreads in quick-changing formations and marches relentlessly upon insects and food plants. During the night the birds roosted in bushes or cacti. Before noon they will rest again in the shade along a desert wash that has been cut by flash floods but is now a dry roadway with flowing sand sculptures left by sweeping brown torrents long subsided. A roadrunner, comic relief in a harsh land, watches for lizards, walking alertly, head forward, and making tentative little half-runs, ready to go at full speed if he surprises a small lizard engrossed in insect hunting.

A cactus wren rustles busily among murderous cholla cactus barbs, and a loggerhead shrike plans the crucifixion

66

Below right: Water hole has produced oasis, excellent location for hunting Mearns', or harlequin, quail. Top, from left: Cluster of pincushion cactus which, like barrel cactus and other globular species, holds much precious water; black vulture, at rest after scavenging foray; sycamore tree, offering roosts and food for birds, browse for animals; and distinctively marked male harlequin quail.

of any tiny creature it can catch, having ample choice of thorns for the most ambitious impalement. A coyote drifts through the mesquite, bound for daytime rest in a shadowed spot that will catch any vagrant midday breeze. He will not hunt again until nightfall. His prey, the jack rabbit, will take to a shaded "form," or "squat," during the hot hours.

Farther down the life scale, the diamondback rattler and the sidewinder make final forays for mice and rats before leaving the sunlight. Already most of the smaller rodents are underground for the day. A chuckwalla lizard moves about for buds or blossoms but stays close to its rock crevice, for it cannot survive long in the open sun.

Ground squirrels are busy, especially before the full midday heat, and a horned toad sits smugly at the entrance to an anthill, greeting the hapless residents with a busy tongue. A herd of grunting, chomping collared peccaries may be eating anything from prickly pear to bull snakes, although if man is near they may feed mostly at night. The peccary usually takes first order at the water holes, and hunters quickly become familiar with their tiny, round hoofmarks and the shredded prickly pear left along their route. They seem to use their musk glands, located on their backs, as trail markers, rubbing

*Near right: High, arid
Arizona canyon, choked with brush,
cactus, and jumbled rocks,
is good habitat for rugged bighorn
sheep. Animals find sufficient
food here and can go without
water during long dry periods. Far
right, from top: collared
lizard dwelling in canyon; saltbush,
which is nutritious food
for sheep; bighorn ram, ewe, and
kid; and close view of ram's
head, displaying impressive curl.*

the strong scent onto overhanging branches as they go. Although the subject of many lurid tales, the javelina is aggressive toward man only to the extent of some ferocious tusk clicking. They can be dangerous when half-tamed or when wounded, but a Central American species, the white-lipped peccary, is much more aggressive. In most of its range the javelina is now classified as a game animal. Many hunters consider its meat to be as tasty as that of the larger wild boar.

The buzzard, riding his high thermals, will see little movement from midmorning until late afternoon but as the sudden dusk arrives, the desert's occupants begin to whistle, squeak, and cluck; crawl, run, and flutter. The little rodents leave their burrows in jerky darts, the skunks move about, engaged in seemingly unplanned hunting. As the stars come on, appearing very near in the clear, cooling air, the coyote pauses at the edge of a shrubby arroyo and gives a rising wail that shatters into brittle barks. Mule deer move slowly toward a water hole, browsing as they go. Horned owls hunt as silent, uncertain shapes against the stars, and the little elf owls go abroad for smaller game.

Upland gunners seldom visit the desert until the heat of summer has gone. They may shoot whitewings and mourning doves in early fall and hunt

for deer in early November, while those who work dogs, searching for quail, prefer the pleasant weather of very late fall and early winter.

Mule deer are found all across the desert, frequently moved from the ravines by horsemen, foot hunters, or four-wheel-drive vehicles, and are usually seen at fairly long range. The little southwestern deer known as the Coues whitetail slips along with fine stealth and when alarmed rarely exhibits the ridge-top gawking habits of the muley. Generally, the whitetails live fairly near evergreen forests and the higher mountains. They are rifleman's game, seen best with a four-power or stronger scope. The little buck, moved from his bed among yucca and mesquite, runs a broken pattern along the canyon's side, and the rifleman feels urgently for a place to sit on the rocky slope. He knows he must have a firm base for his shooting, but despite the risk of landing on prickly pear or cholla balls, he is unwilling to take his eyes from his flickering target. Through the scope he can see the small antlers, probably no more than a fuzzy, moving shadow above the game, yet if his seat is steady, and his elbows braced on knees, he may be able to track the target through the barrel cacti, the mesquite, the yucca, and the dozens of other prickly and scratching plants that somehow do not harm the speeding whitetail.

In early December I halted at an Arizona highway rest stop and allowed my Brittany spaniel to stretch his legs. We were on our way to a desert bird hunt, a new experience for both, and my first identification was uncertain when I heard the piping calls of Gambel's quail on the adjoining cactus flat. But the dog quartered along the rest-stop fence, making game, and I lifted him over. By the time I had scaled the fence myself he had disappeared in barrel cactus, prickly pear, and gleaming cholla clumps. I heard the quail twittering as they moved away unseen, apparently going fast, and then they suddenly became silent. Sure that the dog had pinned the covey, I picked my way after him, mincing to avoid the thorns in my traveling clothes, and found him, not a rigid statue but a pathetic brindle heap, fettered into immobility by

great balls of cholla cactus which he had tried to remove with his mouth. I carried him to the car for a terrible fifteen minutes' work with pliers. I felt certain he would never learn to hunt in the desert, though he had performed admirably in every other kind of terrain that holds upland birds. But two days later he was moving smoothly on the arroyo slopes, coming to me promptly when he collected a stray thorn. His adaptation was quick and almost perfect.

Many dog owners would never hunt cactus country, but I am convinced most dogs will learn the desert's painful lessons quickly. None can always avoid the thorns, and perhaps a wide-ranging pointer should be curbed, but most dogs can work a lifetime in the desert without serious harm.

Gambel's quail, like the scaled quail, will run long distances if cover is skimpy, as it is in much arid country. Even where cover is heavy, the initial flush is likely to be out of range—and sometimes the birds must be pushed hard to fly them at all. Once they have flushed they seldom land in compact groups; individual birds may drop to choice hiding spots, and a covey may scatter widely with individuals holding tightly. A jaunty plume and long tail make the Gambel's appear longer than its actual size, which is nearly that of a bobwhite. It is blended tones of brown and gray with a chestnut crown.

East of Phoenix, we put two dogs into mountainous desert vegetation dominated by saguaro cactus, and followed them into a brushy draw of scrub oak and mountain mahogany. In half an hour, they were on game, moving on a single stratum of the arroyo bank, with birds obviously advancing ahead of them. Here we tried to read their actions, knowing it was unlikely that an unbroken covey would be found under a classic point. The Gambel's broke cover too far ahead to shoot and skimmed the brush tops, fanning out a little as they went over the arroyo bank some hundred and fifty yards away, dropping from sight almost immediately in a low forest of scrub oak. I was with a veteran desert quail hunter who climbed the ridge and guessed the area in which they would put down. Now, he said, we would have some shooting. So we went into another draw two hundred yards from the original flushing site, and both dogs pointed in the thickest cover of the entire depression—facing in opposite directions.

As I walked in, I heard a whir of flight behind me and found myself in the leaden-armed slow motion of the gunner with a surprise target in a surprise direction. It was a dark bird against dark vegetation, scaling the steep slope at what seemed incredible speed as I tried to push my unwilling gun muzzles to cover it in a ragged, forced swing. Somehow I caught the bird in the skimpy edge of the pattern; it was a poor hit but my first Gambel's quail was down and found by a quick dog. The covey was scattered, scent was confused, and the dogs pointed constantly. Only a few birds were exactly where the dogs indicated, but they were close enough for shooting singles and doubles in all directions. One bird flushed would start a chain reaction and others would break out of nearby bushes. Calmer now, I estimated they were somewhat slower than bobwhites, flew with slower wingbeats, and made less noise. But they could be missed for several reasons. They often took off at long range and the course of single birds was unpredictable. It was later in my first day's hunting that I learned of their pattern of driving down steep slopes.

On the crest of a long ridge where vegetation was very thin we saw a quail moving ahead of us, tall with its neat plume, looking back as it moved in a sequence of short runs and pauses. When that bird had disappeared in cover we saw a second quail, also moving swiftly, then a third much closer to us—sure signs that an entire covey was moving. Our dogs followed them hesitantly, trying to point but sensing the changing patterns of scent, and we hurried, hoping to fly the birds before they could slip away. Yet somehow they seemed to soak into the ground like a desert shower. Only two flew, swinging out of range to one side and coasting on set wings into a canyon. The running birds had tolled us away from our planned hunting route, so we retraced our steps, the dogs uncertain and glancing back for instructions. We flushed the lost covey by accident, without their help.

It was probably a young and weak-willed little cock bird that flew first from the base of a yucca, unnerved by our return after we had passed him once. He drove noisily downward over a small cliff. As the speeding betrayer dove past a canyon niche, a second bird flushed. Then the ridge was alive with muttering wings, some fifty Gambel's going down headlong, scattered at first but bunching as they went. Another covey roared from the slope, and two more came from somewhere else, tight wads of birds against the low sun—more than a hundred in all. As they neared the canyon's bottom they spread out again, and chose individual landing spots. In less than a minute their reunion calls came up faintly.

The slope was steep and treacherous with weather-rounded rocks. We climbed down awkwardly and I involuntarily put out a hand for the support of a barrel cactus, then jerked it back. The birds called intermittently. A dog turned abruptly and his game flushed before he could point properly. My companion fired and the bird disappeared, a dark blob lost in tangled brush, leaving a few feathers settling in the still air only inches above the cover. The quail was found after frustrated canine sniffing and a scratchy expedition into the thicket. By then hours of sun had dried the desert air, leaving bird scent a will-o'-the-wisp, and the dogs stared stupidly when close-holders flushed unpointed. One bird left almost at my feet and I came up deliberately for a straightaway shot, but he curved back of a huge saguaro cactus and never appeared again until he was a hundred yards in the distance.

A few miles away we hunted scaled quail—also called blue quail, or "cottontops"—in sparser cover. It is the cover that dictates quail behavior. With poor hiding a quail chooses to run from danger and the scalie does it well. Most frequently the scaled quail is a streaking little blue-gray ghost, scooting with his friends through miniature avenues between prickly pear and thin grass clumps. In desert country the paths are essential—spacings demanded by plants that must divide scant water and require plenty of room for their root systems. Thus, what appears from a distance to be a thicket is split by lanes which are traveled by quail at darting speed.

The scaled quail ranges farther north than the Gambel's and is found in much of the Great Plains as well as in the desert. The topknot is whitish, the overall color gray-blue with scalelike markings. Its habits are almost—not quite—the same as those of the Gambel's, and it runs as well. A cautious dog may follow scooting birds, unable either to pin or flush them, and many are shot running, a system sometimes as difficult as gunning them in the air. Like other runners, cottontops may break up their covey as they race, birds fanning out to take individual hideouts—and the dog's pursuit may end with the scent lost or a single bird flying where a dozen were expected.

With both dog and hunter somewhat subdued, it may be wise to go back the way the covey came and look for single quail. At this point they may hold tightly and give good shooting. There is another system—an undignified sprint after the runners—recommended for the athletic hunter. If he can gain enough ground before tripping over a cactus or running out of wind, he can make them fly, but he must be able to regain his composure instantly if he is to hit anything. Birds will often flush behind him or all around him, but seldom where expected.

In the air the scaled quail has a trait or two of its own. Generally it goes higher than the Gambel's. Computations of "average" covey flights are endless, but two hundred yards might be nearly correct. If a covey spreads out the singles may hold; if it lands in a tight pod they may run with a ground speed only a little less than their air speed. If the cover is thick, the hunter's chances are better. The procedure may change slightly with different types of terrain, but the birds can be hunted with a dog, and sometimes they will hold beautifully.

Since the desert is open country, many a hunter swears by a full-choked gun, although the best choice of all might be a double providing improved cylinder and full choke—a scarce article but available from custom makers. An impatient perfectionist could choose a light factory double, bored modified and full, or full and full, and have one barrel reamed to improved cylinder. One barrel will then give him the wide pattern needed for close, sometimes unexpected shots, while the other will provide the choke needed for longer range.

Going south from Tucson toward the Mexican border, we watched the arid landscape change to grassy hills in winter tan, spotted with green clumps of trees and patches of bear grass. In the distance the mountains rose abruptly. Above 3,500 feet we were out of the true desert, although many such highlands are simply considered a part of the desert community.

We were in another quail country, the grassland of the harlequin, or Mearns', quail which inhabit the border country and farther south and are virtually unknown to American sportsmen, but beloved by a few who use bobwhite methods to hunt them. These birds behave remarkably like bobwhites among live oak trees resembling those of the bobwhite's own southland. Arizona's Mearns' season opens at the beginning of December, a fact little advertised by those who hunt a rather rare bird in very limited surroundings. The grasses are high, knee-high in most of the habitat and up to a man's shoulders in some places. These grasses include a variety of plants, but grama grasses are dominant and the lower stems are separated enough that a gaudy little bird can move among them comfortably and unseen.

There was little standing water in the creek beds. The draw where we camped carried a sandy wash with desert willows along the edges. There were boulders on the grassy banks of dozens of small arroyos that branched from wider canyons. Small live oaks were scattered over the entire landscape, furnishing acorns in good years for industriously foraging quail. When the unpredictable mast crop fails, the harlequins live largely on tubers and bulbs. Chufas are listed as a mainstay and the birds are equipped with very long claws for serious

Author moves in as dog goes on point (above) in high grass near live oaks—fine habitat for Mearns' quail. Desert willow (far left) is also favored by birds. Mourning dove (left) provides early fall gunning in parts of Southwest.

digging. Fresh excavations are much like those made by gray squirrels—a miniature of the javelina's rooting.

We saw English pointers, German shorthairs, Brittanys, and Weimaraners in Mearns' country. One of the dogs we used was a harlequin specialist —a leggy Brittany with a bell, a serious fellow who checked all members of his hunting party regularly and dropped instantly to low gear when he approached a wash where the grass was a little higher or a spot where the fallen top of a dead tree formed a thick shelter. The dog pointed on a hillside where the stand of grass was broken by some small erosions, and I got a glimpse of a harlequin cock with striped head and polka-dot breast. Like bobwhite, the Mearns' is supposed to hold tightly for a dog but often doesn't. We walked out through fifty yards of grass, then heard him fly somewhere in the thick scrub oaks.

One covey held in waist-high grass on the shoulder of a ravine and waited until I was in its midst before buzzing up around me and bulleting into the oaks, followed by two shots that were too hasty to be effective.

When one of the dogs disappeared and his bell fell silent I found him pointing in grass that completely concealed him. Inches from his nose, the single quail bored straight up to clear the grass, leveling out at a little more than head height in a whirring drive for the trees. I managed to wait until the last moment, fired as the bird disappeared, and would not have known it was a hit but for a few feathers that blew clear of the branches.

South of the border the Mearns' lives in still higher country, on 10,000-foot plateaus where a hunter's breath comes short. In the grass country there is little of the hostile vegetation found on the desert floor, but there is scattered prickly pear. This is all coyote country, just as the true desert is. The Southwest was an original home of the

coyote, a species that has spread rather than contracted its range under human pressures. The little wolves are now found from Florida to Alaska, but the greatest numbers still inhabit the deserts and plains. A good varmint caller is likely to have quick success near the Mexican border. While coyotes may kill an occasional game bird, rabbits and small rodents are their chief prey in desert country. In addition to coyotes, a true wolf now and then wanders up from Mexico, but neither the coyote nor the wolf threatens the survival of any southwestern wildlife.

Of all the game of the Southwest none is so prized by the trophy hunter as the desert bighorn sheep, once found in great herds, later reduced almost to extinction, and now brought back to barely huntable numbers through expensive management. Historically the desert sheep grazed the river bottoms, easily hunted by pioneers, and it was the dwindling bands of sheep that fed the stage

stations. Long after sheep hunting was declared illegal, prospectors and settlers killed the animals for food. Where sheep frequented water holes, market hunters built blinds to ambush rams and ewes alike. Survivors moved to the steepest mountains, where they are found today, viewed with mixed feelings by game biologists who question the large expenditures put into sheep management for painfully slow results. Nevertheless, management has been sufficiently successful for the restoration of legal hunting this time on a carefully controlled basis. Although hungry settlers and market hunters no longer pose a threat, areas habitable by the sheep now face other menaces, such as proliferating highways, spreading cities, and domestic livestock that compete with the bighorns.

The yearning of trophy hunters to achieve a "grand slam"—that is, to take each of the four types of American sheep listed in the record books—has made the desert bighorn a disproportionately de-

Desert cottontail (above) is sought by gray hawk (far right) and other predators, such as coyotes. Wild marigold (right) and similar flowers bloom quickly after rainy spell.

sirable trophy. A hunter who has collected the other three (Dall, Stone, and Rocky Mountain bighorn) often will classify the desert sheep as his most difficult challenge. Only a few desert-bighorn permits are drawn for harvest of mature rams, and hunters are carefully briefed. In Nevada, permit-holders must undergo a course in identification so that only older rams, true trophies, will be killed. A dummy sheep, exhibited at considerable distance, is fitted with legal and then illegal horns, and the sportsman must learn to make a quick estimation of the curl.

The hunt itself involves a great deal of scoping and study of terrain before the hard climbing begins. Yet some hunters have complained that their guides lacked experience and expertise (an obvious possibility, since only a few permits are issued and a guide can't generally make a career of hunting desert sheep). On the other hand, some guides have complained—with justification— that a hunter who has waited years for a permit and is now on an expensive trip may feel the completion

of his grand slam is merely a detail to be accomplished with dispatch.

Accounts differ as to the actual difficulty of hunting the rams. Perhaps it is a matter of hunting pressure, for some naturalists say the desert sheep is easily stalked; yet some sportsmen list it as the hardest of all American game to hunt. Certainly hunting is likely to be rigorous in a strange habitat of thorns and jagged rocks. Climbing can be dangerous. There is little desert-sheep country that can be penetrated on horseback, and water will be scarce. Stones may be treacherously slick or may crumble dangerously underfoot.

But curiosity has killed many desert rams. Mexicans are said to attract them by dragging tin cans behind a truck, and hunters who have stalked silently to near where a hidden trophy is known to be bedded may get a shot by luring the animal out of concealment with a judiciously rolled pebble.

A desert ram is likely to be smaller and somewhat paler in color than his more northern relatives, seldom weighing as much as two hundred pounds. He is well camouflaged and is the hardest to see of all the American wild sheep. The horns are nearly as large as those of the Rocky Mountain bighorn. A desert sheep will appear leaner and more muscular. This uniquely adapted animal can go indefinitely without drinking any free water, getting survival moisture from vegetation. Even when water holes are filled, a desert bighorn might drink only once a week. Biologists who have observed the sheep at water holes say that they may appear emaciated after days of abstinence, but fill out visibly as their dried tissues absorb liquid. The animals actually change appearance in minutes. It is the key to desert life—the ability to endure long waits for water and then make thorough use of it when it comes. When there is no free water, sheep take liquid from barrel cactus or saguaro cactus, and a trophy's horns may show scarred and flattened surfaces caused by years of butting over cactus as well as rutting combat. A mounted head may still have cactus thorns imbedded in its corrugations. The upper lip, thickly calloused, seems impervious to any real damage from the thorns.

On the deserts of the Southwest the sheep accommodates its range to a variety of plant life, although the general environment invariably includes tumbled stone, crumbling precipices, and violent weather. In Nevada, the sheep are found primarily in the higher-altitude fringes of Joshua trees and sometimes near ponderosa pines and piñon-juniper growth, but in the lower mountains the animals appear in small and scattered bands where there are no trees at all. The habitat in southern Arizona and western Mexico is shrubby, with paloverde, bear grass, cacti, and sunflower perennials. Like other wild sheep, the desert bighorn prefers grass but will make do with shrubs

When rain comes to the desert it is often spotty as the clouds may have crossed the western mountains ahead of freak winds. Although sheep migrations are generally local, bighorns will appear in numbers on a mountain that has greened up after a local shower.

Lambs are usually born in late winter and early spring, the occurrence fitting desert rain schedules.

This is usually a time of new plant growth, when the desert is on its best behavior. Lamb mortality, adjusted to a range that can support only a small population, is high. While the ewes endeavor to bring their youngsters through a crucial period the rams wander in small groups with an economy of activity. Then, with the rut of early fall, they burn up their hard-earned fat in head-on battles.

Natural competitors for food are of only minor importance—mainly deer, rabbits, and rodents. Domestic livestock has a greater effect, and the wild horses, goats, and burros, castoffs of civilization, use much of the sheep's forage.

There are, of course, desert sheep in Mexico, and otherwise conscientious American sportsmen have sometimes laid elaborate, frequently illegal, schemes for hunting them. Despite the danger of arrest, such practices are encouraged by hints that museum permits can be obtained in Mexico through the proper distribution of "tips." Hunters who are attracted by this prospect might do well to reflect that, in the short time between the giving of a gratuity and the killing of a sheep, local authorities can change their minds and local political situations can also change.

Where hunting and land-use regulations are properly enforced—as they generally are in the American Southwest—wildlife is likely to prosper. The Desert National Wildlife Range in southern Nevada is typically desert in its terraced life zones and thriving, if largely unseen, population. Its busy community lives by the harsh desert rules, and correspondingly there is one very significant man-made regulation for the annual sheep hunt. It proclaims that "camping within a half mile of any spring or water source or the use of any water source for watering horses is prohibited." A reasonable law in a region that sometimes appears desolate, yet is capable—if unmolested—of supporting a secret, teeming array of life.

Man may explore this seemingly brutal ecosystem, and he may even enter as a self-restrained predator without damaging it. But if it is to be preserved he must not interfere with the forces that infuse life into an arid land. ◎

muskeg, meadowland,

forest, moose and caribou

A sophisticated hunter considers the ways to stalk the fine game animals of his well-loved Newfoundland. Text and photography by Lee Wulff

Early October found us in the field, on the Middle Ridge country, lying halfway southward from Gander to the south coast of Newfoundland. Our tent was pitched beside a small lake, actually a long piece of "steady" water in a stream's slow flow from the high, barren country toward the sea. A seaplane had brought us in and a seaplane would take us out. Our canoe was up and overturned on the shore.

As often happens on the first night in camp, we ate bacon and beans. Every meal from then on that didn't include fresh meat would be an added incentive to hunt harder. It's possible now to bring in steaks, but for an old-timer part of the fun is eating the simple, well-remembered foods of the days when the only way to reach the caribou country was to pack in and carry food that didn't require refrigeration.

As we came in we had looked down from the plane at the mixture of meadows, muskeg, lakes, barrens, and timber surrounding us. Newfoundland is an island about the size of the state of Pennsylvania lying sixty miles northeast of Nova Scotia and eleven miles southeast of Labrador, forming the eastern shore of the Gulf of St. Lawrence. Because it is an island its animal species are limited. It has caribou, Arctic hare, lynx, otters, foxes, and beavers, but never a skunk, woodchuck, mink, squirrel, or ruffed grouse. It has salmon and squaretailed trout but lacks pike and lake trout.

Some ten thousand years ago, when the most recent glacial coating finally receded, it scoured the southern slopes and left only a sparse covering on the more slowly melting slopes that drained to the north. As a result, the warmer southern coast, where the sea does not freeze, is relatively barren, while the northwestern and northeastern sides of the island, where the ocean does freeze in winter, are comparatively well-timbered. A long range of mountains, with tops always less than three thousand feet, runs along the island's western side and is made up of either bare rock or timber. The heart of the island, lying to the east, is a mixture of barrens, muskeg, and rocky land covered with low bushes, glades, meadows, and patches of timber. Until this century, the Newfoundlanders sailed along and settled on the coasts only. Except for logging out the island's big white pines and killing off, to a man, the Beothuk Indians, they left the interior of the island to the hunters and trappers.

The early hunters who penetrated the area numbered the caribou at half a million. From their camps, at the times of the migrations, they watched herd follow herd for day after day. Then, at the turn of the century, a narrow-gauge railroad was built on a five-hundred-mile northerly loop across the island from Port-aux-Basques, the year-round port nearest Nova Scotia, eastward to St. John's. As the great migrating herds crossed the railroad in spring and fall, hunters killed them, and their numbers dwindled. By 1923 they were faced with extinction. The season was closed, and no caribou were legally killed until 1937, when a very limited number of licenses was issued.

Lee Wulff fires,
sighting in rifle that
later will kill
fine Newfoundland caribou
stag. Below: Bull
moose crashes his way
to forest freedom

The caribou came back, but their resurgence brought them face to face with a changed countryside. The snowshoe rabbits, or varying hare, introduced before the turn of the century, had spread to every corner of the island. The moose, starting from an introduction in 1904, were spreading, too, browsing along behind the loggers of two great pulp-and-paper mills whose timber rights blanketed the island.

The northern summer is incredibly lush. The days are long with sun and rich with moisture. Shrubs blossom on every soil-filled crevice in the rocks. In every meadow grass grows deep. Then there's food in plenty for countless moose and caribou, but when winter sweeps down from the Arctic, and snow stills and blankets the growing things, there comes the stark reality of bare survival.

Both male and female caribou wear antlers. Some claim this is because the female as well as the male needs brow horns to brush away the snow from the nourishing caribou moss, while the antlers of other deer serve only the male's fighting need. The horns of the doe caribou are small and usually "spikey," while those of the stag are heavy and broadly branched. A distinguishing sign during the early season is the white neck ruff of the male, showing clearly against his brownish coat. Later on in the season, as the caribou's coat becomes lighter, the contrast between neck color and body color lessens. As snow time approaches, the entire coat of both sexes slowly changes toward a uniform creamy gray, much the color of the big lichen-clad rocks that are remnants of the glacial drifts. With his fine coat and graceful carriage—he runs with the stateliness of a pacing horse—the caribou is a strikingly beautiful animal. It takes an exceptionally big caribou stag to weigh four hundred pounds on the hoof; a large doe will go two-thirds as much. A big bull moose will go over a thousand pounds with cows sometimes more than six hundred and fifty.

Moose are essentially animals of the timber, big enough to browse high and survive when the snow is deep. The forests are their homeland and their safety, but they have other, lesser loves. Water attracts them, not only with its rich edge growth of grasses and bushes, but with the roots and stems of water lilies that are favorite foods in summer and fall.

Moose may sometimes travel the highest ridges where caribou moss is plentiful and the shrubs and grass that moose feed on are rare, indeed. In the deepest woods a caribou may still find food, for Newfoundland's forests are broken by wild fields, barren ridges, lakes, swamps, and areas of muskeg. Both animals swim amazingly well and tend to cross water rather than take a long way around, and both travel bog and muskeg with ease. The hoofs of a caribou are designed to spread on soft ground and stay contracted on hard terrain. While moose are basically animals of the forest and caribou animals of the open country and the forest fringes that edge it, there is no spot in Newfoundland's wilds where either animal might not be encountered. They have different survival foods and the limited populations there now can share the island.

Hunting a moose in timber is a tough proposition. He moves like a shadow; in spite of his spreading horns, he travels between the tree trunks with little or no difficulty. His hearing is better than man's and his sense of smell is as acute as that of a whitetail deer. In the mottled light and dull background of the forest he's almost impossible to see and stalk. His speed, when he really turns it on, seems to rival that of a race horse, and the sloppy, swampy country that he travels in minutes can take a man several hours to traverse.

When he moves out of the forest into the

grassy glades or open country, or into the lakes or slow streams, he's quite conspicuous because of his huge bulk. Most stalking hunters seek him there. On the waterways or in the grassy wild meadows or brush-covered barrens, the hunter's chances are good. He may laze along in a canoe scanning the shores, or he may climb to look out over the open country and locate moose with the help of binoculars. Like all animals the moose develops habit patterns of rest and feeding when not disturbed by the rut. Usually he stays within an area of only a few miles and will tend, under similar wind and weather conditions, to reappear in a favored area day after day.

The bull moose has one weakness that hunters may take advantage of. He falls in love easily. When the rut is on, he's fairly likely to respond to any sound that even remotely resembles the call of a lovesick cow or the challenge of another bull. If he's lonely he'll come toward the call, which most guides make by grunting through a birch-bark horn. He may come rushing up, throwing caution to the wind. More often he'll come quietly, pausing to listen and scent the air. If the calls are good and the hunter's hideout well chosen, the odds are long against the moose. It is, incidentally, an unforgettable thrill if, by chance, the unsuspecting hunter finds himself in the path of a rutting moose, and sees the big bull suddenly materialize, moving toward him and towering over him, antlers looming and eyes flashing, red and wild. In this circumstance men have let their guns fall to the ground; some have climbed trees and been proud later of their presence of mind. However, in spite of their orneriness in rut, moose are rarely dangerous. These animals have developed a fear of man which can be counted on to make them stop short of contact. The rule is that a man who stands his ground is safe.

Caribou in rut are much more cautious. They do not love and leave; they collect and cherish their does.

Newfoundland's caribou country in its purest sense is the open, high plateau. The Middle Ridge is such a place. Standing on a hilltop there a hunter can see to the horizons. The land wrinkles like a great spread of rawhide draped and weathered on an uneven floor. A few patches of timber are black accents on a general pattern of red, yellow, brown, and caribou gray. One can sit on such a vantage point for hours knowing that most successful caribou hunters spend a good deal of time on lookouts, sweeping the surrounding country with binoculars. Six-power magnification is good; eight is better, if the hands are steady.

The hunter spotting a moving animal at a distance must stalk. He must estimate the course and intercept the caribou, unless by rarest chance it comes directly to him. To look at a point a mile away, know it is a mile, and be able to walk right to it is an ability that takes experience and judgment, for from the moment the hunter leaves his lookout and loses sight of the game, he must travel around swamps and through timber, staying in the twisting valleys and gulches and downwind of the traveling caribou.

The caribou hunter has one great advantage: Traveling caribou follow a pattern. Looking down from the air, one sees a network of paths, dark ribbons meandering through the wet fields. Where caribou traveled last year they will move again this year. Thus, when a hunter feels he is close to the route of the oncoming stag he looks for a trail, chooses one and sits downwind, in good range, behind some cover or at least where his silhouette will not show against the sky. Even if he has done everything right, things may turn out wrong. Another animal, moving up from a hidden dip of land behind him may blunder into his scent

Bull moose on alert; author advises hunters to stand their ground if huge animal charges.

and, spooking, also spook the hunter's quarry just as it nears him. Game has the habit of doing the unusual.

If, on the other hand, the hunter spots a stag and his herd, they'll be moving slowly or not at all. He must stalk to within good viewing distance, select his animal, and make his shot. He must close in slowly. The sure course is to wait long enough between moves, or to move so slowly that any animal in a position to see him will give itself away first. He is the stalker and though the sod may appear soft, more often than not there will be dried branches or loose gravel to cross. All too often one of the many listen-

ing ears of a herd will pick up an unusual sound, or the wind, eddying up a valley, will give the trespasser away. But if the hunter can reach a point of vantage he may see caribou at ease.

He may watch the young stags engage in immature fights, tolerated by the herd stag, since they offer no threat to his domain or prerogatives. He may see a jealous stag of lesser proportions make his bid for attentions from one of the harem, fleeing at the first approach of the herd stag. He may, if he's very lucky, see a serious challenge between well-matched stags and if he does, he'll have witnessed the core of existence and survival in the animal world.

If, when he has finally seen his stag and judged him, he decides to shoot, he will have time to place his bullet in a vital spot— so that death comes like a breath of wind —and on the morrow another stag will rule.

What about cartridges? More moose and caribou have been killed with the old .30-.30 cartridges than with any other, but flatter-shooting rifles have an advantage for caribou, and those with a heavier wallop for moose. Where the shooting is more open, the .270 and .268 Magnum are excellent; where moose are to be hunted, a heavier cartridge like the 7mm Magnum and .300 Magnum are excellent choices. The .30/06 and the .308, however, have enough power for both animals.

Out of recognition of the pure majesty of the animal, you may want a moose. Because of the trim beauty of the caribou, I wanted a stag on this trip, and a good one. My search took me high on the open ridges. The caribou stags were still expanding their harems, although the rut for the moose was well on the wane. There were opportunities but, except for sighting my rifle, I did not fire a shot the first three days. That evening, another hunter passed our camp. He had shot his moose, he said, and caribou came next. Here is his story.

He had moved from one glade to another, vision limited on occasions to the width of the game tracks he traveled; opening at others to cover both sides of the valleys. Several times he saw moose in the distance, but on approaching the spot, found they'd vanished. In late afternoon of the first hunting day hope had waned, when he came abruptly into a small glade in which a moose lay, half hidden in the tall meadow grass. Only the tips of his horns showed, but suddenly he rose with more speed than majesty. Before the hunter could overcome his surprise and work a cartridge into the chamber, the bull was only a shadow among the other shadows of the forest.

On the second day, the hunter saw a bull swimming and might have taken an easy shot from the canoe but chose instead to wait till the animal stood on solid ground. It was a sporting gesture and the moose took full advantage of it, splashing up from the water to a screen of bushes so swiftly there was no time for a precise shot.

On his third day the man passed up another shot—this time at a going-away bull— for fear he would wound, rather than kill. It was with these missed opportunities behind him that he began the fourth afternoon of his hunting. A hundred yards along the way, he heard a crashing in the bushes ahead. A bull came running through—appearing for an instant—and, had he not reacted swiftly with the pent-up frustration of holding his fire on the preceding days, the bull would have passed into the woods.

According to him, it was all one motion— the working of the bolt, the pointing of the gun, and the detonation as the gun butt touched his shoulder. The bullet shattered the bull's spine midway in the neck. He fell and lay still. It was a clean, sure shot, and in the warmth of the firelight that night after moose liver, onions, and hashed-browns, he was glad he had waited and happy with his accomplishment. It's a strange thing about big-game hunting, but the killing shot is a culmination of all the things that lead up to it. Without the errors or misfortunes, the final situation might not be so wonderful.

I'd chosen the Middle Ridge area for my hunt because in previous seasons I had found more symmetrical antlers in that area than in any other. A caribou's antlers have three main branches: the high crown, the "bez" or intermediate palm branching forward from the main shaft, and the low, forward-sweeping horns or "shovels" that end just above a stag's nose. The upper and central horns usually follow a roughly symmetrical pattern because if the weight on one side or the other were out of balance the stag would be less efficient in fighting and in winning a harem. The brow horns are on the centerline and balance is not so important. They vary greatly from one side to the other.

The part of heredity in the development of antlers is often overlooked. Biologists tend to refer to the food available and indicate simply that food and horns go together. They forget that big horns and uniform spreads are affected as much by heredity as by the food an animal eats.

As more and more of the perfect heads have been taken by hunters, fewer stags with balanced horns have bred and fewer and fewer double brow horns are to be found. The norm is now a full brow horn on one antler and a slender spike roughly paralleling it on the other side. In seeking a head to mount, I wanted a well-matched set of double brow horns. There was little hope that I'd find such an animal but I'd made up my mind that I wouldn't settle for anything less.

I saw several good stags and was sorely tempted. I found one great stag weary and bleeding from a battle with another of his kind. I came upon him on an open marsh—head down, breathing heavily, flecks of blood on the white coat around his head and neck from a cut above one eye. He was mad—furious at himself, perhaps—and made a menacing start toward me as I stood quiet and alone in a natural buckskin shirt and drab trousers. Then he turned away and trotted, limping, into the scrub. I spent the rest of the day in the area looking for the stag that had subdued him, knowing that he must have been a magnificent animal and that his brow horns could have equalled his fighting ability and been perfectly matched.

At one time I heard the clash of antlers. Topping a ridge, I saw through glasses two bull moose squared off across a meadow. As I watched they came together and again the sound of antler meeting antler carried across the glade. It sounded like the head-on crash of two automobiles but we were far from cars or roads and in the stillness the sound only emphasized the power of their meeting. They were not machines but living creatures of flesh and blood, as powerful as machines and more determined. They shuddered from the shock, separated, recovered, and within seconds charged again. I left my vantage point then to try to get a closer view and, as I moved in, I startled a cow—the prize they fought for.

I heard the cow move off and heard no more. When I reached the turf on which they fought they had gone, leaving a torn-up battleground and a single ten-inch tine torn from an antler that an ax blow would scarcely have dented.

Seven times in my hunt I saw mature stags with horns that were big enough but unbalanced. Only one was able to sneak off without giving me a good glimpse of his head. I saw his body clearly; had I been a casual hunter I could have shot him, too, when he stood for a moment behind a dead birch, his horns half hidden, just as I could have killed the others I had studied carefully and let go on their way.

When I finally found the one I wanted it was story-book stuff. I saw the light-colored spots a herd of caribou makes on the rich, dark blend of muskeg moss and berry bushes, at a distance of nearly a mile. The wind blew into my face from their direction. They were scattered on the far edge of the open area, tight to the deep shadow of a tall stand of evergreens. A single spur of scrub spruce and tamarack poked its way out from the timber on my side, withering gradually from full height to stunted bushes a foot or two above the marsh. Down this narrow avenue of cover I crawled.

To reach the last dwarfed tamarack, a slender wisp of branches with needles turned to gold by sun and frost, I slid along the muskeg on my belly. The wet moss and the puddles soaked me to my skin. Reaching it I rested on left haunch and elbow, waiting for my breath to steady, moving slowly as I drew out the small binoculars that hung within the neck opening of my shirt. The day was cool and overcast.

From my earlier view I had been able to count the herd which numbered thirty-one. Here I was lower and could see only those nearest me on a slight rise of land. Between them and the forest the land sloped downwards and the rest of the herd was hidden from view. The nearest animals were does, about two hundred and fifty yards away. About ten were in full view—some lying down, some standing to feed. Off to my right a stag approached them. He was a good stag but when the binoculars brought his antlers close, I found to my regret that he, like all the others, had unbalanced antlers. Relaxed, I watched him move up toward the nearest doe.

Suddenly from behind the ridge came a magnificent stag, horns flashing, to meet the intruder and drive him back and away. Once he had him on the run, he dropped out of sight behind the ridge. I could still see the herd stag's great antler tips as he swung back toward the does and then they, too, disappeared. The movements had been so rapid I'd been taken by surprise and then, when I had finally glimpsed the perfect double brow horns, I had not wanted to risk a careless shot.

The does were placid, watching—always watching—and I dared not move up. To go back and circle to their forest side would run the risk of having my scent come to them downwind. I could only wait where I

was and hope that a varying wind would not carry my scent to one of them or, more likely, that their period of rest and slow feeding would end and they'd move off toward the evergreen depths before the big stag came into full view again. Half a dozen times, I saw his antlers and part of his head and back as he wandered among his does. Once more the lonely stag approached and was chased off but this time the action was half hidden by some brush and there was, again, no chance to shoot.

A long two hours later, my trophy stag came over the slight rise. He'd been completely out of sight for twenty minutes and only the knowledge that he wouldn't leave as long as the does remained had kept me rooted to my bed of wet moss. First his horn tips glinted and I could see their breadth; then his head came up and I could see his antlers in their entirety. The earlier glimpses had only indicated double brow horns. Now I was sure of symmetry.

During the long wait, I'd guessed the distance at two hundred and fifty yards. With my four-power scope sighted at one hundred yards, I centered just below the ridge of his back, above the chest cavity, and squeezed the trigger. At the report, the stag made a great leap forward and fell.

Now, the does in full stampede raced toward me, then veered away across the open stretch of bog. Up over the ridge from behind came the love-lorn stag. Racing, flat out, with the stately pace only a caribou has, the challenger came on to merge with the moving mass, his horns lifting higher and flashing, crown-like, among the lesser points of light from the small horns of the does. They disappeared behind the trees and when the last was out of sight I turned toward the gray shape on the bog. The tiniest speck of blood rested beside the small hole, low in the chest, leading directly to the heart. ◉

Nahnook

The Great White Hunter by Jack Denton Scott

Photography by Frederick Baldwin

The most remarkable hunter in the animal kingdom spends eighteen months of his early life learning his art from his parent. And a highly developed art it must be, if he is to survive in the most barren region on earth. Moving on hair-soled ghost feet, circumpolarly in Arctic North America from the northwestern coast of Alaska to northern Labrador and the islands and drifted pack ice of the Arctic Ocean, the great white bear —called "Nahnook" by the Eskimos—must have incredible skills and amazing armor. He must make sprints on ice up to twenty-five miles an hour; he must blend his yellow-white fur with an ice hummock and lie motionless for hours, finally converting his body into a sled, slowly, patiently sliding toward his prey, inches at a time. He has only seconds to make his move and he must be a master of timing and as quick as a leopard. He does not have a second chance. Only his skill determines whether he lives or dies of starvation. That skill requires the ability to swim six miles an hour in water that freezes on his coat. It demands that he make sudden fifteen-foot plunges while swimming, that he dive and swim with great speed underwater. It demands that he be able to lie motionless atop the water for long periods. It requires that he disappear on ice or in water in seconds like an object in a magician's trick.

To develop these skills requires special physical assets. He has air spaces in his fur, oil glands in his skin, and a thick layer of fat which enable him to float like a boat. His legs are jointed in such a way that he can swing his legs in a wide angle, this maneuverability making him a superb swimmer. Nictitant membranes (virtually built-in sunglasses) protect his eyes from the blinding glare of ice and snow. He is

Preceding pages: Amid ghostly ice fields of Spitsbergen a lone polar bear rests between hunts.
Left: On Kong Karls Land three bears hungrily pace shore. Warm weather had caused ice — and seals — to recede, forcing bears to subsist on seaweed. Above: Bears are remarkable swimmers. Here two-year-old female knifes smoothly through freezing sea in search of seals, mainstay of polar bear diet.

Superb hunting skill of polar bears is captured in photo sequence proceeding clockwise from left: Large (1,200-lb.) male sights seal and flattens himself in snow during advance. Here he has raised head, but dark nose is kept hidden in snow for most of stalk. The seal caught, the bear wastes no time eating it. Arctic fox lives on carrion left behind.

the only bear with feet webbed for the water, and he has a peculiar growth of hair on the bottom of his feet which makes them as effective as snowshoes. Long, unretractable claws grow so that his constant walking on ice hones them to knife-sharpness.

As the only carnivorous bear (all others are omnivorous), the white hunter has only one prey. He is a true predator, but one without much choice: Seals, especially the clever hair seal, are what he hunts. Life in the bear's world is keyed to a variety of planktonic sea organisms, called krill, which gather where icebergs melt in the sea, attracting feeding fish. The fish in turn draw the seals and the seals the polar bears.

It is probably the polar bear's diet of seal blubber that allows him to survive in weather that forms icicles on his coat. This pure fat is handled by an amazing digestive system. In a matter of hours, all that remains of the blubber of an entire seal is about a quart of green bile in the stomach. The fat has been turned into body heat.

Not least of the great white hunter's attributes is his brain. He has discovered (or was taught by his mother during his apprenticeship) that good hunting is often found where ice action has broken old ice and caused a thin new surface to form. Storm tides sometimes open cracks two feet wide and miles long in heavy ice; the exposed water freezes slightly and is then retarded from deep freezing by light snow. These fissures create breathing spaces for the seals, who stick their heads through the thin ice. For this kind of hunting, the polar bear again needs a special technique. He has learned to skate his thousand pounds-plus over ice so thin that it would be unsafe

for a man. Humped like a small berg beside the skim of ice, the bear waits until a seal surfaces. Then Nahnook slashes out swiftly, always with his left paw, hooking the seal, and flipping it out. Next, with a quick surgically skillful bite, he kills it. If he misses with the first swipe, the seal vanishes.

The white bear does have a few alternatives if his daily search for seals over a seventy-five-mile range proves fruitless: birds. Eider ducks are sharp-eyed and fast, but the bear has learned that he can approach a rafted flock by swimming slowly, with only his black nose showing above water. Then, a sudden fifteen-foot lunge puts him among them. They dive, so does he—often surfacing with a flapping duck. The white hunter also has learned that he can suddenly stand like a man amid a flock of low-flying snow buntings and, by clap-

ping his paws like hands, sometimes snare a small meal. On some of the islands of the Bering Sea, polar bears have been seen using those versatile claws to dig puffins out of their burrows, and they are effective in hooking spawning fish out of tundra streams. The bear is also fond of young walruses and sometimes can flash in and get a very young one before the mother screams for the herd to come to the rescue. Good as he is, the polar bear has learned that he is no match for a great walrus in the water, so he restricts his hunting of them to the ice where his speed and agility save him.

But superb as his hunting skills and physical attributes may be, perhaps the best is his sense of smell.

I witnessed an example of this fine sense in action while on a ship in the Barents Sea. With a crew of five, my wife and I were cruising near the five islands of Spitsbergen, a barren, mountainous arctic archipelago north of Norway.

There were several objects to the trip: fishing for char in a lake no man had visited for a dozen years; reaching the North Pole, or, at least, trying to; and making a study of the polar bear in his natural habitat. The boat we chose for the trip was the forty-ton, fifty-seven-foot, 150-horsepower *Havella*, built along the lines of the famed Norwegian rescue boat, with a special ice-cleaving double hull, and—if we needed it—1,178 square feet of sail area. The crew—captain, mate, ice pilot, engineer, and cook—were out of Tromsö, the last outpost of civilization in Norway, two hundred miles beyond the Arctic Circle.

On one particular afternoon, as the offshore arctic breeze lazily lifted smoke from the deck, my wife and I puzzled as we watched the mate arranging pieces of seal fat in a charcoal brazier. As it sizzled, smelling fishy, we looked at each other. I turned to our tow-headed captain, Haakon Godlieb-

sen. We weren't going to have seal for lunch; we'd had reindeer stew a few hours ago. "What's happening?" I asked.

The captain grinned. "My secret," he said, in his heavy accent. "We send signal. You wait and see..."

We had nothing else to do but wait. Even so, the guessing game was annoying. Alf Olsen, the mate, kept putting seal blubber on the charcoal and the stench was becoming unpleasant. We walked aft to avoid it and stood watching terns fly shoreward, going like hurled darts.

My wife saw it first. She pointed at a V-shaped wave coming toward us from shore, perhaps two miles away. Starting as a small rippling wave like those created by a sudden wind, it grew as it neared.

"Hey, Alf," I said, "what's this?"

He hurried over, smelling like a barbecued seal. He looked. He grinned. He whooped. The captain came. He did the same. Then the engineer and the ice pilot and the cook came. They whooped together.

Seeing that I wasn't sharing their excitement, the captain said, *"Isbjørn,"* which I knew was the Norwegian word for ice bear or polar bear.

Now I, too, watched with interest. The V of the wave became sharper as it came nearer. When it was thirty yards away it suddenly took form and definition: a black nose poking ahead, the head with long pointed muzzle, rear legs hanging motionless like a rudder, front legs cleaving the water as skillfully as an Olympic swimmer.

This was my first view of a wild polar bear. He looked more like a great hairy fish than a mammal. But he quickly became a mammal when he pulled himself up on a nearby ice floe like some huge old man in a white fur coat. Then he turned and faced us. His fur was thick and yellow-white, his head long and snaky, his eyes cold and black. He didn't make a sound. I judged he was nine feet long and weighed a thousand pounds.

Demonstrating his strength and intelligence in one quick movement, he grabbed the anchor rope and pulled himself and the floe closer to the *Havella*. Alf was ready. He had placed snowy pieces of seal blubber on boat hooks and given one each to my wife and me, showing us with another what to do. As he reached over with the boat hook, the bear stood like a man. He *was* nine feet tall. And with an easy flick of a paw he swiped the blubber off the hook. We stood hypnotized, feeding him until we ran out of seal blubber. When we stopped he began acting peculiarly, pacing as if caged, going to the far end of the floe, then making a rush to the side near us. When he repeated this three times, the captain said, "Up anchor!" The engineer and Alf heaved the anchor out of the water and we chugged off, the bear still pacing.

Alf explained that in their last encounter with a bear they hadn't acted quickly enough. The bear had leaped on deck, and they had had to kill him. He also said that our bear had probably scented the burning seal blubber from three miles away and could actually scent it from five times that distance.

"But that nose get him in trouble," Alf said. "Trappers use it to kill him. They burn blubber, then tie more blubber to a bell rope outside a cabin. When the bear come and eat the blubber and ring the bell, the trapper put his rifle through hole in cabin and shoot him...."

We saw thirty-five more bears on that arctic adventure in an area that has more than any place on earth. We saw them hunting seals, cavorting in the water, swimming miles from shore. We saw them with cubs sleeping in the sun on the ice, playing, sliding down icy hummocks like children on a playground slide.

"Do polar bears deliberately attack man?" is a question some still consider unsettled. Some old North hands like Bud Helmericks do not think so. But I have a friend who was attacked by one; I believe that the bear, having no natural enemies, seeing only other bears, seals, walruses, and foxes in his far North, attacks as a hunter, searching for food. Anything that moves is fair game to a polar bear.

Norwegian Henry Rudi, who has spent twenty years in the Arctic and holds the world's record with over seven hundred kills, reports being trailed over fifty miles, escaping only by injuring the bear and reaching the shelter of a cabin.

F. J. De Gisbert, who has probably had as much experience with polar bears as anyone, having killed more than four hundred, shares my belief. He told of the time he was trying to take one alive for a zoo. He and his companions were moving through ice floes when they saw a bear. "He was evidently searching for his breakfast, as he repeatedly stood up on his hind legs, stretching himself to his full height to have a look around. He soon caught sight of us and came along at a lively gait to meet us. Our intentions were to get him into the water, but unfortunately our boat got jammed between two floes, and before we could release it, he charged.

"I have never seen a bear charge so rapidly. I was in the bow ready with the rope when we struck the floes, and he was about fifteen yards away. He covered that distance giving me scarcely time to drop the rope, pick up the rifle, shove the muzzle against his head and fire. Next moment I found myself pinned to the seat, over which I had stumbled, by the weight of a paw on my thigh. The explosion had blown away part of his head and he had fallen stone dead over the bow of the boat."

But if polar bears sometimes hunt us, we

often hunt them, going after them in diverse ways, by dog sled, boat, airplane, and by stalking them in their own territory. I consider it most sporting, once the bear has been spotted by plane or boat, to go after him by foot, trailing him—for hours if necessary—along a *jøkel*—a long, slippery, frigid glacial tongue. Following that in sporting excitement is a hunt by dogsled on landfast ice—of course accompanied by a guide who knows the country and the dogs. Since a bear *can* move seventy-five miles in a day, going after him by foot or sled is a rugged business. The way that many hunters prefer, I am sorry to say, is to get him by plane, herding him with low swoops and shooting from the plane or only walking a few feet after landing. Another is to tag him from a boat while he is at a disadvantage in open water. Either of these "sports" is akin to walking out in a meadow and shooting a Jersey cow. Planes can be sporting though, if they are just for *spotting* the bear from a distance, putting the hunters down and then letting them off to take after the game on foot.

The laws of polar bear hunting vary. Although the bears have protection off Canadian shores, the killing of them by natives is allowed. Greenland, Norway, and Sweden have spotty restrictions, with residents generally free to hunt. Sealers, whalers, fishermen, trappers, and hunters kill polar bears whenever they see them, selling their skins for prices ranging from $100 to $600, depending upon size and condition. I saw a dozen bloody polar bear skulls aboard a cod boat off King's Bay where we had anchored to take on water just before making our cruise into Spitsbergen. Russia does not permit polar bear hunting. Now that Alaska is a state, it costs $150 for a polar bear permit there, and only one bear is allowed per hunter, the season running from January 1 to April 30.

Man alone threatens the polar bear's survival.

The trouble with all of the laws is that the polar bear has no protection beyond the three-mile limit in the seas where he is often found. Currently there is a strong movement which is trying to form an International Marine Animals Act, similar to our Migratory Bird and Whaling Acts. Its backers hope not only to protect polar bears, but sea otters, walruses, hair seals, and white foxes, with both Federal and international control of the high seas. In my opinion, it is time the nations got together to protect the polar bear. Expert estimates of the remaining world population range from twenty-five thousand down to ten thousand. If any nation is allowed a free hand with them, extinction seems imminent.

Given a chance—even though they live in the coldest, most barren place on earth—polar bears can take care of themselves. They are loners, the males and females not associating except in the midsummer mating season. The female mates when she is fully mature and, with the approach of winter, she looks for a den. Pressure ice, an area where ice has been forced into high ridges and hummocks, is the spot she usually seeks. She digs an entrance and hollows out a home about three or four feet deep, five feet wide, and seven feet in length. There she settles down and is promptly sealed in by drifting snow. Outside, the weather may dip so low that a normal thermometer cannot show it, but within her den the white bear is snug. Although polar bears do not truly hibernate, as do all other bears, the female stays in the ice-den until the cubs are born, usually in January.

The offspring, often twins, a male and female, are born blind and naked, ten inches long, weighing two pounds. (As adults the males will reach nine and one half feet in length, and weigh up to 1,600 pounds.) The cubs survive the cold by snuggling into the fur of their mother's belly. Soon they begin to grow their own woolly, protective fur. In six weeks their eyes open.

Polar bear milk is incredibly rich. The cubs grow swiftly and by late March or early April are large enough to face the frigid outside world. With one massive heave, the female breaks loose from the den, freeing herself and cubs of their cocoon of ice. Then the cubs' long period of instruction begins.

The ice pilot of the *Havella*, Sigurd Dal, told of seeing a mother teach her two cubs to swim. "I was watching them through glasses," he said. "The cubs were lying on the ground. The mother stood at the edge of the water, looking back at them. Then she walked into the water and stood until they joined her. She struck out for deep water, swimming slowly as if instructing them. They followed clumsily—splashing, obviously having trouble. She went under them and came up with the two clinging to her back, turned around and headed back to shore. About twenty feet out she dumped them into the water, then made for shore and just stood watching as they splashed toward her."

Some explorers believe that the cubs' long apprenticeship is necessary in order for them to master the all-important task of seal-stalking. The mother shows them how to move on the ice, how to stalk the prey. While she hunts a seal the cubs watch the procedure intently.

The problem is that the hair seal is a quick, intelligent creature with remarkable vision, whip-fast reflexes—and an escape hatch. They have blowholes in the ice, just large enough for their bodies. Every few seconds they come up through the blowholes for air, or to stretch in the sun. The polar bear stalks them, trying to strike before they vanish into the blowhole. The procedure requires infinite patience.

We witnessed a stratagem that was evidence of just how well this skill is taught—and learned. Evidently a bear, swimming at some distance, had spotted a seal on the ice. We saw him move in from hundreds of yards away, then swim underwater to the entrance of the blowhole. There he scratched his claws on the ice, and waited. The seal, atop the ice, apparently heard him, and, frightened, made for the blowhole. The white bear was there with open arms.

So richly endowed is the polar bear that he can afford to be prodigal with his energy. This unpredictable beast has been known to spend days on a shifting platform of floating ice on its way to the open ocean; then, having either made a seal-kill or having had enough of his free ride, he will plop back into the frigid water and swim a hundred miles to shore—a feat that probably could not be equaled by any other land animal.

Certainly in the arctic wastes no other creature, save man, challenges Nahnook. The great and canny white bear is undisputed master of his frozen world. ◉

A CRAFT FOR ALL WATERS

*Since the days
of birchbarks and dugouts,
the swiftly gliding
canoe has been ideal for
navigating America's
lakes and streams.*

**BY
JOHN GARDNER**

Once again the song of the voyageur is heard in the North. It is summer and the canoes are moving out, more this year than last, paddles flashing or dipping silently, trending into wilderness ways where the skies are bright, the waters clean, and the air tangy with balsam.

In selecting a canoe these days, one can investigate a variety of materials: aluminum, fiberglass, polypropylene, time-tested canvas, and a rubber-based plastic. But in essential shape all these modern canoes are closely alike, deriving from birchbark prototypes which have not substantially changed in design since the Old Stone Age.

Perhaps aluminum or some of the new plastic materials are tougher than bark, and will stand up to more abuse on flinty gravel or jagged boulders; yet each has its disadvantages. Aluminum is noisy, tends to hang up on rocks, and takes dents which refuse to pound out cleanly. Fiberglass is heavy. And so on. According to all accounts, the best of the old bark canoes would go just as far and just as fast as anything we have today, besides carrying just as big loads. The feats accomplished in birchbark canoes have been numerous and extraordinary.

Canoes are ancient in origin, worldwide in occurrence, and all but infinite in their variety. There are dugouts of every sort contrived from hollowed logs, a variety of frames covered with bark or hide, and still other species of canoe formed from bundles of buoyant reeds or rushes—papyrus on the upper Nile and balsa on Lake Titicaca in Bolivia and Peru. Size also varies greatly. The tiny cypress dugouts no more than eight feet long, twenty inches wide, and eight inches deep used by Creole frog hunters in Louisiana swamps, contrast with Haida war dugouts of cedar sixty-five feet long, with six to eight feet of beam, which once were not uncommon on our northwest coast. Even larger war canoes, worked out of gigantic logs of kauri pine with wash strakes added to increase the freeboard, were once used by the Maori warriors of New Zealand.

When white settlers first reached the eastern shores of North America, they found log

Frederic Remington

VICTOR SMITH

Left: Time-tested wood and canvas canoe is poled over shallows of Allagash Lake in Maine. Below: Flyfisherman casts from old birchbark. Bottom left: Fiberglass model competes in race. Bottom right: Latex canoe is maneuvered over beaver dam obstructing river.

HANSON CARROLL

PETER MILLER

LEONARD LEE RUE III

CHARLES STEINHACKER

105

dugouts, as well as bark canoes, with the former in common use along the entire Atlantic Coast. Such native craft were immediately adopted, though log canoes eventually were replaced by planked boats.

Robert B. Roosevelt in his book, *Some Game Fish of the North*, published in New York in 1862, mentions the white-pine dugouts of thirty feet favored by the salmon fishermen on the St. John River near Fredericton, New Brunswick. More than two hundred years earlier in Salem, Massachusetts, every household, according to Wood's *New England Prospect*, had one or more "small Cannowes, which were made of whole pine trees being about two foot & a half over, and 20 foote long." The villagers used these dugouts principally for going back and forth to their farms, but also "in these likewise they goe a-fowling, sometimes two leagues to sea," probably to hunt ducks among the outer islands of Marblehead Harbor, as their descendants still do.

About this same time, Roger Williams was becoming acquainted with the dugout canoes of the Indians near Narragansett Bay, which craft he accounted crank and treacherous, having nearly drowned on more than one occasion while using them. When the first English settlers arrived at Southold and Southampton at the eastern end of Long Island in 1640, they found the local Indians carrying on a flourishing whale fishery in log canoes. Some of these were large. One dugout belonging to Chief Wyandanch

*Photograph of New England sportsmen
shows that occasionally dugouts were still used by
anglers late in nineteenth century.*

reportedly was capable of carrying forty men on sea voyages as far as Massachusetts Bay.

Log dugouts were particularly well suited to the needs of the oyster fishery, being so employed along the Connecticut shore almost down to the present day. Two such pine oyster dugouts, approximately thirty feet long, still survive at Mystic Seaport.

To increase dugout capacity, their sides were sometimes built up by the addition of planks, or they might be split down the center lengthwise, so that planks could be inserted between the two sides.

Craft derived from Indian log dugouts attained their ultimate development, as sailing canoes, brogans, and bugeyes in the Chesapeake in the late nineteenth century. Somewhat more than a hundred years previous to this, the Rev. Robert Rose, rector of St. Ann's Parish in Albemarle, in the Virginia tidewater, is credited with the invention of a "tobacco boat" consisting of two large dugout canoes placed side by side and overlaid with a stout platform for transporting tobacco casks.

Curiously, a nearly exact duplicate of this craft crops up a century or so later on the upper Missouri for tranporting bales of furs downriver. Log dugouts were a principal means of transportation on the upper Missouri in the early years. Immense cottonwood trees found in the rich river bottoms provided logs as large as thirty feet long and two-and-a-half feet across. In hollowing these, thin transverse sections were sometimes left in to serve as bulkheads, producing several separate tight compartments. Shipments of wild honey were sent down to St. Louis in them, as well as bear's grease, which served as cooking fat in place of lard, since bears were more plentiful on the upper Missouri than hogs.

Besides log dugouts, now all but forgotten, birch canoes were employed in New England from earliest times. Hunters, woodsmen, and explorers borrowed the birch from the Indians, yet never adopted it for commercial transportation to the same extent as dugout craft, nor did the white settlers ever undertake to build bark canoes themselves.

One of the first accounts of the birchbark canoe in New England is by Martin Pring, who commanded the *Speedwell* from Bristol, England, when that vessel visited Plymouth Harbor seventeen years before the landing of the Pilgrims. "Their Boats, whereof we brought one to Bristoll, were in proportion like a wherrie of the River of Thames, seventeen foot long and four foot broad, made of Barke of a Birch-tree, farre exceeding in bigness those of England; it was sowed together with strong and tough Oziers or twigs, and the seams covered over with Rozen or a Turpentine little inferior in sweetness to Frankincense, as we made trial by burning a little thereof on coals at sundry times after our comming home; it was also open like a Wherrie, and sharp at both ends, saving that the beake was a little bending roundly upward. And though it carried nine men standing upright, yet it weighed not at the most above sixtie pounds."

Of all the Maine rivers the Penobscot is most noted for its canoes. At Old Town, above Bangor, canoes are still manufactured, although no longer of birchbark by Indians. Here at Indian Island (which, by the way, is still tribal territory and not a reservation) Henry David Thoreau engaged Joe Polis for a trip to Moosehead Lake and the Allegash in 1857. Joe, a wealthy Indian who lived in a fine white house and was reputed to be worth $6,000, a fortune acquired from moose hunting, agreed to go for a dollar and a half a day, and fifty cents a week extra for his canoe. Newly built by Polis himself, the canoe, according to Thoreau, was neatly and stanchly put together with stout ribs and extra-thick bark. It looked small to Thoreau for three men and 166 pounds of

dunnage, and getting out his ever-ready "black ash rule," Thoreau took its dimensions for the benefit of posterity: eighteen feet three inches long, two feet six inches at its greatest beam, and one foot deep amidships. Indeed, this canoe was somewhat smaller than a Penobscot River canoe still to be seen at the Peabody Museum of Salem, the oldest surviving birchbark canoe known, having been donated to the East India Marine Society in 1826.

The weight of Polis' canoe Thoreau estimated to have been about eighty pounds. In any case, Polis, who was stoutly built and slightly over middle height, evidently lugged it easily enough when required, sometimes on the run. And if it at first seemed small to Thoreau, it carried his party of three safely enough, even during very rough weather on Moosehead Lake.

The name Passamaquoddy, according to Frank Speck, means "Those whose occupation is pollock fishing." The Passamaquoddy, a Malecite tribe formerly occupying the valley of the St. Croix River and the shores at the mouth of the bay to which they have given their name, developed an ocean-going bark canoe of outstanding ability in rough water. The ends of the canoe were low to cut windage, and pointed, yet full enough for good lift. The raking stem and cutaway forefoot, together with the rising bottom rocker toward the ends, allowed the canoe to be swung quickly by a strong and skillful paddle to meet oncoming waves, to backwater, or to run down a breaking crest.

Not only did the Passamaquoddy take pollock in these bark canoes, but they were accustomed to going miles offshore at the mouth of the Bay of Fundy in all kinds of weather, winter and summer, to shoot porpoise. At one time the sale of porpoise oil was the chief source of income for this tribe. Two Indians commonly hunted together, one to steady the pitching canoe as best he could with the paddle, while the other stood up to throw the spear.

Beyond the territory once occupied by the

New Brunswick Malecite lies the ancient hunting range of the Micmac, extending from eastern New Brunswick across Nova Scotia to Newfoundland and the coast of Labrador. Micmac canoes were built in a number of models—light wood canoes for easy portaging, river canoes with rounded bottoms for fast paddling and running rapids—but most distinctive were the deep rough-water, or ocean-going, canoes, otherwise known as "humpbacks." The gunwales of these canoes rose amidships, producing a decided hump in the sheer at the center of the canoe, giving additional freeboard at the point where cresting waves were most apt to curl aboard when seas were running high.

In these humpbacks the Micmacs often ventured far to sea, porpoise hunting or on journeys. Canoes crossed from Digby to St. John, New Brunswick. Abram Toney, former chief of the Yarmouth Micmacs, once paddled as far as Grand Manan, and on another occasion claimed to have spent the night on a whistling buoy twenty-one miles off Yarmouth, having been caught offshore in his canoe by a sudden blow while porpoise hunting.

The Micmacs were not the only northeastern tribe to venture long distances at sea in birch canoes. Regularly each summer from time immemorial, the now extinct Beothuk Indians of Newfoundland visited the Funk Islands forty miles offshore by open sea from Cape Freels to fill their canoes with seafowl eggs which they dried in cake form to enrich their winter diet.

The materials used in constructing the Beothuk canoe were the usual ones, birchbark sewn and served with flexible spruce roots and sealed with tempered pitch, ribbed and reinforced with thin splits of spruce, substituting for cedar which does not grow in Newfoundland. But in its shape this unique canoe was unlike any other Indian craft. Its crescent profile was aptly likened by one early explorer to the "new moone." Its sheer line was in actuality two crescent arcs meeting in a peak amidships which stood nearly as high as the slim, upturned ends. In thwartships section the slightly curved sides opened upward in a narrow V, so that the canoe sat deep in the water and required ballast to keep it upright. Yet these canoes seem to have been excellent sea boats, both able and fast, and of ample capacity. It has been suggested that the influence of Norsemen, visiting America long before Columbus, may account for the odd shape of these vessels. The canoes bear some resemblance to small fishing boats used along the west coast of Norway for more than a thousand years.

Our modern canoes derive directly from the aboriginal birch canoes of the Algonquian-speaking tribes of northeastern America. These earliest migrants from Asia are believed to have come as sub-Arctic hunters across the wide land bridge now submerged under the Bering Strait, possibly thirty thousand years ago, or even earlier. Probably they did not bring canoes with them in any developed form, although birchbark canoes of an inferior sort occur in Siberia. Indeed, crude bark canoes in great variety are found throughout the world.

Not until the Algonquian tribes had crossed the continent and established themselves where the white men found them is it likely that the birchbark canoe was perfected. Nature put materials of superlative quality in one area only—that is to say, in the region extending south of Hudson Bay to the Great Lakes, thence east through the watershed of the St. Lawrence and its tributaries, and across northern New England and the Canadian Maritimes to the sea.

Here the canoe birch, or paper birch, sometimes attains a height of a hundred feet and a diameter of thirty inches or more at the butt. Its bark is one-eighth to three-six-

Algonquian-style birchbark canoes are still built by a few Indian craftsmen, employing traditional methods, black-spruce servings, and white-cedar ribs.

teenths of an inch thick. Not only is such bark tougher than any other but, being impregnated with natural oils, it neither absorbs water nor rots. To sew such bark and to bind it with servings about the gunwales and stems, the fibrous, flexible roots of the black spruce are ideal. These roots will be found in damp ground, close to the surface, under moss, sometimes as long as twenty feet, with a uniform diameter hardly larger than a lead pencil. Such roots were carefully prepared, split, and sometimes quartered, and kept damp to retain their original pliability. Melted spruce gum, expertly tempered with fat and powdered charcoal, produced excellent pitch for sealing.

The wood of large, clear, straight-grain, white-cedar butts was also essential. The wood of the northern white cedar is extremely lightweight, yet adequately tough and strong, as well as bendable. Straight-grain white cedar can be split, if one knows how, into thin, uniform strips. Other timber, in particular black spruce, can also be split, but not with equal precision and facility.

Even after the Indians acquired steel axes and crooked knives, building a canoe remained an extended and laborious operation, requiring numerous skills and specialized knowledge. Canoe birches of large size and superior bark were never plentiful. One might search for weeks before finding a suitable tree. Winter bark is the best, but getting it off the tree in one piece in the winter was a slow, precarious process best accomplished with hot water. Felling a large tree so that it might be more easily worked on presented difficulties, too, and there was the risk of damaging the bark. Cedar splits best when dry. Thus it was desirable to cut or girdle selected trees long enough in advance to permit seasoning. After the materials were assembled, an earthen building bed had to be formed and staked; gunwales cut and bent; bark shaped, cut, and sewed; nu-

Top: At meeting of canoe enthusiasts in 1880's, kayak-like decked canoes predominated. Above: Canoe shown at Lake George in 1881 had sun canopy. Right: American Canoe Association member W. M. Carter sails his racer, "Singara."

merous wooden parts worked to shape and size; and so on.

In the beginning, before trails had been chopped through the wilderness, one mighty, natural thoroughfare led into the heart of America—the St. Lawrence River, its tributaries, and connecting waterways. The river extends a distance of two thousand miles to Lake Nipigon, beyond Lake Superior, and drains some four hundred thousand square miles. This was Algonquian territory, canoe territory. In this vast region the birchbark canoe played out its final spectacular role. For more than two hundred years, fur-trade canoes hauled their annual cargoes of wilderness riches to Montreal. Well into the nineteenth century, the great birch canoes of the voyageurs continued to make their annual circuit from Montreal to Grand Portage at the height of land on the northern extremity of Lake Superior, and back again before the winter freeze-up.

Each year, when passage opened on the St. Lawrence through the spring ice, the canoe brigades set out, hundreds of huge canoes bound west, for *le pays d'en haut*. Brigade after brigade of big canoes, bright with color and gaily blazoned insignia, departed upriver in orderly formation. The red-shirted voyageurs in their tasseled stocking caps and fringed, varicolored sashes, flashed vermilion-tipped paddles, dipping vigorously to the rhythm of old French paddling songs.

Canoes of the largest size, *canots des maîtres*, ran to thirty-six feet in length, were manned by crews of fourteen, and needed four men on the portage. *Bâtards*, the slightly smaller version of the canots des maîtres, required a crew of twelve. On the lesser inland waters west of the Grand Portage were found the smaller North canoes, *canôts des nord*. Generally not more than twenty-five feet in length, these canoes were worked with crews of six to eight, and were easily carried by two men.

According to one qualified witness, U.S. Boundary Commissioner Major Joseph Delafield, whose diary for 1823 survives, the French Canadian was a superior woodsman, more hardy than the Indian. The elite of the voyageurs were the *hivernants*, the "winterers." They lived the year around in the back country and were contemptuous of the ordinary voyageurs who returned to Montreal for the winter. But whether a canoeman wintered in the wilderness or not, he had to be incredibly tough.

There was not only paddling, but innumerable portages, as well. The paddlers jumped into rapid water up to their waists, armpits, or necks when necessary, to hold the canoe off the rocks until it could be unloaded. On the carry, two hundred pounds was accounted a fair load—two kegs of pork of ninety-six pounds each, or three bushels of corn weighing about as much. With such a load on his back tied to the two ends of a long strap, or tumpline, across his forehead, the bearer, leaning well forward and with knees slightly bent, was off at a fast walk or slow trot. Usually it was necessary to return several times before everything had been carried across.

The birchbark canoe declined with the aboriginal Indian. Such craft were never built by whites, and were used less and less by them as the nineteenth century advanced. Even before 1840, white trappers and market hunters in the Adirondack wilderness had adopted crude precursors of the celebrated guide-boat.

The open canoe, managed with the single-bladed paddle and modeled on the birch, but constructed of other materials, achieved only limited popularity before 1900. About that time, however, the demand for the open, canvas-covered canoe jumped quite spectacularly. Meanwhile, for the three previous decades quite a different canoe held the cen-

113

ter of the stage. This was a small decked-over craft resembling the Eskimo kayak more than it did the Indian birch, and lightly planked with wood, usually varnished white cedar. Most of these were fitted for sailing, often with intricate rigs. Otherwise they were propelled with the double-bladed paddle. Originated for cruising, they were sailed more than they were paddled, and evolved rather quickly into ever more specialized racing machines.

It all started with John MacGregor, a British missionary, sportsman, author, and lecturer, who visited North America in 1859. He tried canoes, presumably the birch, on the Ottawa River, and continuing across the continent experimented with Eskimo kayaks in the Arctic. Returning to Britain, MacGregor built his first fourteen-foot Rob Roy cruising canoe on the kayak idea, but planked like a boat with wood. It weighed about seventy pounds. In this canoe and in succeeding Rob Roys, MacGregor cruised through the British Isles and a great part of Europe, eventually going as far afield as Scandinavia and the Holy Land. As a popular writer and lecturer, MacGregor converted Britain to the gospel of the cruising canoe. His most famous book, *A Thousand Miles in the Rob Roy Canoe on Twenty Rivers and Lakes of Europe*, was first published in 1866, the same year the Royal Canoe Club was founded in London.

America was ready to follow suit. A new urban class with increasing leisure and means had begun to turn to nature and to sports for recreation. In 1871 the New York Canoe Club, modeled after the Royal Canoe Club, came into being with sixteen members, each of whom had a sailing canoe.

Canoeing received some marvelous publicity. In 1874, Nathaniel Holmes Bishop paddled his *Maria Theresa*, a fifteen-foot paper canoe made by the Waters Paper Boat Company of Troy, New York, all the way from that city down the Hudson and the length of the Atlantic coast to Florida. His book, *The Voyage of the Paper Canoe*, was an immediate best-seller.

In 1879 three cruising enthusiasts reached Elk Lake at the source of the Mississippi with Rob Roy canoes. Two years later another canoeist-explorer returned from the headwaters of the same river to paddle from Aitkin, Minnesota, to the Gulf of Mexico, according to his claim, a distance of 3,184 miles in one hundred and seventeen days. Even longer was the five-month cruise of Charles A. Neidé in the *Aurora*, a Rushton Princess canoe, in the company of his friend Captain Samuel D. Kendall in a home-made canoe, *Solid Comfort*. They traveled from Lake George in the Adirondacks to the Gulf of Mexico.

J. Henry Rushton, born and raised in northern New York at the edge of the Adirondack wilderness, was the foremost American canoe-maker of this period. He helped to found the American Canoe Association in 1880, and he became world-famous for his Rob Roy and Indian Girl models in both lapstrake and "smoothskin" versions. His canoes more or less followed the contours of the aboriginal birchbarks but with refinements and were constructed entirely of cedar. (Some late Rushton models were canvas-covered in deference to the public's changing tastes.) He and a few fellow-craftsmen were chiefly responsible for the resurgence of the classic canoe which remains in use today.

A cedar canoe that came from the Rushton Boat Shop in Canton, New York, circa 1912, is now in the possession of Atwood Manley, author of *Rushton and His Times in American Canoeing* (published jointly by the Adirondack Museum and Syracuse University Press in 1968). Manley's Rushton is a fifteen-footer named *Vayu*—for the Hindu god of the winds—and is still perfectly stanch. Its owner was caught in it by a nasty gale in 1967 on Blue Mountain Lake. "There were three-foot waves," he recalls, "but my little canoe rode them like a duck."

The Rushtons were light, maneuverable, graceful, seaworthy, and very durable. Probably the lightest craft ever cruised in successfully were the five pint-sized lapstrake cedar canoes Rushton built for the diminutive and sickly woodsman-author, George Washington Sears, who signed his many contributions to *Forest and Stream*, Nessmuk. *Wood Drake*, the first of the Nessmuk miniatures, measured ten feet and weighed but fifteen pounds, nine-and-one-half ounces before painting, which added another two pounds. She carried her owner dry and safe over Adirondack waterways in the summer of 1880. The smallest and most remarkable of the five was *Sairy Gamp* (which never took water), weighing ten-and-a-half pounds for her nine-foot length. Her builder was afraid she might crack apart like an egg shell, but after a successful six-week cruise Nessmuk pronounced her dry and safe, and as good as new. After many years at the Smithsonian Institution, the *Sairy Gamp* is now on display at the Adirondack Museum.

As the racing fad subsided, and with it the sailing canoe, the open paddling canoe—today's basic design—grew ever more popular. Its form continued to recapitulate the Indian birch except for a watertight covering of painted canvas over a wooden hull. Rushton would have much preferred to go on building the beautiful varnished all-wood cedar canoes for which he was—and still remains—famous, but he was a businessman and he did what had to be done to save his business. The public was demanding canvas-covered paddling canoes. After designing his canvas-covered Indian models, in 1902 he turned over production to an experienced canoe-builder brought in from the Penobscot River where the Indians had been building superior birchbarks for countless generations. Thousands of canvas canoes were built and sold, keeping the shop open during the last years of Rushton's life.

Since then, the paddling canoe has had its ups and downs. For a time competition with the automobile as well as the outboard motor cut into the demand for canoes. But more recently canoes have come back strong and continue to gain. During the last couple of decades, wood-and-canvas construction has given way to aluminum, plastic, and hardened rubber, yet the basic design remains constant. Though aluminum has the drawbacks of being noisy and taking dents, it is obviously durable and requires minimal maintenance—no calking, painting, or varnishing. Moreover, an aluminum canoe does not easily swamp. Fiberglass is heavier than aluminum, but just about as durable, and hardened latex has the same advantages with a little less weight. To repair the canvas covering of an old canoe, one needs Ambroid glue, unbleached muslin patches, and sandpaper to roughen the edges for a good bond. A small rip or puncture in an aluminum canoe can be quickly repaired with nothing more than a tube of liquid solder, and there are tough, fast-setting epoxy-resin glues for plastic and latex craft. Modern canoes are so maneuverable, stable on the water, and easily repaired that they remain the best means of travel on remote waterways.

Despite the variety of materials and models now available, all are close copies of the original Indian birch. Increasing numbers of campers and sportsmen are turning to canoes. Longer vacations, earlier retirement, and the general movement away from polluted cities and off congested and deadly highways combine to swell the demand. There is still a primeval wilderness in the North to escape to, and nothing quite equals the paddling canoe to enjoy it in. ◉

SWIFT, WILD AND ELUSIVE

by Bert Popowski
When a pronghorn
antelope flashes
his danger signal
and the herd races
over the nearest ridge,
a hunter grasps
the difficulty of
stalking this perpetually
alert animal—
North America's
fastest quadruped.
Photography
by Bill Browning

*Preceding pages: Pronghorn races over prairie.
During long run, animal keeps mouth open for maximum
intake of oxygen. Below: Mature buck is relatively
small but has impressive horns. Right:
Buck escorts two does in flight from intruder.*

The pronghorn antelope is of strictly North American origin. He is a separate genus, the sole survivor of a mammalian form which, eons ago, evolved into several subspecies. Thus, he dimly resembles some lightly built cloven-hoofed quadrupeds, but is not closely related to them. He is a creature of odd physical characteristics and habits. For instance, like deer and cattle, he has two hoofs on each foot, but, like the giraffe, he has no dewclaws. Like sheep and goats, he has hollow horns. He is the only horned animal to shed his headgear annually, as deer and wapiti shed their antlers, but the outer shells alone are discarded; the inner cores are permanent and serve as foundations around which the new horn-shells grow. Both sexes have horns, but those of the does are token nubbins, ranging from two to four inches in length, and lack the buck's characteristic prongs—from which the species derives its descriptive name.

The pronghorn is easily the fastest North American quadruped and, very probably, is second only to the African cheetah throughout the world. The animal's smooth and floating gait eliminates waste effort and motion; there is no bobbing or bouncing as an antelope swoops gracefully and easily down a hillside, across a wide draw, and up the facing hill almost as if flying.

Forty miles per hour, a speed that no deer can match, is merely cruising for pronghorns. Occasional sprints of 50 miles per hour aren't unusual, and under pressure they can reach a mile a minute or better. No one really knows just how fast a thoroughly spooked pronghorn can travel in an

Left: Does and young trot along at comfortable but swift pace. Below: Band of thirteen antelope has been alarmed; on some of the animals, rump patches are erect to signal danger. Buck keeps to rear of his harem, carefully herding does.

Above: Five kid antelope have been startled. Rump-hair rosettes are raised and spread, but curiosity has conquered nervousness as two animals pause to look at photographer. Far right: Female kid has typical profile of immature antelope. Near right: Despite coltish build and spindly legs, very young kid is swift runner.

emergency, because no reliable tests have ever been made. Countless antelope have run away from saddle horses as if the mounts were picketed, and many have left rough-country vehicles in their dust in easy half-mile sprints.

Such speed requires highly specialized physical equipment. The windpipe is double the diameter of a human trachea, the heart is twice the size of a sheep's, and the lungs are also oversized. Finally, the species makes use of a supercharged type of breathing. Unlike other big-game animals, pronghorns seldom use just their nostrils for air intake beyond the first fifty yards or so of a fast run. Thereafter, they open their mouths and gulp air in rhythm with their flowing leaps.

Young pronghorns do not approach peak speed until they're eighteen to twenty months of age, or what are called "long yearlings" in the second hunting season after their birth. But compared to the young of other North American big game, they develop astonishing fleetness at an early age. Within a fortnight after birth, the kids abandon their camouflaged hideouts and begin following their mothers. By the time pronghorn youngsters are six weeks old they can give a good saddle horse a dandy race, and at three months of age they can outrun the best cow ponies. By the time they're long yearlings, they run as well as mature adults.

Some observers have claimed that the fastest pronghorns are mature does. I don't agree. During the rut, when the does break out of a harem—an instinctively calculated ploy, I believe, to inflame the bucks—the bucks are never outdistanced.

An even surer proof of the comparative speeds of the two sexes occurs when spooked herds are running. A mature doe almost invariably leads off, while the harem boss brings up the rear of the herd. But that's simply male possessiveness, allowing him to keep an eye on the harem and chase any doe that might stray. While herding his laggards, the buck frequently swerves from one flank to the other. He therefore covers more ground than the rest of the band, yet keeps up rather easily.

If shot at during such runs, when fleetness may mean the difference between life and death, the running superiority of bucks is very convincing. I've observed hunters trying to down a trailing buck, but they never got any more than one open shot. The supposedly slower-footed buck accelerated, so that he was almost instantly in the center of his harem or running at the far side of his band. It is true, however, that an overage male may abandon harem chasing to live a slower, more solitary life.

Pronghorns obviously enjoy racing; even when not spooked by gunfire, they often test their speed against a horseman or motor vehicle. They're also very stubborn about going where they want to go despite any efforts to turn them. They'll amble along at a good pace paralleling a vehicle and then, when some land feature offers them a slight advantage, they'll turn on the speed and cut ahead, often with only a few yards of passing margin.

They virtually never jump over obstructions, no matter how narrow the depression or low the obstacle. They won't jump fences which deer clear with ease, nor will they broad-jump dry washes. Woven-wire fences stop them, but they'll dive through or under

barbed wire. In some cases, they'll slide under the bottom strand like a baseball player stealing second, then spring up to continue their run. If a dry wash is so steeply banked that they can't run down into it and climb out the opposite bank, they'll turn parallel to it until a suitable crossing is found.

The name antelope is a misnomer for the pronghorn. Like some other American animals, the species was named by slightly confused Old World biologists. The pronghorn is no more an antelope than the American bison is a buffalo, or our largest deer a moose, or the wapiti an elk. Common usage has so firmly fixed the pronghorn's alias in our big-game terminology that any attempt to replace it with a scientifically correct name would be wasted effort. But the fact remains that the American pronghorn bears no close relationship to any of the true antelopes of Africa or elsewhere.

His scientific name is *Antilocapra americana*—in translation, the American goat-antelope. When the natives of pronghorn areas call him a goat they're closer to being correct than those who think he is an American cousin of the extensive Old World antelope family. Modern biologists suspect that he may be distantly related to the American mountain goat, the chamois of Europe, and the serow of Tibet and eastern Asia. But the predecessors of the pronghorn were flourishing in North America long before our now-native wild goats crossed the land bridge from Asia. Early pronghorn remains have been found over a broad stretch of North America, as far east as Illinois and Wisconsin, ranging across the Great Plains of Canada, the United States, and Mexico, and as far west as the coastal plains sloping toward the Pacific Ocean.

The Paleozoic era marked the development of the major groups of animals. The mammalian forms, including the pronghorn, originated near its close about 230 million years ago. Evolution then produced a number of species and subspecies, including pronghorns of jack rabbit size and others as large as today's pronghorns and larger.

Fossils of the more recent Pleistocene epoch, which began one million years ago, include pronghorn remains from such widely separated parts of the United States as the Rancho La Brea tar pits of southern Califorina, Fossil Lake of Oregon, and Hay Springs of Nebraska. But it is significant that most fossils found in the far western states are only a few thousand years old, while those from Nebraska and other mid-continental areas indicate that pronghorns lived there several hundreds of thousands of years ago.

Today's antelope subspecies are five in number: *americana*, the form found throughout the Great Plains; *oregona*, found in a limited area along the boundaries of Oregon, California, Idaho, and Nevada; *peninsulara*, of Baja California; *sonora*, of Mexico's Sonora Province and adjacent southern Arizona; and *mexicana*, ranging through the Chihuahua and Coahuila provinces of Mexico, and occasionally cropping up in the southeastern fringes of New Mexico and Texas. These subspecies designations mean very little to the hunter, for they do not indicate great variations in size, coloration, or habits. Except for the *sonora* subspecies, the smallest and palest of the lot, the trophy potential of all these antelope is about the same, even though certain habitat pockets may produce more than their share of large bucks.

The pronghorn's coat consists of very brittle outer hair, underlaid with much finer fur. The animal has the unusual ability to move its hair by a complex system of muscles beneath the hide; it can clamp down its outer sheath to fend off icy winter blasts or loosen it so that cooling breezes can play on its skin during sweltering summer days. The coat is fawn-colored on the back and sides. A broad band of creamy-white hair extends in a series of slashes across the front of the neck and throat, and the belly is the same hue. The facial coloration of does and bucks varies considerably. Females wear tannish hair across the bridges of their noses, while bucks have a dark brown mask.

The most spectacular pelt feature of the pronghorn is the rosette-like rump patch. This is immaculately white and composed of hair which may run up to six inches in length. When the animals are alerted or excited they erect and spread this much longer hair until it extends inches beyond the width and height of the rump. Then this rosette reflects an astonishing amount of light, and literally flashes its message of warning to pronghorns. It is actually an animal heliograph, regularly used to alert distant bands of some disturbance or danger. On sunny days in the clear air of wide-open pronghorn range, those flashes twinkle like tiny mirrors. I've glimpsed them thousands of times, often from miles away without using my binoculars. Whenever I saw them, I knew those bands had already identified some intruder.

The eyesight of antelope is equally marvelous. It is their primary protection against predators and hunters. They can sight and identify objects, especially moving ones, that are far beyond the range of unaided human eyesight.

The intrusion of anything new attracts their instant attention and curiosity. Bucks are generally bolder than does in inspecting strange things and dealing with them. The need to drive rivals away from their harems during the rut makes them naturally bold, and of course they have better offensive weapons than females.

Coyotes are the primary predators which beset pronghorns. If they are numerous they may sniff out and kill the kids before the

Photographed from helicopter, Montana pronghorn swoops over slope with smooth, effortless gait.

baby antelope have gained their running legs. Does keep a wary eye on the places where they hide their kids, but one doe can't always cope with a pair of meat-hungry coyotes determined to dine on her young.

Spring is also the time when golden eagles patrol the kidding areas, hoping to spot easy meals. Eagles do not seriously deplete a region's antelope population, but they are a menace until kids are able to run with their mothers. When an eagle appears then, a kid will run under its mother's belly and the doe may rear and thresh the air with her forelegs if the bird tries to threaten her young. That usually is enough to drive away the eagle.

Pronghorn bucks sometimes get into trouble because of their aggressiveness during the rut. In the old muzzle-loading days, a favorite hunting trick was to tie a bandana to the ramrod and stick it like a flag into the prairie sod. As the wind fluttered the bandana the antelope would see it and the buck of the herd would frequently approach to investigate. The hidden hunter could be sure that curiosity would bring the buck within close range. But such tolling seldom works on today's pronghorns, because they have become accustomed to strange objects on their ranges. A far more productive method is to crawl up as close as possible, get into a prone shooting position, and then raise one foot, waggle it, and let it drop out of sight. Its alternating appearance and disappearance has tolled a dozen aggressive bucks within range for me.

One year my younger son Jerry and I drew licenses for an area of wide valleys, many of them a half-mile or more in width. We scouted the area thoroughly in our hunting car and spent two frying days looking for a shot at reasonable range. Then we spotted a good herd in a valley with a meandering thread of green crossing it. I knew that meant there was a waterway, probably dry at this time of year, but offering some chance of a closing stalk.

We drove our hunting car along a trail to intersect the line of greenery and found that the crossing was deep enough to hide the vehicle, so we left it there and started toward the band on foot. At that point we were a mile away from the herd, far enough to avoid spooking the animals, and we could remain concealed as we made our way closer by way of the dry wash. We took our time, walking upright along the deeper parts of that little ravine and crawling in shallower spots, until we were opposite the herd. We snaked along on our bellies for another hundred yards until we got to the last of the sagebrush cover. Jerry was behind a scrawny bush and I was behind another. But that left a fearsome 400-yard shot to make.

We were discussing the trajectory of Jerry's .308, which was zeroed point-blank for two hundred yards, when the harem boss spotted us and came toward us at a dead run. He came so fast that I was afraid he'd get close enough to identify us and then offer a tough running shot. So I thrust one hand above the sagebrush and waggled my fingers at him. He pulled up short and stared at us. That pause was all Jerry needed. He put a bullet just under the buck's chin, killing him in his tracks. Moments before he had been four hundred yards away, but he fell just forty-nine paces from us.

Such incidents do not mean that pronghorn hunting is easy. Because of their superb eyesight, the successful stalking of antelope approaches a fine art. In my long hunting career, I've killed a good many of the wily creatures and I can't recall any two stalks that were exactly alike. A man has to study the country and the behavior of each herd, and then suit his approach to the conditions of the moment. Most of my stalks were made after sightings from eight hundred yards to a mile away. If the animals were drifting, I tried to check the lay of the land, guess where they would go, and place myself far enough ahead of them so that I could shift position to compensate for any changes of course. The average shot, I would say, is taken at two hundred yards.

In my experience, only one factor has remained constant in pronghorn stalking: A hunter has the best chance of putting himself within rifle range if he approaches the animals from below their level. Most big-game animals expect danger to come at them from below, but antelope keep a close watch on the skyline and expect hunters to show up above their location. Probably a great part of the success in approaching from below lies in the fact that it permits a cautious hunter to camouflage himself better amid surrounding vegetation.

For this kind of stalking a hunter must be willing to develop callouses on his belly, elbows, and knees; and, occasionally, his body will be pincushioned by cactus spines. He must crawl like a snake, employ cover like an Apache, shoot with minute-of-angle precision, and maneuver until his targets aren't screened by bullet-deflecting brush.

Since the average mature buck will weigh perhaps a hundred to a hundred and fifteen pounds, the target is small and a 200-yard shot may be quite a challenge. My preferred shot is broadside, not only because it provides the largest possible lung, heart, or liver target, but also because—if well placed in the chest—it damages the least amount of excellent meat. A frontal or rear shot is often a messy one, even if it results in a clean kill. And since pronghorns are comparatively narrow targets, the chance of a crippling hit is greatly increased.

Pronghorns have such smooth ground gaits that it would seem they'd be easy to hit on running shots, but that is seldom the case. The difficulty is two-fold: First, the shooting range is long; and second, the animals have many running speeds, all of them deceptively difficult to gauge. The hunter who misses on his first shot, usually because he failed to lead the animal sufficiently, may think he can very easily correct his aim for a successful second shot. But the target has increased its speed, the range has lengthened—and the subsequent shot is often just as far off its mark as the first try. It takes a lot of experience to gauge correctly the increasing range and running speed, and then neatly mesh them with fading bullet velocity.

Hunters unaccustomed to shooting at long ranges frequently fail to appreciate the enormous reduction of velocity which a bullet undergoes in traversing several hundred yards. As an example let's take the .270, a grand plains-land caliber of high velocity, flat trajectory, and excellent killing potential. Using 130-grain commercial loads, it delivers over 3,100 feet per second of velocity at the muzzle, 2,850 at one hundred yards, 2,600 at two hundred yards, 2,350 at three hundred yards, and 2,100 at four hundred yards. In four hundred yards of flight, then, there is a loss in velocity of a thousand feet per second, with a proportionate reduction of killing effect. While such bullets are slowing up, the antelope is speeding up, thus widening the lead required to score a hit.

The trajectory of a 130-grain .270 load is equally significant. If the rifle is zeroed in to hit at point of aim at two hundred yards, its bullets will strike an inch - and-a-half high at a hundred yards, seven inches low at three hundred yards, and twenty inches low at four hundred.

Because pronghorns offer little resistance to bullet penetration, rapidly expanding bullets are best. I recommend varmint-type soft-points wearing thin jackets over soft cores. Hard-cored and thick-jacketed big-game bullets will not mushroom rapidly enough. They'll fatally wound antelope, but the animals' great speed may carry them far beyond easy finding and retrieving. I've seen many well-hit antelope lost by inexperienced hunters because they didn't follow up far enough.

Other factors being equal, if you can choose between two or three bullets, you should select the heaviest. Antelope country is often breezy, and the longer the shot the more the bullet is blown off course. Light bullets drift too easily and slow up too soon.

A good pair of 7x35 or 9x50 binoculars is an invaluable aid in antelope hunting. Glasses of the lower power are ideal for examining trophy potential while stalking and should be carried on a short neck strap. The 9x50 glasses are too clumsy for carrying, but are excellent for glassing from motor vehicles. The dedicated trophy hunter can also save himself miles of walking and crawling by using a quality spotting scope.

A rifle scope is even more important, and it should provide from four- to six-power magnification. Variable scopes of the 2-7X or 3-9X range are ideal. If you use a variable scope, you may want to crank it up to high power for a close inspection of horns, but for actual aiming it will probably serve you best if you use a setting from 3X to 6X. A moderate magnification lessens the effect of mirage and the wavering of the sight picture caused by a hunter's involuntary movements.

Trophy horns, incidentally, do not take long to develop. In comparison to other big-game species, pronghorns are short-lived. They reach peak vigor and size at a mere four-and-a-half to five-and-a-half years. Bucks continue annually to grow more impressive headgear thereafter, but at seven-and-a-half years they're nearing the end of the line. A rare few reach nine years of age.

Good pronghorn country is always sagebrush country, since this drought-resistant plant provides their main food. Although they'll eat spring grasses, they much prefer forbs of that season, and if grasses are the only available foods they decline rapidly. Thus, they offer only minor competition to cattle on the wide pastures of the West. They compete strongly with sheep, however, which will eat anything, down to and including the roots of virtually all plants. If ranchers continue to destroy sagebrush by bulldozing and applying broad-leafed plant poisons in order to grow more grass for their livestock, the denuded areas which result will be death to pronghorns, which have no more suitable range to move to.

The savior of modern-day pronghorn hunting was Paul Russell of New Mexico. Antelope were once abundant in his state, but had been reduced to a few random herds when—some thirty years ago—he originated and perfected the live-trapping methods which are still in use. In an astonishingly few years, all antelope-producing states were copying his methods, trapping and transplanting mixed-age pronghorns from marginal range to habitat where they could again prosper.

Until Russell developed his trapping technique, transplanting had been done by capturing juveniles, bottle-raising them for some months, and then releasing them on suitable range. But these kids became so tame in the process that, when freed, they were as likely to run toward predators as to avoid them. It was believed that the adults' nervous temperament would cause them to die of fright if captured, but Russell proved otherwise. He also proved that trapping bands of bucks, does, and kids of all ages preserves herd identity; when released together the older animals continue to teach the kids to avoid predators and other hazards.

Paul Russell's first catch consisted of thirty-four head of mixed age captured in the spring of 1937. Russell then improved his techniques and traps so that two hundred and fifty-six were captured in 1938. Twelve of these were trucked to the Wichita Mountain Federal Wildlife Refuge in Oklahoma, in exchange for twelve elk which were used to start New Mexico's San Antonio mountain herd. The pronghorns were loaded and hauled in an eighteen-hour nonstop drive and all were delivered in excellent condition.

Other antelope-hungry states promptly showed keen interest in expanding the range of their own native pronghorns. After passage of the Pittman-Robertson Act of 1937, when Federal funds were made available to game departments, such transplanting projects were shifted into high gear. The Pittman-Robertson funds originated from an excise tax which sportsmen asked to be imposed on the sale of firearms and ammunition. Through P-R funds the nation's sportsmen have largely financed the enormous interstate swapping of wildlife species and improvement of habitat.

The trapping techniques which Paul Russell originated—now often including such modern refinements as herding by aircraft—are the basic reason for today's resurgence of pronghorn hunting. A 1923 Bureau of Biological Survey census set the continental antelope population at a mere 30,326 head, thinly scattered from Canada to Mexico. By 1957, hunting harvests had risen to around 54,000 head out of a continental population of 370,000. These figures remain reasonably stable today, and if sound conservation practices are maintained, the pronghorn antelope should continue to be numbered among this nation's great game animals. ◉

October Journal

by Nelson Bryant

In New Hampshire's hills,
the flaming colors of autumn
mark a short, perfect
time when seasons overlap and a
man can hunt grouse
or fish for brook trout.
Photography
by Hanson Carroll

When autumn's colors flare on New Hampshire's hills I think of mountaintop ponds where male brook trout are wearing their gaudy spawning colors, and they and their mates are feeding voraciously in anticipation of winter. I think also of the world's most glorious game bird, the ruffed grouse, or partridge as he is called by northern New Englanders, his battering wings carrying him through the red-gold forest.

There is no lovelier time of year in the North Country. It is a time of profound change, a change that gains impetus from each cold night. In lakes and ponds the water clears as plankton growth slows, and one can see generations of leaves lying on the bottom, fifteen or twenty feet down. On shore the birches show pale yellow, the beeches yellow and brown, and the dark-green conifers stand like exclamation points. Soon the essential shape of the forest will emerge as weakening sunlight streams through its broken roof.

For several weeks, if there are no storms, the dying leaves remain aloft, slowly losing their brilliance as winter approaches, but one gale can strip the forest in a few hours.

It is harvest time. Beechnuts, hazelnuts, hickory nuts, butternuts, and acorns litter the ground where they are sought by grouse, squirrels, porcupines, and deer. Some of the white-striped green needles of the hemlocks fall into the water and the hungry trout eat them in the belief they are insects tumbled from pond-side bushes.

Right: Bryant admires handsome banded fan of a partridge's tail feathers. Far right: His setter pauses at stream's edge, nose high for bird scent. Ruins of farms, like the one below, with their tumbled buildings, overgrown fields, and abandoned orchards, are often good hunting spots.

Witch-hazel bushes are festooned with trailing yellow flowers, and when the cold—and, I think, the heat of the sun after a cold night—opens their swelling pods, the twin seeds burst forth like buckshot, flying as far as ten feet. On a windless day one can hear the seeds pattering on the dry leaves. Sometimes the woods are full of grackles chattering as they feed on the sprinkled fruit of this bush, which is a tree in the southern states. Witch-hazel liniment still has its devotees. Its essence, distilled from the bark or leaves of the bush, is sweet and astringent, an excellent after-shave lotion, and some people find it helpful in treating mosquito bites. If one is so inclined, he can gather witch-hazel leaves in late summer or early fall and distill his own liniment. (There is a good description of how to do this in Euell Gibbons' *Stalking the Wild Asparagus*. This book and a companion volume, *Stalking the Blue-eyed Scallop*, are excellent for those who enjoy foraging for food and medicinal plants.)

The air in the mountains is never clearer than in the fall. From a high and rocky ledge one can look down on a lake marked by the dimple of an occasional rising trout or the V of a beaver patrolling his domain. From such a place, mountains and ridges in the distance are soft and blurred, as are yesterday's problems. Here and there, if the day is cold, a thin column of wood smoke rises from a farmhouse chimney in the far valleys. Wood smoke has the headiest aroma in all Creation, containing all the sweet-sadness of summer's lost and golden promise. If in some great city in winter, when all is gray and glum and damp, I came upon a woman wearing essence of wood smoke as a perfume, I would fall at her feet and worship her.

In New Hampshire, as in some other New England states, there is a short time when the grouse and trout seasons overlap. The blending in early October of perhaps the best trout fishing of the year with the start of grouse hunting is almost more than some men can bear. A choice is impossible. The only thing is to do both. From the day after Labor Day until October 15, New Hampshire has a fly-fishing-only season for trout, while the grouse season opens October 1. Fall trout fishing in New Hampshire is largely limited to lakes and ponds. Most of the streams are very low and many have only a few fish remaining, being managed on a put-and-take basis. But the state's still-water (pond and lake) trout fishing in the fall is another story, particularly in the seldom-visited remote ponds.

Nestled in the hills and forests and mountains of New Hampshire are more than seventy trout ponds labeled remote by the Fish and Game Department, because they can be reached only on foot, or, in some cases, by a four-wheel-drive vehicle. Most of these ponds are stocked with brook trout fingerlings from a low-flying airplane. These are the waters that offer the best fall fishing, and the trails to them lead through good grouse cover.

If one does not plan to camp overnight at one of the trout ponds, it is wise to arrive at dawn or shortly thereafter. I recall one fall morning when Vic Pomiecko, of Claremont, New Hampshire, and I reached a mountaintop lake before the sun was up. Glass-thin ice had formed in the shallows, the air temperature was perhaps twenty-six degrees, and the water was covered with swirling mist through which ghosts of trees across the nearby cove could be seen. As we dropped our packs, Vic spotted trout rising just beyond the ice in front of us and we raced to get ready. I have never been able to assemble a fly rod as rapidly as Vic. Twice, my cold, fumbling fingers lost the leader, and the entire rig slithered down out of the guides. Vic was roll-casting from shore before I tied on my fly.

We launched the best of three old boats that were tethered to hemlocks on the shore and pushed out through the fragile ice. We had carried in a two-man inflatable life raft, a precaution we always take, even if we know that the pond we plan to fish has

boats. It is always possible that they have rotted, that porcupines have chewed holes in them, or that they are being used.

In two or three casts, each of us was fast to a trout of about eleven inches. We were using flies of our own creation which we have found effective in the fall. Both are tied on a long-shanked #12 hook. Vic's has a body of red fluorescent floss, a butt of peacock herl, peacock tippets for a tail, and gray squirrel-tail hair on top. My fly substitutes orange floss for the red, and brown-and-black bucktail for the squirrel tail. Dried by false casting, these flies provided a short float, but the fish would probably have hit almost anything that morning, on or below the surface.

We were hampered by ice clogging our rod guides. After half a dozen casts our lines were immobilized and the only way to get back into action was to submerge the rod in the relatively warm waters of the pond. A half hour and a dozen fish later, the feeding ended. We continued to cast but raised no fish. The excitement over, the cold began to reach us and we waited impatiently for the sun to rise over the forest and cut through the chill mist. Being less of a Spartan than my companion, I fired up a small hiker's stove on the center seat of the boat and brewed a cup of coffee. Before we finished drinking it, a breeze came down off the ridge to the west, blowing the mist away in ragged streams, and the sun rose red over the woods.

In the summer on such waters there is no real problem about the plan of action when the dawn activity is done. Trout come up at sunrise and in the cool of evening to feed, then retreat to the cold depths where they can be reached with sinking lines. But in the fall they may be ranging at any depth and they will often gather in the sun-warmed shallows.

There is not, to my knowledge, any text

devoted to the art of fly fishing for trout in still waters, and one is needed. Unlike a stream, a pond offers no fast water, eddies, or pools, only deeps and shallows, shadows and bright sunlight. A sinking line often makes the difference between success and failure when the fish are down.

Emerging from their summer doldrums, still-water trout often feed recklessly in the fall, but I have gone after them too many years to offer this as any more than a generality. There are times, even on a crisp October day, when one has to find the right fly, and it is then that a companion fisherman is a great help. By consistently using different patterns and sizes until the right one is found, the experimentation time is cut in half. One of the common failures in pond or lake fishing for trout is to fall into a drowsy routine of offering the same fly in the same way for hours at a time. The fly should be changed often and fished at all depths, and the speed of the retrieve should be constantly varied.

Fall fly fishing in northern New England often tests even the hardiest souls. Several years ago Vic Pomiecko and I went forth on the last day of the season. The wind was from the northwest, blowing half a gale, and intermittent snow squalls came down out of the heavy skies. Arriving at Pleasant Lake in New London, New Hampshire, we looked out over a welter of tumbling waves and wind-driven snow. We launched our big Old Town canoe and anchored a few hundred feet from shore. The canoe bounced and wallowed in the waves and a mixture of freezing spray and snow soon covered it and us. The water was six to eight feet deep. We fished our brown bucktails right on the bottom and the fish, brook trout averaging nearly a pound each, were there. Two or three times motorists stopped on the highway to gaze incredulously at the snow-covered apparitions throwing fly lines in a

near-blizzard, and we obligingly took fish while they watched.

One further peculiarity of fall fly fishing for trout should be mentioned. The aquatic insects that hatch at that time of year are often very small and nothing but a tiny #22 fly on a twelve- or fourteen-foot leader tapered to a gossamer-thin 4X will tempt trout. At such a time a fisherman can be driven mad by hundreds of fish rising all about him that reject all but the tiniest offerings. I have found that the size of the fly, not its pattern, is all-important, although grays and blacks seem to produce best. A good fly for such an occasion can be made by rolling a bit of Canada goose quill around a #22 hook, leaving two little ends sticking up as feelers. No more dressing is needed.

Although October marks the end of fly fishing for trout, both logically and legally, in most of New England, one may still use his fly rod if he is able to transfer his attentions to the lowly chain pickerel and yellow perch. Both of these species will readily hit a fly. I have taken a nice string of pickerel on white and yellow bucktails in mid-November when the trees were bare and waterfowl were on the move. Pickerel put up a good fight on a light fly rod, often leaping out of water. Their sharp teeth raise havoc with flies, and I always try to use summer's trout-fishing rejects on them.

When combining trout fishing and grouse hunting in the fall, one should not ignore the chances for birds sometimes offered on the trail to and from a remote pond. All of the fishing and camping equipment must be carried in packs, so both hands are free to handle the gun. My first trail grouse fell on Mount Sunapee in Newbury, New Hampshire. My two boys and I and two other trout fishermen had begun the forty-five-minute climb up rocky Andrews Brook trail to Lake Solitude early in the morning. Just before we reached the halfway mark where the brook crosses the trail for the third time, the grouse beat his way off a hemlock perch on my left, heading across a ravine. When I shot he was no longer visible, having gone behind the hemlock. The others were sure I had missed and continued on. Clambering down the slope I found twigs cut off by the pellets. Then, a few feet farther, I saw a tiny feather resting on the forest floor. It took five minutes to find another feather at the edge of the brook, where I sat down, stoked my pipe, and looked about me. Eventually, what I had taken for a collection of leaves turning slowly in an eddy at my feet assumed the shape of a floating grouse and I had my bird. At the lake, my oldest son Steve prepared the bird for campfire cooking. He even retrieved a handful of beechnuts from its crop and opened and ate them.

The difficulty of finding some downed birds is the main drawback to hunting without a dog. Good grouse dogs are rare, however, and most pointers, for example, range too wide for thick grouse cover.

Windy days make for difficult grouse hunting. Many birds are heard before they are seen, and some not seen at all. A few years ago, while walking up grouse in Newport, I spent a half hour following a bird I could not see before putting him in the game bag. I first flushed him from a stand of young white pines. He thrashed his way out of the heavy cover, and, a few seconds later, I heard him land less than a hundred yards away. I went toward where I had last heard him and flushed and followed him twice more before I had a chance to shoot. This particular bird cooperated by not running very far after landing. Without a dog, a running grouse is often lost after the first flush. He may land in a tree, and it is a good idea to search the trees for roosting birds.

Always remember that grouse often jump when you stop walking, so always stop with your feet in shooting position. It may be that the grouse has been watching you, and if your approach is not directly toward him he will let you go by. Stopping may be interpreted by the bird as meaning you have spotted him.

If one wishes to divide his time equally between grouse and trout, he should stop fishing in midmorning and go for birds until an hour or two before sunset. Grouse usually feed from daybreak until shortly before noon, then resume again in midafternoon, breaking off at dusk to roost. The birds are easier to find in early morning and late afternoon, but that unfortunately conflicts with the prime trout-fishing time.

Trout and grouse are not the only delights available to the fall sportsman. Vic and I never pass a batch of edible mushrooms on our way through the woods without harvesting them. Vic was instructed in the art of wild-mushroom gathering by his father, who came to Vermont from Poland as a young man. Vic still uses one of the split-willow mushroom baskets made by his father twenty-five years ago. I received my first lessons from Vic, then expanded his list of perhaps a dozen edible fungi to thirty by delving in textbooks.

If possible, we gather our mushrooms on our way to a trout pond and place them in the shade while we fish. We keep a few trout alive on a stringer and make our noon meal of wild mushrooms and brook trout.

The true taste of a brook trout can never be known until the fish is eaten within a few minutes of its demise. This can be partially attributed to the magic of the woods and a hunger whetted by the out-of-doors, but there is a sweet and delicate flavor in a just-caught trout that is gone a few hours later. Although gourmets will shudder, we fry them in bacon fat along with the mushrooms. It is necessary to sever the backbones of the fish in one or two places to stop them from curling in the pan.

In summer, if it has been a wet one, there are usually more mushrooms available. Among our favorites at this time are the *Boletus edulis* and the *Suillus granulatus*. The latter species is also prevalent in September and sometimes early October. Shortly before mid-October and continuing into November in northern New England, the oyster mushrooms, or *Pleurotus ostreatus*, can be found in great quantities on scarred or dead areas of sugar maples. Another fall mushroom, and one that can survive alternate freezing and thawing, is the *Flammulina velutipes*, which is found on dying elms or their stumps, and which resembles the oyster mushroom.

Frequently the clumps of *Pleurotus ostreatus* are high above the ground, making it necessary to climb for them. I used to carry a long pole on top of my car when driving about the New Hampshire countryside in the fall, and with its help dislodged many oyster mushrooms.

A New England fall hike is also a practical lesson in history, on the decline of the small farming homestead. Old England has its castles and crumbling ruins, New England its ubiquitous stone walls and abandoned, broken farmhouses, barns, and outbuildings. Often, beyond the tumbled, weathered boards and beams, gnarled apple trees, as tough as the man that planted them, fight with the other trees of the forest for their share of sunlight and water. And sometimes, even after seventy-five years, the trees still bear fruit, small misshapen apples, that are sought by deer, grouse, and porcupine when fall winds shake them loose.

While hunting or hiking, I have followed up my noon meal of a sandwich and a cup of tea brewed over a small fire with two or three of these apples. Even when frozen, they are good. Your teeth ache when you bite into them, but they are often sweet and firm-fleshed.

Not all of interior New England's early settlers chose the flatlands and the river and stream valleys for homesites. There were some who, having moved that far from the towns and cities of the seacoast, moved still farther and built their homes on the slopes of mountains. The remnants of such a farm may be found halfway up the Johnson Brook trail on Mount Sunapee, and another is near the summit on the west slope of Green Mountain, in Claremont. In both locations, pure drinking water from a brook was and is available. Water was the first requisite of a good homesite. Coming on such a place, perhaps attracted by the bright red of apples against the dark surrounding trees, one marvels at the hardiness of the men and women who chose to live alone and so far above their nearest neighbors.

Sometimes enough of the house or barn or outbuildings remains for the wandering hunter to take shelter from a rain squall, and I have often shared their drafty interiors with a grunting porcupine or scampering wood mouse. Caught in such a spot, with nothing to do but wait out the storm, one can shut his eyes and imagine the place as it was, and the wind in the broken eaves is the sound of a woman singing as she cleans house on a sunny June morning.

There is an aura of sanctity about these abandoned farms. One can feel the presence of the people long dead who spent their lives shaping a bit of the land to their desires. One can hear the father telling his young sons of his plans for them to take over when he is gone. But often the force that drove him was not transferred to his sons, and the people and the lights and mills and wages of the towns and cities pulled them away until the old man and his old wife were left alone in a decaying house while the ranks of the trees closed in. ◉

A TOUR ON THE PRAIRIES

By Washington Irving

The untamed land that was Indian Territory
in the 1830's is vividly portrayed in
passages from the hunting and scouting narrative of a
great American writer, and in contemporary
watercolors by Alfred Jacob Miller.

"Bull-boating" by Alfred Jacob Miller. Irving describes his crossing of the Arkansas River by this same technique.

In the often vaunted regions of the Far West, several hundred miles beyond the Mississippi, extends a vast tract of uninhabited country, where there is neither to be seen the log house of the white man, nor the wigwam of the Indian. It consists of great grassy plains, interspersed with forests and groves, and clumps of trees, and watered by the Arkansas, the grand Canadian, the Red River, and their tributary streams. Over these fertile and verdant wastes still roam the elk, the buffalo, and the wild horse, in all their native freedom. These, in fact, are the hunting grounds of the various tribes of the Far West. Hither repair the Osage, the Creek, the Delaware and other tribes that have linked themselves with civilization, and live within the vicinity of the white settlements. Here resort also, the Pawnees, the Comanches, and other fierce, and as yet independent tribes, the nomades of the prairies, or the inhabitants of the skirts of the Rocky Mountains. The regions I have mentioned form a debatable ground of these warring and vindictive tribes; none of them presume to erect a permanent habitation within its borders. Their hunters and "braves" repair thither in numerous bodies during the season of game, throw up their transient hunting camps, consisting of light bowers covered with bark and skins, commit sad havoc among the innumerable herds that graze the prairies, and having loaded themselves with venison and buffalo meat, warily retire from the dangerous neighborhood. . . . It is the purport of the following pages to narrate a month's excursion to these noted hunting grounds, through a tract of country which had not as yet been explored by white men.

It was early in October, 1832, that I arrived at Fort Gibson, a frontier post of the Far West, situated on the Neosho, or Grand River, near its confluence with the Arkansas. I had been travelling for a month past, with a small party from St. Louis, up the banks of the Missouri, and along the frontier line of agencies and missions, that extends from the Missouri to the Arkansas. Our party was headed by one of the Commissioners appointed by the government of the United States to superintend the settlement of the Indian tribes migrating from the east to the west of the Mississippi. In the discharge of his duties, he was thus visiting the various outposts of civilization.

And here let me bear testimony to the merits of this worthy leader of our little band. He was a native of one of the towns of Connecticut, a man in whom a course of legal practice and political life had not been able to vitiate an innate simplicity and benevolence of heart.

Another of my fellow-travellers was Mr. L., an Englishman by birth, but descended from a foreign stock; and who had all the buoyancy and accommodating spirit of a native of the Continent. Having rambled over many countries, he had become, to a certain degree, a citizen of the world, easily adapting himself to any change. He was a man of a thousand occupations: a botanist, a geologist, a hunter of beetles and butterflies, a musical amateur, a sketcher of no mean pretensions, in short, a complete virtuoso; added to which, he was a very inde-

Both Miller and Irving participated in successful buffalo hunts. This painting is entitled "Taking the Hump Rib."

Miller's "Escape from the Blackfeet" depicts a common experience in the 1830's, when hostile bands roamed the West.

"*Capture of Wild Horses by Indians.*" Irving notes that a half-breed member of his party was adept at this procedure.

"*Trappers' Encampment on the Big Sandy River.*" Stops were made at such spots so frontiersmen could pursue game.

fatigable, if not always a very successful sportsman.

My third fellow-traveller was one who had accompanied the former from Europe, and travelled with him as his Telemachus; being apt, like his prototype, to give occasional perplexity and disquiet to his Mentor. He was a young Swiss Count, scarce twenty-one years of age, full of talent and spirit, but galliard in the extreme, and prone to every kind of wild adventure.

Having made this mention of my comrades, I must not pass over unnoticed, a personage of inferior rank, but of all-pervading and prevalent importance: the squire, the the factotum, and, I may add, the universal groom, the cook, the tent man, in a word, meddler and marplot of our party. This was a little, swarthy, meagre, French creole, named Antoine, but familiarly dubbed Tonish; a kind of Gil Blas of the frontiers, who had passed a scrambling life, sometimes among white men, sometimes among Indians; sometimes in the employ of traders, missionaries and Indian agents; sometimes mingling with the Osage hunters. We picked him up at St. Louis, near which he has a small farm, an Indian wife, and a brood of half-blood children. According to his own account, however, he had a wife in every tribe; in fact, if all this little vagabond said of himself were to be believed, he was without morals, without caste, without creed, without country, and even without language; for he spoke a jargon of mingled French, English, and Osage.

Our route had been a pleasant one, quartering ourselves, occasionally, at the widely separated establishments of the Indian missionaries, but in general camping out in the fine groves that border the streams, and sleeping under cover of a tent. During the latter part of our tour we had pressed forward in hopes of arriving in time at Fort Gibson to accompany the Osage hunters on their autumnal visit to the buffalo prairies. Indeed the imagination of the young Count had become completely excited on the subject. The grand scenery and wild habits of the prairies had set his spirits madding, and the stories that little Tonish told him of Indian braves and Indian beauties, of hunting buffaloes and catching wild horses, had set him all agog for a dash into savage life. . . . It was amusing to hear his youthful anticipations of all that he was to see, and do, and enjoy, when mingling among the Indians and participating in their hardy adventures; and it was still more amusing to listen to the gasconadings of little Tonish, who volunteered to be his faithful squire in all his perilous undertakings; to teach him how to catch the wild horse, bring down the buffalo, and win the smiles of Indian princesses;—"And if we can only get sight of a prairie on fire!" said the young Count—"By Gar, I'll set one on fire myself!" cried the little Frenchman.

→≫≫≫≪≪≪≪

Our march continued parallel to the Arkansas, through a rich and varied country; sometimes we had to break our way through alluvial bottoms matted with redundant vegetation, where the gigantic trees were entangled with grape-vines, hanging like cordage from their branches; sometimes we coasted along sluggish brooks, whose feebly trickling current just served to link together a succession of glassy pools, imbedded like mirrors in the quiet bosom of the forest, reflecting its autumnal foliage, and patches of the clear blue sky. Sometimes we scrambled up broken and rocky hills, from the summits of which we had wide views stretching on one side over distant prairies diversified by groves and forests, and on the other ranging along a line of blue and shadowy hills beyond the waters of the Arkansas.

The appearance of our troop was suited to the country; stretching along in a line of upwards of half a mile in length, winding among brakes and bushes, and up and down the defiles of the hills: the men in every kind of uncouth garb, with long rifles on their shoulders, and mounted on horses of every color. The pack-horses, too, would incessantly wander from the line of march, to crop the surrounding herbage, and were banged and beaten back by Tonish and his half-breed compeers, with volleys of mongrel oaths. Every now and then the notes of the bugle, from the head of the column, would echo through the woodlands and along the hollow glens, summoning up stragglers, and announcing the line of march. The whole scene reminded me of the description given of bands of buccaneers penetrating the wilds of South America, on their plundering expeditions against the Spanish settlements.

At one time we passed through a luxuriant bottom of meadow bordered by thickets, where the tall grass was pressed down into numerous "deer beds," where those animals had couched the preceding night. Some oak trees also bore signs of having been clambered by bears, in quest of acorns, the marks of their claws being visible in the bark.

As we opened a glade of this sheltered meadow we beheld several deer bounding away in wild affright, until, having gained some distance, they would stop and gaze back, with the curiosity common to this animal, at the strange intruders into their solitudes. There was immediately a sharp report of rifles in every direction, from the young huntsmen of the troop, but they were too eager to aim surely, and the deer, unharmed, bounded away into the depths of the forest.

In the course of our march we struck the Arkansas, but found ourselves still below the Red Fork, and, as the river made deep bends, we again left its banks and continued through the woods. We encamped in a beautiful basin bordered by a fine stream, and shaded by clumps of lofty oaks.

The horses were now hobbled, that is to say, their fore legs were fettered with cords or leathern straps, so as to impede their movements, and prevent their wandering from the camp. They were then turned loose to graze. A number of rangers, prime hunters, started off in different directions in search of game. There was no whooping nor laughing about the camp as in the morning; all were either busy about the fires preparing the evening's repast, or reposing upon the grass. Shots were soon heard in various directions. After a time a huntsman rode into the camp with the carcass of a fine buck hanging across his horse.

Just as the night set in, there was a great shouting at one end of the camp, and immediately afterwards a body of young rangers came parading round the various fires, bearing one of their comrades in triumph on their shoulders. He had shot an elk for the first time in his life, and it was the first animal of the kind that had been killed on this expedition. The young huntsman, whose name was M'Lellan, was the hero of the camp for the night, and was the "father of the feast" into the bargain; for portions of his elk were seen roasting at every fire.

THE WESTERN MASTERPIECES OF WASHINGTON IRVING
AND ALFRED JACOB MILLER

In 1832, when he was forty-nine years old, Washington Irving had become a literary idol in his native country and was one of the few American writers to have earned foreign acclaim. He was also a respected diplomat who had lived abroad for seventeen years, the last half-dozen of them in Madrid, where he had been attached to the American embassy. Soon after returning to the United States, he decided to see something of the West, and in the summer of 1832 he booked passage on a steamer to Detroit.

With him were two friends, an Englishman named Charles Joseph Latrobe and a young Swiss nobleman, Count Albert-Alexandre de Pourtalès. Aboard the steamer, the three men became acquainted with Henry Leavitt Ellsworth, who had just been appointed commissioner to deal with the western Indians and was about to journey to Fort Gibson, west of Arkansas, in the Indian Territory that is now Oklahoma. When Ellsworth invited Irving to accompany him, the famous author was delighted, for here was a chance, as he said, "to see those fine countries of the 'far west,' while still in a state of pristine wildness."

Arrangements were soon made for Irving, Latrobe, and Pourtalès to go with Ellsworth and a company of Rangers on a scouting expedition — a circuit that took them westward from Fort Gibson on the Arkansas River to the Canadian and Cimarron rivers, over a hundred miles into the Indian Territory. In addition to the commissioner, the Rangers, and a camp surgeon, Irving's party secured the services of a halfbreed hunter named Pierre Beatte and a halfbreed retainer, Antoine (also called Tonish).

Finding the West even wilder and more exciting than he had hoped, Irving made copious notes on everyone and everything he saw—the game, the landscape, the Indians, trappers, hunters, and Rangers. From these notes he compiled his famous *Western Journals* and in 1835 he published *A Tour on the Prairies*, which has become a minor American classic. (An excellent edition is in print, published by the University of Oklahoma Press.)

The scouting trip began in early October—when the savage grandeur of the wilderness was enhanced by fiery autumn foliage—and lasted just over a month. Passages from *A Tour on the Prairies* convey the flavor of the forests and plains, the exhilaration of the hunt, the dangers of exploring a region frequented by hostile tribes, and the personalities of the frontiersmen.

Accompanying these excerpts are watercolors by Alfred Jacob Miller (1810-1874), one of the most notable American artists who painted western scenes. In 1837, only five years after Irving's excursion, a wealthy Scottish tourist and hunter named Captain William Drummond Stewart hired Miller to accompany him on a trip even farther west than Irving had gone—across the prairies, into the Rocky Mountains beyond Fort Laramie, and finally into the Oregon Territory. Stewart commissioned the artist to record the trip in oil paintings, which afterward adorned the walls of Stewart's castle in Scotland.

These oils were painted from hundreds of on-the-spot sketches and watercolors executed during the long western journey. Later, Miller painted many watercolor duplicates of the same scenes, and in doing so showed a genius for retaining the spontaneity of the rough sketches while producing more finished landscapes, and narrative paintings. Today, his watercolors are considered superior to his oils.

For years, Miller's work was all but forgotten, but during the last two decades his artistic reputation has been resurrected, and he is now represented in virtually every major exhibition of art concerned with the Far West. The paintings appearing in these pages have been selected from more than two hundred of his works at the Walters Art Gallery in Baltimore. The same wild scenes depicted by Washington Irving's prose are captured in these watercolor masterpieces of prairie life by Alfred Jacob Miller.

The other hunters returned without success. The Captain had observed the tracks of a buffalo, which must have passed within a few days, and had tracked a bear for some distance until the foot-prints had disappeared. He had seen an elk, too, on the banks of the Arkansas, which walked out on a sand-bar of the river, but before he could steal round through the bushes to get a shot, it had re-entered the woods.

Our own hunter, Beatte, returned silent and sulky, from an unsuccessful hunt. As yet he had brought us in nothing, and we had depended for our supplies of venison upon the Captain's mess. Beatte was evidently mortified, for he looked down with contempt upon the rangers, as raw and inexperienced woodsmen, but little skilled in hunting; they, on the other hand, regarded Beatte with no very complacent eye, as one of an evil breed, and always spoke of him as "the Indian."

Our little Frenchman, Tonish, also, by his incessant boasting, and chattering, and gasconading, in his balderdashed dialect, had drawn upon himself the ridicule of many of the wags of the troop, who amused themselves at his expense in a kind of raillery by no means remarkable for its delicacy; but the little varlet was so completely fortified by vanity and self-conceit, that he was invulnerable to every joke. I must confess, however, that I felt a little mortified at the sorry figure our retainers were making among these moss-troopers of the frontier. Even our very equipments came in for a share of unpopularity, and I heard many sneers at the double-barrelled guns with which we were provided against smaller game; the lads of the West holding "shotguns," as they call them, in great contempt, thinking grouse, partridges, and even wild turkeys as beneath their serious attention, and the rifle the only fire-arm worthy of a hunter.

After riding a short distance [the next] morning, we came upon a well-worn Indian track, and following it, scrambled to the summit of a hill, from whence we had a wide prospect over a country diversified by rocky ridges and waving lines of upland, and enriched by groves and clumps of trees of varied tuft and foliage. At a distance to the west, to our great satisfaction, we beheld the Red Fork rolling its ruddy current to the Arkansas, and found that we were above the point of junction. We now descended and pushed forward, with much difficulty, through the rich alluvial bottom that borders the Arkansas. Here the trees were interwoven with grape-vines, forming a kind of cordage, from trunk to trunk and limb to limb; there was a thick undergrowth, also, of bush and bramble, and such an abundance of hops, fit for gathering, that it was difficult for our horses to force their way through.

—»»»»»×≪≪≪←

We had now arrived at the river, about a quarter of a mile above the junction of the Red Fork; but the banks were steep and crumbling, and the current was deep and rapid. It was impossible, therefore, to cross at this place; and we resumed our painful course through the forest, dispatching Beatte ahead, in search of a fording place. We had proceeded about a mile further, when he rejoined us, bringing intelligence of a place hard by, where the river, for a great part of its breadth, was rendered fordable by sandbars, and the remainder might easily be swam by the horses.

Here, then, we made a halt. Some of the rangers set to work vigorously with their axes, felling trees on the edge of the river, wherewith to form rafts for the transportation of their baggage and camp equipage. Others patrolled the banks of the river farther up, in hopes of finding a better fording place; being unwilling to risk their horses

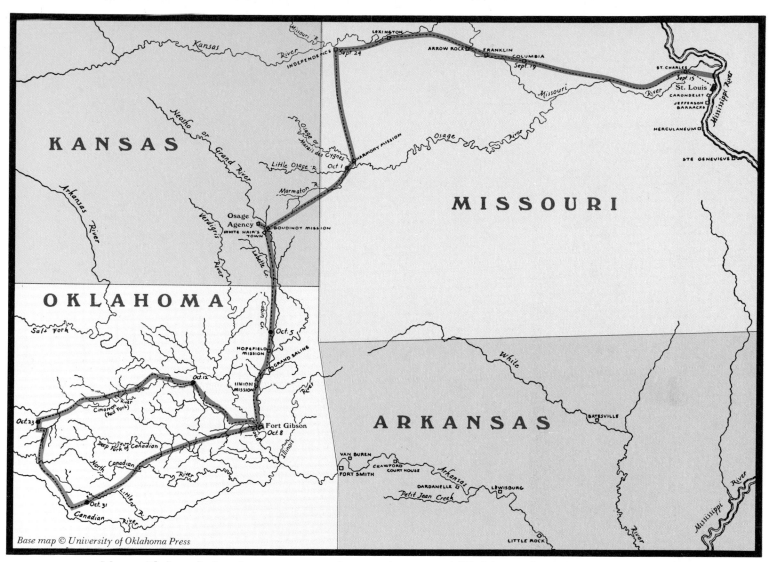

Map, with boundaries of present states, shows entire route of Washington Irving's western tour.

in the deep channel.

It was now that our worthies, Beatte and Tonish, had an opportunity of displaying their Indian adroitness and resource. At the Osage village which we had passed a day or two before, they had procured a dry buffalo skin. This was now produced; cords were passed through a number of small eyelet holes with which it was bordered, and it was drawn up, until it formed a kind of deep trough. Sticks were then placed athwart it on the inside, to keep it in shape; our camp equipage and a part of our baggage were placed within, and the singular bark was carried down the bank and set afloat. A cord was attached to the prow, which Beatte took between his teeth, and throwing himself

into the water, went ahead, towing the bark after him; while Tonish followed behind, to keep it steady and to propel it. Part of the way they had foothold, and were enabled to wade, but in the main current they were obliged to swim. The whole way, they whooped and yelled in the Indian style, until they landed on the opposite shore.

The Commissioner and myself were so well pleased with this Indian mode of ferriage, that we determined to trust ourselves in the buffalo hide. Our companions, the Count and Mr. L., had proceeded with the horses, along the river bank, in search of a ford which some of the rangers had discovered, about a mile and a half distant.

Our men having recrossed with their cockle-shell bark, it was drawn on shore, half filled with saddles, saddle-bags, and other luggage, amounting to a hundred weight; and being again placed in the water, I was invited to take my seat. It appeared to me pretty much like the embarkation of the wise men of Gotham, who went to sea in a bowl: I stepped in, however, without hesitation, though as cautiously as possible, and sat down on the top of the luggage, the margin of the hide sinking to within a hand's breadth of the water's edge. Rifles, fowling-pieces, and other articles of small bulk, were then handed in, until I protested against receiving any more freight. We then launched forth upon the stream, the bark being towed as before.

It was with a sensation half serious, half comic, that I found myself thus afloat, on the skin of a buffalo, in the midst of a wild river, surrounded by wilderness, and towed along by a half savage, whooping and yelling like a devil incarnate. To please the vanity of little Tonish, I discharged the double-barrelled gun, to the right and left, when in the center of the stream. The report echoed along the woody shores, and was answered by shouts from some of the rangers, to the great exultation of the little Frenchman, who took to himself the whole glory of this Indian mode of navigation.

Our voyage was accomplished happily; the Commissioner was ferried across with equal success, and all our effects were brought over in the same manner.

→»»→»×«←«←

Having passed through the skirt of woodland bordering the river, we ascended the hills, taking a westerly course through an undulating country of "oak openings," where the eye stretched over wide tracts of hill and dale, diversified by forests, groves, and clumps of trees. As we were proceeding at a slow pace, those who were at the head of the line descried four deer grazing on a grassy slope about half a mile distant. They apparently had not perceived our approach, and continued to graze in perfect tranquillity. A young ranger obtained permission from the Captain to go in pursuit of them, and the troop halted in lengthened line, watching him in silence. Walking his horse slowly and cautiously, he made a circuit until a screen of wood intervened between him and the deer. Dismounting then, he left his horse among the trees, and creeping round a knoll, was hidden from our view. We now kept our eyes intently fixed on the deer, which continued grazing, unconscious of their danger. Presently there was the sharp report of a rifle; a fine buck made a convulsive bound and fell to the earth; his companions scampered off. Immediately our whole line of march was broken; there was a helter-skelter galloping of the youngsters of the troop, eager to get a shot at the fugitives; and one of the most conspicuous personages in the chase was our little Frenchman, Tonish, on his silver-gray; having abandoned his pack-horses at the first sight of the deer. It was some time before our scattered forces could be recalled by the bugle, and our march resumed.

Two or three times in the course of the day we were interrupted by hurry-scurry scenes of the kind. The young men of the troop were full of excitement on entering an unexplored country abounding in game, and they were too little accustomed to discipline or restraint to be kept in order.

After a march of about fifteen miles west we encamped in a beautiful peninsula, made by the windings and doublings of a deep, clear, and almost motionless brook, and covered by an open grove of lofty and magnificent trees. Several hunters immediately started forth in quest of game before the noise of the camp should frighten it from the vicinity. Our man, Beatte, also took his rifle and went forth alone, in a different course from the rest.

For my own part, I lay on the grass under the trees, and built castles in the clouds, and indulged in the very luxury of rural repose. Indeed I can scarcely conceive a kind of life more calculated to put both mind and body in a healthful tone. A morning's ride of several hours diversified by hunting incidents; an encampment in the afternoon under some noble grove on the borders of a stream; an evening banquet of venison, fresh killed, roasted, or broiled on the coals; turkeys just from the thickets and wild honey from the trees; and all relished with an appetite unknown to the gourmets of the cities. And at night—such sweet sleeping in the open air, or waking and gazing at the moon and stars, shining between the trees!

On the present occasion, however, we had not much reason to boast of our larder. But one deer had been killed during the day, and none of that had reached our lodge. We were fain, therefore, to stay our keen appetites by some scraps of turkey brought from the last encampment, eked out with a slice or two of salt pork. This scarcity, however, did not continue long. Before dark a young hunter returned well laden with spoil. He had shot a deer, cut it up in an artist-like style, and, putting the meat in a kind of sack made of the hide, had slung it across his shoulder and trudged with it to camp.

Not long after, Beatte made his appearance with a fat doe across his horse. It was the first game he had brought in, and I was glad to see him with a trophy. . . . He laid the carcass down by our fire without saying a word, and then turned to unsaddle his horse; nor could any questions from us about his hunting draw from him more than laconic replies. If Beatte, however, observed this Indian taciturnity about what he had done, Tonish made up for it by boasting of what he meant to do. Now that we were in

a good hunting country he meant to take the field, and, if we would take his word for it, our lodge would henceforth be overwhelmed with game. Luckily his talking did not prevent his working, the doe was skilfully dissected, several fat ribs roasted before the fire, the coffee kettle replenished, and in a little while we were enabled to indemnify ourselves luxuriously for our late meagre repast.

The Captain did not return until late, and he returned empty handed. He had been in pursuit of his usual game, the deer, when he came upon the tracks of a gang of about sixty elk. Having never killed an animal of the kind, and the elk being at this moment an object of ambition among all the veteran hunters of the camp, he abandoned his pursuit of the deer, and followed the newly discovered track. After some time he came in sight of the elk, and had several fair chances of a shot, but was anxious to bring down a large buck, which kept in the advance. Finding at length there was danger of the whole gang escaping him, he fired at a doe. The shot took effect, but the animal had sufficient strength to keep on for a time with its companions. From the tracks of blood he felt confident it was mortally wounded, but evening came on, he could not keep the trail, and had to give up the search until morning.

>>>>>><<<<<

With the morning dawn, the prime hunters of the camp were all on the alert, and set off in different directions, to beat up the country for game. The Captain's brother, Sergeant Bean, was among the first, and returned before breakfast with success, having killed a fat doe, almost within the purlieus of the camp.

When breakfast was over, the Captain mounted his horse, to go in quest of the elk which he had wounded on the preceding evening; and which, he was persuaded, had received its death wound. I determined to join him in the search, and we accordingly sallied forth together, accompanied also by his brother, the sergeant, and a lieutenant. Two rangers followed on foot, to bring home the carcass of the doe which the sergeant had killed. We had not ridden far, when we came to where it lay, on the side of a hill, in the midst of a beautiful woodland scene. The two rangers immediately fell to work, with true hunters' skill, to dismember it, and prepare it for transportation to the camp, while we continued on our course. We passed along sloping hillsides, among skirts of thicket and scattered forest trees, until we came to a place where the long herbage was pressed down with numerous elk beds. Here the Captain had first roused the gang of elks, and, after looking about diligently for a little while, he pointed out their "trail," the foot-prints of which were as large as those of horned cattle. He now put himself upon the track, and went quietly forward, the rest of us following him in Indian file. At length he halted at the place where the elk had been when shot at. Spots of blood on the surrounding herbage showed that the shot had been effective. The wounded animal had evidently kept for some distance with the rest of the herd, as could be seen by sprinkling of blood here and there, on the shrubs and weeds bordering the trail. These at length suddenly disappeared. "Somewhere hereabout," said the Captain, "the elk must have turned off from the gang. Whenever they feel themselves mortally wounded, they will turn aside, and seek some out-of-the-way place to die alone."

There was something in this picture of the last moments of a wounded deer, to touch the sympathies of one not hardened to the gentle disports of the chase; such sympathies, however, are but transient. Man is naturally an animal of prey; and, however changed by civilization, will readily relapse into his instinct for destruction. I found my ravenous and sanguinary propensities daily growing stronger upon the prairies.

After looking about for a little while, the Captain succeeded in finding the separate trail of the wounded elk, which turned off almost at right angles from that of the herd, and entered an open forest of scattered trees. The traces of blood became more faint and rare, and occurred at greater distances: at length they ceased altogether, and the ground was so hard, and the herbage so much parched and withered, that the foot-prints of the animal could no longer be perceived.

"The elk must lie somewhere in this neighborhood," said the Captain, "as you may know by those turkey-buzzards wheeling about in the air: for they always hover in that way above some carcass. However, the dead elk cannot get away, so let us follow the trail of the living ones: they may have halted at no great distance, and we may find them grazing, and get another crack at them."

We accordingly returned, and resumed the trail of the elks, which led us a straggling course over hill and dale, covered with scattered oaks. Every now and then we would catch a glimpse of a deer bounding away across some glade of the forest, but the Captain was not to be diverted from his elk hunt by such inferior game. A large flock of wild turkeys, too, were roused by the trampling of our horses; some scampered off as fast as their long legs could carry them; others fluttered up into the trees, where they remained with outstretched necks, gazing at us. The Captain would not allow a rifle to be discharged at them, lest it should alarm the elk, which he hoped to find in the vicinity. At length we came to where the forest ended in a steep bank, and the Red Fork wound its way below us, between broad sandy shores. The trail descended the bank, and we could trace it, with our eyes, across the level sands, until it terminated in the river, which, it was evident, the gang had forded on the preceding evening.

"It is needless to follow on any further," said the Captain. "The elk must have been much frightened, and, after crossing the river, may have kept on for twenty miles without stopping."

Our little party now divided, the lieutenant and sergeant making a circuit in quest of game, and the Captain and myself taking the direction of the camp. On our way, we came to a buffalo track, more than a year old. It was not wider than an ordinary footpath, and worn deep into the soil; for these animals follow each other in single file. Shortly afterward, we met two rangers on foot, hunting. They had wounded an elk, but he had escaped; and in pursuing him, had found the one shot by the Captain on the preceding evening. They turned back, and conducted us to it. It was a noble animal, as large as a yearling heifer, and lay in an open part of the forest, about a mile and a half distant from the place where it had been shot. The turkey-buzzards, which we had previously noticed, were wheeling in the air above it. The observation of the Captain seemed verified.

->>>->>X<<-<<<-

The capture of the wild horse is one of the most favorite achievements of the prairie tribes; and, indeed, it is from this source that the Indian hunters chiefly supply themselves. The wild horses which range those vast grassy plains, extending from the Arkansas to the Spanish settlements, are of various forms and colors, betraying their various descents. Some resemble the common English stock, and are probably descended from horses which have escaped from our border settlements. Others are of a low but strong make, and are supposed to be of the Andalusian breed, brought out by the Spanish discoverers.

Some fanciful speculatists have seen in them descendants of the Arab stock, brought into Spain from Africa, and thence transferred to this country; and have pleased themselves with the idea, that their sires may have been of the pure coursers of the desert, that once bore Mahomet and his warlike disciples.

The habits of the Arab seem to have come with the steed. The introduction of the horse on the boundless prairies of the Far West changed the whole mode of living of their inhabitants. It gave them that facility of rapid motion, and of sudden and distant change of place, so dear to the roving propensities of man. Instead of lurking in the depths of gloomy forests, and patiently threading the mazes of a tangled wilderness on foot, like his brethren of the north, the Indian of the West is a rover of the plain; he leads a brighter and more sunshiny life; almost always on horseback, on vast flowery prairies and under cloudless skies.

I was lying by the Captain's fire, late in the evening, listening to stories about those coursers of the prairies, and weaving speculations of my own, when there was a clamor of voices and a loud cheering at the other end of the camp; and word was passed that Beatte, the half-breed, had brought in a wild horse.

In an instant every fire was deserted; the whole camp crowded to see the Indian and his prize. It was a colt about two years old, well grown, finely limbed, with bright prominent eyes, and a spirited yet gentle demeanor. He gazed about him with an air of mingled stupefaction and surprise, at the men, the horses, and the camp-fires; while the Indian stood before him with folded arms, having hold of the other end of the cord which noosed his captive, and gazing on him with a most imperturbable aspect.

Commenting on his portrayal of elk hunt, artist noted that elk were easier to stalk than deer.

Beatte, as I have before observed, has a greenish olive complexion, with a strongly marked countenance, not unlike the bronze casts of Napoleon; and as he stood before his captive horse, with folded arms and fixed aspect, he looked more like a statue than a man.

If the horse, however, manifested the least restiveness, Beatte would immediately worry him with the lariat, jerking him first on one side, then on the other, so as almost to throw him on the ground; when he had thus rendered him passive, he would resume his statue-like attitude and gaze at him.

The whole scene was singularly wild; the tall grove, partially illumined by the flashing fires of the camp, the horses tethered here and there among the trees, the carcasses of deer hanging around, and in the midst of all, the wild huntsman and his wild horse, with an admiring throng of rangers, almost as wild.

Afterward . . . when [Beatte] was seated by our fire, I readily drew from him an account of his exploit; for, though taciturn among strangers, and little prone to boast of his actions, yet his taciturnity, like that of all Indians, had its times of relaxation.

He informed me, that on leaving the camp, he had returned to the place where we had lost sight of the wild horse. Soon getting upon its track, he followed it to the banks of the river. Here, the prints being more distinct in the sand, he perceived that one of the hoofs was broken and defective, so he gave up the pursuit.

As he was returning to the camp, he came upon a gang of six horses, which immedi-

154

ately made for the river. He pursued them across the stream, left his rifle on the river bank, and putting his horse to full speed, soon came up with the fugitives. He attempted to noose one of them, but the lariat hitched on one of his ears, and he shook it off. The horses dashed up a hill, he followed hard at their heels, when, of a sudden, he saw their tails whisking in the air, and they plunging down a precipice. It was too late to stop. He shut his eyes, held in his breath, and went over with them—neck or nothing. The descent was between twenty and thirty feet, but they all came down safe upon a sandy bottom.

He now succeeded in throwing his noose round a fine young horse. As he galloped alongside of him, the two horses passed each side of a sapling, and the end of the lariat was jerked out of his hand. He regained it, but an intervening tree obliged him again to let it go. Having once more caught it, and coming to a more open country, he was enabled to play the young horse with the line until he gradually checked and subdued him, so as to lead him to the place where he had left his rifle.

>>>·>>|<<·<<<

After riding a few miles, Beatte, who kept parallel with us, along the ridge of a naked hill to our right, called out and made signals, as if something were coming round the hill to intercept us. Some who were near me cried out that it was a party of Pawnees. A skirt of thickets hid the approach of the supposed enemy from our view. We heard a trampling among the brushwood. My horse looked toward the place, snorted and pricked up his ears, when presently a couple of huge buffalo bulls, who had been alarmed by Beatte, came crashing through the brake, and making directly toward us. At sight of us they wheeled round, and scuttled along a narrow defile of the hill. In an instant half a score of rifles cracked off; there was a uni-

versal whoop and halloo, and away went half the troop, helter-skelter in pursuit, and myself among the number. The most of us soon pulled up, and gave over a chase which led through birch and brier, and break-neck ravines.

After riding a few miles further, we came to a fine meadow with a broad clear stream winding through it, on the banks of which there was excellent pasturage. Here we at once came to a halt, in a beautiful grove of elms, on the site of an old Osage encampment. Scarcely had we dismounted, when a universal firing of rifles took place upon a large flock of turkeys, scattered about the grove, which proved to be a favorite roosting-place for these simple birds.

In the height of the carnage, word was brought that there were four buffaloes in a neighboring meadow. The turkeys were now abandoned for nobler game. The tired horses were again mounted, and urged to the chase. In a little while we came in sight of the buffaloes, looking like brown hillocks among the long green herbage. Beatte endeavored to get ahead of them and turn them towards us, that the inexperienced hunters might have a chance. They ran round the base of a rocky hill, that hid us from the sight. Some of us endeavored to cut across the hill, but became entrapped in a thick wood, matted with grape-vines. My horse, who, under his former rider, had hunted the buffalo, seemed as much excited as myself, and endeavored to force his way through the bushes. At length we extricated ourselves, and galloping over the hill, I found our little Frenchman, Tonish, curvetting on horseback round a great buffalo which he had wounded too severely to fly, and which he was keeping employed until we should come up.

We now made repeated shots at the buffalo, but they glanced into his mountain of flesh without proving mortal. He made a slow and grand retreat into the shallow river, turning upon his assailants whenever they pressed upon him; and when in the water, took his stand there as if prepared to sustain a siege. A rifle ball, however, more fatally lodged, sent a tremor through his frame. He turned and attempted to wade across the stream, but after tottering a few paces, slowly fell upon his side and expired. It was the fall of a hero, and we felt somewhat ashamed of the butchery that had effected it; but, after the first shot or two, we had reconciled it to our feelings, by the old plea of putting the poor animal out of his misery.

Two more buffaloes were killed this evening, but they were all bulls, the flesh of which is meagre and hard, at this season of the year. A fat buck yielded us more savory meat for our evening's repast.

[Later] we perceived two buffalo bulls descending a slope, toward a stream, which wound through a ravine fringed with trees. The young Count and myself endeavored to get near them under covert of the trees. They discovered us while we were yet three or four hundred yards off, and turning about, retreated up the rising ground. We urged our horses across the ravine, and gave chase. The immense weight of head and shoulders, causes the buffalo to labor heavily up hill; but it accelerates his descent. We had the advantage, therefore, and gained rapidly upon the fugitives, though it was difficult to get our horses to approach them, their very scent inspiring them with terror. The Count, who had a double-barrelled gun loaded with ball, fired, but it missed. The bulls now altered their course, and galloped down hill with headlong rapidity. As they ran in different directions, we each singled one and separated. I was provided with a brace of veteran brass-barrelled pistols, which I had borrowed at Fort Gibson, and which had evidently seen some service. Pis-

tols are very effective in buffalo hunting, as the hunter can ride up close to the animal, and fire at it while at full speed; whereas the long heavy rifles used on the frontier, cannot be easily managed, nor discharged with accurate aim from horseback. My object, therefore, was to get within pistol shot of the buffalo. This was no very easy matter. I was well mounted on a horse of excellent speed and bottom, that seemed eager for the chase, and soon overtook the game; but the moment he came nearly parallel, he would keep sheering off, with ears forked and pricked forward, and every symptom of aversion and alarm. It was no wonder. Of all animals, a buffalo, when close pressed by the hunter, has an aspect the most diabolical.

It was with difficulty I urged my horse sufficiently near, when, taking aim, to my chagrin, both pistols missed fire. Unfortunately the locks of these veteran weapons were so much worn, that in the gallop, the priming had been shaken out of the pans. At the snapping of the last pistol I was close upon the buffalo, when, in his despair, he turned round with a sudden snort and rushed upon me.

Three or four bounds of the horse carried us out of the reach of the enemy; who, having merely turned in desperate self-defense, quickly resumed his flight.

After pursuing my way for some time, I descried a horseman on the edge of a distant hill, and soon recognized him to be the Count. He had been equally unsuccessful with myself; we were shortly after rejoined by our worthy comrade, the Virtuoso, who, with spectacles on nose, had made two or three ineffectual shots from horseback.

We now formed our plan to circumvent the herd, and by getting on the other side of them, to hunt them in the direction where we knew our camp to be situated: otherwise, the pursuit might take us to such a distance as to render it impossible to find our way back before nightfall. Taking a wide circuit, therefore, we moved slowly and cautiously, pausing occasionally, when we saw any of the herd desist from grazing. The wind fortunately set from them, otherwise they might have scented us and have taken the alarm. In this way, we succeeded in getting round the herd without disturbing it. It consisted of about forty head, bulls, cows, and calves. Separating to some distance from each other, we now approached slowly in a parallel line, hoping by degrees to steal near without exciting attention. They began, however, to move off quietly, stopping at every step or two to graze, when suddenly a bull that, unobserved by us, had been taking his siesta under a clump of trees to our left, roused himself from his lair, and hastened to join his companions. We were still at a considerable distance, but the game had taken the alarm. We quickened our pace, they broke into a gallop, and now commenced a full chase.

As the ground was level, they shouldered along with great speed, following each other in a line; two or three bulls bringing up the rear, the last of whom, from his enormous size and venerable frontlet, and beard of sunburnt hair, looked like the patriarch of the herd; and as if he might long have reigned the monarch of the prairie.

For some time I kept parallel with the line, without being able to force my horse within pistol shot, so much had he been alarmed by the assault of the buffalo in the preceding chase. At length I succeeded, but was again balked by my pistols missing fire. My companions, whose horses were less fleet, and more way-worn, could not overtake the herd; at length Mr. L., who was in the rear of the line, and losing ground, levelled his double-barrelled gun, and fired a long raking shot. It struck a buffalo just above the loins, broke its back-bone, and brought it to

the ground. He stopped and alighted to dispatch his prey, when borrowing his gun, which had yet a charge remaining in it, I put my horse to his speed, again overtook the herd which was thundering along, pursued by the Count. With my present weapon there was no need of urging my horse to such close quarters; galloping along parallel, therefore, I singled out a buffalo, and by a fortunate shot brought it down on the spot. The ball had struck a vital part; it could not move from the place where it fell, but lay there struggling in mortal agony, while the rest of the herd kept on their headlong career across the prairie.

Dismounting, I now fettered my horse to prevent his straying, and advanced to contemplate my victim. I am nothing of a sportsman; I had been prompted to this unwonted exploit by the magnitude of the game, and the excitement of an adventurous chase. Now that the excitement was over, I could not but look with commiseration upon the poor animal.

It became now an act of mercy to give him his quietus, and put him out of his misery. I primed one of the pistols, therefore, and advanced close up to the buffalo. To inflict a wound thus in cool blood, I found a totally different thing from firing in the heat of the chase. Taking aim, however, just behind the fore-shoulder, my pistol for once proved true; the ball must have passed through the heart, for the animal gave one convulsive throe and expired.

While I stood meditating and moralizing over the wreck I had so wantonly produced, with my horse grazing near me, I was rejoined by my fellow sportsman, the Virtuoso; who, being a man of universal adroitness, and withal, more experienced and hardened in the gentle art of "venerie," soon managed to carve out the tongue of the buffalo, and delivered it to me to bear back to the camp as a trophy. ◉

Winter on the Trapline

The vivid experiences
of a fledgling naturalist
in the vast expanse
of Minnesota's
Big Bog.
by
Paul L. Errington
Photography
by
Charles Steinhacker

❧ This is the story of a young man's winter tending traplines in a vast, primeval area of northern Minnesota nearly fifty years ago. The muskrat, mink, and weasel pelts he laboriously gathered in the course of a frigid and solitary season helped finance his education and start him on a distinguished career as one of America's outstanding biologists. At his death in 1962, after thirty years on the faculty of Iowa State University, Paul L. Errington was internationally recognized for his work in population phenomena of vertebrates, and had received many awards both for academic achievement and service to wildlife conservation.

❧ "Winter on the Trapline" has since been published in *The Red Gods Call* by Iowa State University Press. In a prefatory note to the manuscript, Professor Errington summarizes, simply and briefly, the satisfaction of a man fulfilled: "I am glad to say that I have been able to spend a large part of my life where wild things lived in freedom, in northern scenes where they belonged."

160

As I settled down alone in my trapping headquarters, I felt a little scared. I did not know what to expect of the cold as winter progressed. The cabin on the Tamarack River needed a stove, so an old oil barrel was transformed into a stove. The boiler door of a small derelict steamer on Upper Red Lake served for a stove door. I recall shooting the rivets out of the hinges of the boiler door with a deer rifle, and having the problem of standing sufficiently close to center the bullets on the rivets offhand and, at the same time, sufficiently far back to be safe from flying metal. This oil barrel sat in a log-boxed foundation of sand on the floor.

I worked to rehabilitate the cabin, chinking and nailing. I cut and carried and piled firewood and put things where I could find them after the snows came. I prowled the woods and did some loafing while I had the chance before the fur season began. Some unharvested onions remained in what had been a garden during the summer, and these I gathered one day as snowflakes came out of the sky.

For a bed, I spread a small tent over a layer of wild hay and I lay on that with woolen blankets over me. I weighted down the blankets with logs piled along the bottom and one side and in that way had a makeshift sleeping bag —not as nice, I admit, as an eiderdown, but I did not have and could not afford the eiderdown.

As fall turned into winter, I tried some psychological resistance to the North Woods cold. My reasoning was that if I postponed changing from cotton to woolen underwear as long as possible, I should be better acclimated to the cold when it really did become severe. All that this idea did was to keep me shivering for about a week and to encourage thoughts that the northern cold must have a unique penetrating power even before it had brought along much

163

more than hard frosts at night. Finally, I put on my woolens and the climate seemed to moderate.

A tremendous amount of wood-cutting had to be done to keep the oil-barrel stove putting forth heat while I was in camp. This cutting required every precaution to prevent the ax from glancing. If the ax glanced in very cold weather, a piece of frost-brittle steel might break from the blade. Once after chipping away a little half-moon I had to work for hours to get the bit sharpened so that it would cut again.

For night logs, I used slow-burning green aspen, and the burning resulted in creosote draining through the joints of the stove pipe. The creosote would dry and accumulate and sometimes it smoked as the pipe heated. On a cold night it glowed on the red-hot pipe.

I did not like this glowing residue and tried to keep the excess creosote scraped off. But the night came when the creosote accumulation blazed, filling the upper part of the room with smoke. After that I tried to keep the creosote scraped off and always to be watchful when there was a hot fire.

One midwinter afternoon I was across the river cutting wood and happened to look over at the cabin. The roof was on fire around the chimney. I went back as fast as I could run with snowshoes, ran into the cabin with snowshoes still on, grabbed a pail of water, and heaved it up at the blazing roof. The water came down on me. I got the snowshoes off and ran outside. My wet clothes froze, but I could not be bothered by that. I climbed up on the roof and put out the rest of the fire with snow. The fire had burned a yard-wide hole in the roof.

I went back across the river and cut down an aspen that must have been a foot and a half in diameter at the level of the snow. Out of this, I chopped two rough planks about four feet long and four inches thick. Later,

looking at the mess inside, I began to work out a compromise with physics and chemistry. After the fire burned low in the oil barrel and the stove pipe cooled, I took down the pipe and replaced it in an upside-down position, so that the creosote would drain back into the stove instead of outside through the leaky joints. The pipe took a bit of forcing in places, but, when the job was done, I could rebuild the fire with more confidence than I had known for weeks.

Admittedly, my experience with cold never did compare with the experience of polar explorers or others to whom sixty below zero might be commonplace; and I feel like a novice when I read of people enduring temperatures of a hundred below zero. That these people may have electrically heated garments and similarly modern comforts does not detract from the fact that they know an intensity of cold that I find difficult to imagine. I shall have to be satisfied with my memories of cold on a much more modest scale.

Nevertheless, the weather I knew when trapping in northern Minnesota in my late teens could be cold. During three months of thickening ice and deepening snow, I do not recall having seen anything melt in the outside air without the warmth of body heat or fire. Temperatures got down to twenty to forty degrees below zero almost every night from late December until the first of the spring thaws. Twice I was told the minimal daily temperatures observed at Waskish, on Upper Red Lake. One of these minima was thirty-three below, on what felt like a slightly colder-than-ordinary day. The other minimum was forty-two below, and that day was much colder. It was a day I spent cutting cordwood. My outer garments were frosted over like the fur on the horses pulling the bobsled. One day felt so much colder than the day of forty-two below that I guessed it must have been about fifty-five below.

By early winter, I was wearing four pairs of heavy woolen socks inside of lumberjack-style leather-topped rubbers. If one sock had an unmended hole, a cold foot usually reminded me. When needing to do an open-air job with bare hands—such as tying the laces of snowshoe bindings—I would kneel, determine where to put my mittens so I could grab them in a hurry, jerk off the mittens and put them there, tie the laces before my fingers stiffened, and jam my hands back into the mittens. I did not do much shooting, and when I did it had to be without long aiming. Manipulating picture-wire rabbit snares had to be with mittens on.

When making a start on a trapline before sunrise, I held the mittens to freezing cheeks and nose until circulation speeded up and I became accustomed to the outside cold. If I anticipated exceptional cold, I might stick fresh pieces of skin from a snowshoe hare—flesh side down—on my cheeks and the sides of my nose, and these seemed to prevent my face from actually freezing.

My snowshoes were a three-dollar investment I had made when the snow became knee-deep early in the winter. They were Indian-made and I rigged up bindings to fit them to my boots. Walking straddle-legged and with that unaccustomed weight on my feet, I quickly learned that I had some sets of muscles to train. It did not take long to gain proficiency with showshoes, however, and I soon had trails packed for the length of my traplines and to all of the places I visited regularly.

It is true that travel with snowshoes is not as easy or convenient as travel without them in the absence of snow, and that with snowshoes one may have mishaps from time to time. The webbing or frames sometimes caught on twigs, snowshoes sometimes tangled with each other, or something else

happened to plunge me into the snow—gun, packsack, and all. Once I lost balance and fell while breaking a trail over very deep, soft snow, and I hung suspended by the snowshoes without finding anything solid to get hold of from beneath until I could free my feet from the snowshoe-bindings. Another time, early one evening, when I was far from camp and in no position to repair a snowshoe, I learned what it was to wade, when already tired, through a couple of miles of four- to five-foot soft snow. I carried both snowshoes on my shoulders and alternately pushed along and rested, probably for about three hours.

But the shoes were the only way to move in deep snow. I recall how they would creak as I moved along the packed snow of the trapline, finding a frozen weasel in a trap or a frozen snowshoe hare in a snare. Red squirrels would be out in the trees and chickadees would flit and fluff and dee-dee.

During a period of intense cold the balance would be so fine between comfort and discomfort that I seldom could stop to rest for more than a few minutes. At the same time, I felt that I had to avoid sweating, or breathing in the dangerous air too fast or too deeply, but now I suspect that I may have overestimated the danger of freezing my lungs.

I forgot to be careful about breathing only once during the winter—on the one occasion when I found anything alive in a trap or snare. A snowshoe hare was alive and uninjured in a snare, probably having run into it as I approached. It was lively and looked like an animal that might make a pet. My snare line was within a mile of the cabin, so I held the hare between my knees, removed the noose from its neck, and used the wire to bind its hind legs together. All this I did with mittened hands, merely winding the snare wire, untied, around and around the captive's legs. A short distance farther along the snare line, a snare with slipped noose dangled over a runway. To have my hands free to adjust the noose, I put my captive down in the snow.

It started crawling off, ineffectually at first. The wire about its hind legs began to loosen. That was when I started after it, off through a dense stand of young jack pines. The hare stayed barely out of my reach, and I ran through the brush on snowshoes, breaking trail and running humped up to clear the boughs and branches overhead. Finally, the hare kicked loose the rest of the binding, and away it went. I was panting and my lungs were hurting. I was scared and held my breath as long as I could and drew in what air I had to through my nostrils. The pain gradually subsided.

It was here, incidentally, near the far end of my snare line that I found myself lost in an extensive block of forest. A light snow was falling. Even where I could look up through the trees at the sky, I could not see the sun. I did not realize that I was lost until I had walked for about an hour, heading in what I thought was the direction of the river. There had been nothing frightening about this experience, only annoyance, for I knew broadly where I was with respect to the river, and, if necessary, I could always backtrack. The odd thing was that I did not believe my compass and kept walking in the direction where I thought the river had to be rather than where the compass indicated. After another half hour of this nonsense, I obeyed the compass and came out on the river some two miles upstream from where I had expected to be.

Within my cabin, as winter temperatures went down, crystals formed on the water in a pail in the corner of the room, despite the oil barrel. The oil barrel and stove pipe would redden, and I would watch the hot places, to judge when to shut the damper in the pipe and bank the stove door with sand. At bedtime I filled up the oil barrel with slow-burning green aspen logs and tightly banked the stove door. The great outer cold would press in, and everything freezable would freeze.

I went to bed with a stocking cap and most of my clothes on, except my mackinaw and leather-topped rubbers, and on the coldest nights I put on everything I wore outside. Over me would be the substantial weight of fourteen woolen blankets alternated with layers of newspapers. Whenever I shifted positions, the mass crackled, but weighted down by logs, as it was, along one side and the bottom, it never slipped off to expose me to the subzero temperatures.

Early morning routine was to push away the sand with which the door of the oil-barrel stove was banked and so let the draft in on the smoldering shells of aspen logs. As the blaze caught, I put in hot-burning dry tamarack or spruce or white cedar. By lantern light, I chopped through the inches of ice on the water pail, whittled or hacked off some frozen venison, mixed baking powder and wheat flour for pancakes or biscuits. Sometimes I warmed up whatever happened to be in the stew kettle and ate that for breakfast.

In the evenings, while writing letters or reading or reinforcing the thinning places in socks, I sat beside a lantern some five to eight feet from the alternating glowing and cooling oil barrel. At that distance, I opened my mackinaw or shirt collars and buttoned them again almost automatically.

About once a week, I had a bath and washed clothes. The upper part of the cabin would be wet with steam, and the log surfaces nearest the stove would glisten, while the inner cracks between the logs and the angles deep in corners stayed frosted and gathered more frost. Underwear, shirts, and socks hung as close to the stove as I dared put them, and I felt the drying clothes to make sure nothing became too hot.

I ate when hungry, as much as I wanted to eat, as much as my developing eighteen-year-old body needed. I ate ruffed-grouse meat while I still liked it, butter and jam on pancakes, dried fruit. I drank hot cocoa mixed with canned milk. Soon, I found I liked to watch the grouse much more than I liked to eat them. The piquant flavor of fried grouse, which initially I found delightful, later made my jaws ache. About the only way I could still enjoy grouse meat was to use it as a base for stew, when the flavor was diluted and modified. Old but edible remnants of mustard and horseradish left in the cabin helped me to eat grouse meat when I could hardly tolerate it and yet still needed it for nourishment.

There was also venison to eat. I packed a winter supply in layers of ice in a barrel outside of the cabin. That assured me of always having game, which, together with flour, meant the energy-giving essentials for a trapper's diet.

At times I craved unobtainable sweets and luxuries. Once I ran out of sugar and dried fruit and for five or six weeks ate large quantities of wheat-flour pancakes—just as they came out of the pan—for what little sweetness I could imagine in them. When I next could buy sugar, I cooked up a granular fudge that a schoolgirl would have thrown out, and this I ate not only in chunks but also as frosting on biscuits.

I did my baking in an improvised oven consisting of a rusty frying pan kept for this purpose, some nails in the frying pan, a greased pie tin on top of the nails, and, finally, an outer pan upside down over pie tin and frying pan. The nails simply raised the pie tin enough so that hot air could circulate below it, thus turning the whole device into an oven rather than just a top-of-the-stove utensil.

The dough was placed in the pie tin to bake, and the bread or biscuits emerged with charred bottoms. After the charred bottoms were trimmed off, the rest was fairly good, especially with butter or syrup. If there was nothing to go on top, the bread or biscuits were still food for one hungry enough not to be finicky.

Snowshoe hares were always fat and delicious and a staple food of which I never tired, but I did not always have the hares to eat and often had to depend on the venison. With a single exception, no venison that I cooked could be called delectable. The exception was a rib roast baked in the frying-pan oven. This was good, but it made such a sticky mess of the pie tin and the old frying pan that I did not feel another roast justified the work of cleaning up the utensils. Hence, I continued to fry the venison or stew it. The meat was very wholesome, very nourishing. It was eaten, strictly as food, for my body's sake and for the warmth and energy required by the cold, by the snowshoe trails, and by the axwork. I ate the venison with mustard and horseradish, thankful that venison could be made to taste less like venison. Toward spring, I thawed out and "jerked" (salted and dried) the rest and ate it when I had to.

For variety in meat, I sometimes had porcupine. I had read in an outdoor magazine that porcupine flesh should be fried in hot grease. Therefore, I fried it in hot grease, at arm's length and with mittens protecting my hands.

My one expensive food item was dried fruit. I would ration a newly opened box but never could make rationing work with anything so lusciously different from venison and my wheat-flour products. I had no trouble eating a pound or two of dried fruit a day—which, while good for me, sometimes could become financially burdensome. A pound of prunes or peaches at forty or fifty cents cost about one weasel pelt or, if I needed cash to the extent of taking a job cutting cordwood for the Chippewa Trading Post at Waskish, about three hours of axwork and lifting logs on a bobsled.

Porcupines not only added variety to my diet but also variety to the cabin's surroundings. My first glimpse of one against a background of sky and dark greenery behind the cabin suggested a small bear, as did its heavy flat-footed trail in the snow. But in their gnawing away at the raw patches of bark of upper limbs and trunks and in their prickly displays while bunched up and alarmed, the porcupines revealed themselves as most peculiar animals adapted to live when and how they did. Their quills had a menacing fascination for me, especially the quills on that awful weapon, the tail. Somehow it seemed that every time I skinned a porcupine, I got a few of the quills in my woolen outdoor clothing and into the bedding, to work through later.

Among the other wild ones about the cabin was a horned owl that gave me some competition for the local snowshoe hares early in the winter. On the cabin roof and about the garbage heap, chickadees and Canada jays sat and flew and searched and pecked. One of the little nostalgic fragments that stays with me relates to a creature of the wilderness that established its headquarters in the cabin with me. I had heard the whistling and rustling of a mouse for several evenings. Then one morning, as I tried to put on one of my leather-topped rubbers, I discovered that it lacked the room for both my foot and a cache of prune pits. So in the evenings, as I lay on the bed finishing dessert, I tossed prune pits into the wood-pile corner from which the sounds came. Gradually, I began tossing pits along the wall, nearer and nearer to me. The mouse worked nearer and nearer to the light, gathering the pits, until I could see that my

companion was a deer mouse. I could see its white underparts and watch its squirrel-like foraging before it went scampering off into the darkness with another pit.

My very gradual maturing did not lead to exclusively serious thoughts or behavior. I remember with satisfaction some kid-trapper nonsense involving a red squirrel on my northern Minnesota trapline. This squirrel was nearly always at its station in a big Norway pine, from which it would address me in the most scolding tone as I traveled my snowshoe trail below. I came to anticipate my scolding and was glad the squirrel was there to give it to me, yet felt a peculiar malice toward it. One day the squirrel was in a little pine tree out of jumping distance from any other tree, and I ran up to see what might be done.

The squirrel clung to the top of the little tree, notably subdued. I found that I could move the tree top, in a wider arc with each push and pull, until the squirrel was waving back and forth from the top like a pennant, hanging on with his front feet. The squirrel shook loose and dropped into the snow, bounded to the big pine, and ran up to its customary perch at the base of a limb. I do not think that I have ever seen any other nonhuman creature so enraged as that squirrel. It jumped up and down on its perch, it choked and sputtered, and burst into the nearest equivalent of a sustained roar of which a red squirrel would seem capable. Thereafter, it started scolding me well before I appeared in sight of the big pine, and it scolded as long as I remained within hearing distance.

I had good mink trapping along the Tamarack River early in the winter, but after the weather became very cold the minks were not at all easy to catch. In part this was because of my relative inexperience as a trapper. I was not as clever at it as I might have been, not sufficiently discriminating to see what were the most promising trap sets. In part this was because of the special wariness of some of the minks, which could detect traps no matter how carefully I concealed them, even after a new snowfall obliterated all signs of my having made the trap sets. As winter came on with its deeper and deeper snow, the minks came out on the snow surface only now and then, as out of a hole in a bank or a hole in the side of a beaver lodge. Finally, they came outside no more, and I had to dig and chop to find where they were; and after I had done the digging and chopping, they would no longer use such a disturbed place.

There were places where I frequently scooped away loose snow with a snowshoe to try to explore what was at the water's edge. I could see why the minks did not have to come out in the bitter temperatures of the outer air: They were living right with the wintering muskrats. Ice shelves had their leavings of mink and muskrat food—the particles of vegetation and fish skin, the blood stains and clam shells, the remains of thin muskrats that both minks and other muskrats fed upon.

The weasels were the most indefatigable runners over the snow and the best tunnelers through it. Their trails went bounding, quartering over meadows, swamps, stream edges, and through the forest. When I found a hole in the snow with several weasel trails going in and out, I might dig down to see what could be found. Mostly, when I could trace a weasel's tunnel without snow falling into my digging and covering up everything, all I found was a hole leading into the frozen ground.

There was not much I could do about some of the animals I especially coveted. Fisher tracks appeared at the far end of one of my traplines, great bounding trails in the powdery snow. The fishers were really worth money then, and I considered trying to track one down as the Indians were said to do; but I did not know how I could safely undertake spending two or three days and nights camping outside.

I have many memories of the snowshoe hares upon which I subsisted. Despite the disinclination of the hares to be active during daylight, their "sign" showed well what they did at night. They beat some most convenient trails for snare-setting through the thickets and from one favored feeding ground to another. They ate on the twigs and smaller branches of the green aspens that I cut for night wood in the hardwood fringe along the river. Sometimes they left impressions of their sitting bodies in the alders or willows at the edge of the woods, though without tracking up open snow very much. They obviously did not like to get out in the open and seldom did anything so rash as running across the river. My snaring reduced the population of hares in the vicinity of the cabin so far down into the numerical range of diminishing returns that I discontinued it before winter was over. From the approximately square mile that was most convenient for me to cover, the snares probably yielded a hundred hares.

The exploitation of fur bearers—my economic justification for wintering in northern Minnesota's Big Bog—turned out to be of almost minor importance for me, though it took a great amount of time and effort. I worked hard at the trapping, from which my returns in cash were modest, indeed. Mostly, I caught weasels, along with some minks. In a seven-month stay I did a little better than to make expenses, with much living off the country and a good deal of doing without things that cost money—the same as everyone else did up there. But I have many memories—of northern terrain, of cold, of deep-snow traplines, of wild creatures, wherever, whatever they were. In memories, the Big Bog paid off handsomely. ◉

WHEN THE GAME OUTNUM

The golden age of Western hunting comes to life

BERED THE HUNTERS | *by Paul A. Rossi*

again in the paintings of the Gilcrease collection.

HERD ON THE MOVE by Wm. Jacob Hays (previous pages). Over 60,000,000 buffalo are estimated to have roamed the Great Plains in the 1840's. By the end of the century the species was virtually extinct. Before the coming of the white men, with their horses and guns, the Indians hunted these great, shaggy beasts on foot, sometimes driving whole herds over cliffs, sometimes stalking them singly. When the Plains Indians finally acquired horses, they quickly combined their own tracking ability with the mobility of their mounts to get close to the buffalo. The Indians' weapons were designed for close-in work: the average plains bow was approximately 34 inches long—ideally suited for work on horseback. But, as the Remington painting illlustrates (below), such close work could be very dangerous.

EPISODE OF THE BUFFALO HUNT *by Frederic Remington*

The immense herd of bison portrayed in William Jacob Hays' "Herd on the Move" effectively evokes the awesome abundance of Western game and wildlife that existed at the start of the nineteenth century. The seemingly endless stretches of plain and mountain teemed with animals—bison, elk, antelope, deer, bear, sheep, goat, moose, cougar, and myriad smaller species. The hunter of those days was a colorful figure in the public imagination, and paintings depicting his adventures have maintained consistent popularity over the past hundred years. One of the finest collections of such works is that of the Thomas Gilcrease Institute of American History and Art in Tulsa, Oklahoma. There a visitor can clearly follow the great pageant of Western hunting as illustrated by artists who had usually witnessed the scenes they painted. For the present-day sportsman, these pictures recall some of the purer pleasures that hunters of this era have forfeited by their acceptance of mechanical advantages. Old-time hunters were mightily practiced in the virtues of patience and determination, and they fervently studied the habits of their quarry. For them no high-powered, telescopic-sighted rifle diminished the length—or the excitement—of the track and stalk. They savored the country to the fullest, moving by foot and horseback rather than four-wheel drive, sleeping on the ground rather than in camper trucks. They experienced hunting in a way that is shared by only a small minority of hunters taking the field today. So, if this art serves no other purpose than to inspire some present-day or future hunters to recapture part of the sporting spirit of the past, the efforts of those artists who devoted their lives to portraying hunting scenes will be rewarded. Much of the Western big-game country is still unspoiled and—with a good horse—can be seen as Alfred Jacob Miller, Frederic Remington, Charles M. Russell, and other American artist-sportsmen saw it.

173

THE BUFFALO HUNT *by Charles M. Russell*

Within a comparatively short time after the Spaniards had introduced the horse to America in the 1500's, the Plains Indians—armed with bows, arrows, lances, and rifles—became the best horseback hunters the world had ever known. Their most common method of hunting buffalo was "running" them. They would approach the herd as quietly as possible from one direction and stay alongside it during the chase. Each hunter's horse would bring him up on the "off," or right, side of the buffalo selected. At the sound of the arrow released or the shot of the gun, the horse was trained to veer away from the wounded animal to avoid being hooked by its horns. This dangerous and exciting form of hunting later became popular with American and European sportsmen hunting buffalo on the plains.

THE CONTESTED GAME *by William de la Montaigne Cary*

WHERE TRACKS SPELL MEAT *by Charles M. Russell*

The mountain men, or trappers, of the early nineteenth century were the first white men to hunt the then virgin areas west of the Mississippi. Armed with their one-shot, smooth-bore guns and their long knives, they were intrepid explorers as well as hunters. Miller's fine watercolor (bottom right) is a good portrayal of such a Western fur trader in the 1830's. With the advent of high-powered, repeating rifles in the last third of the century, the game began to retreat from the plains and hills into the less accessible mountains. The wintry scene shown in Russell's painting (above) was one familiar to that hunter-artist. He knew that elk, when jumped and shot, will waste little time putting distance behind them in their peculiar mile-eating stride. The hunter who did not get his meat in his first shots often found himself in for a long ride into high, rough country before he got another opportunity. Pronghorn antelope (top right) were such curious animals that they often were easily killed and almost became extinct in some areas. Many pioneer Western families supplemented their meager diet with antelope meat.

BETTER THAN BACON *by Charles M. Russell*

THE LOST TRAPPER *by Alfred Jacob Miller*

The scene below was and is a common dilemma in hunting bighorn sheep. Russell, always the situation-artist, was a great storyteller with his paintings, ever conscious of the country. Here he depicts the area north of Glacier National Park, Montana. Few big game animals in the world have inspired the hair-raising stories and lies that the grizzly bear has. At one time grizzlies had inhabited the plains (Lewis and Clark encountered them and they did kill buffalo as seen in the picture on page 45), but were soon forced into the remote mountains (right). Livestock men blamed the great bears for many deaths that actually came about through natural causes, but showed bear feeding signs when discovered days or weeks later.

MEAT'S NOT MEAT 'TIL IT'S IN THE PAN *by Charles M. Russell*

persimmon

wild strawberry

wilderness

sedge

a

c

acorn

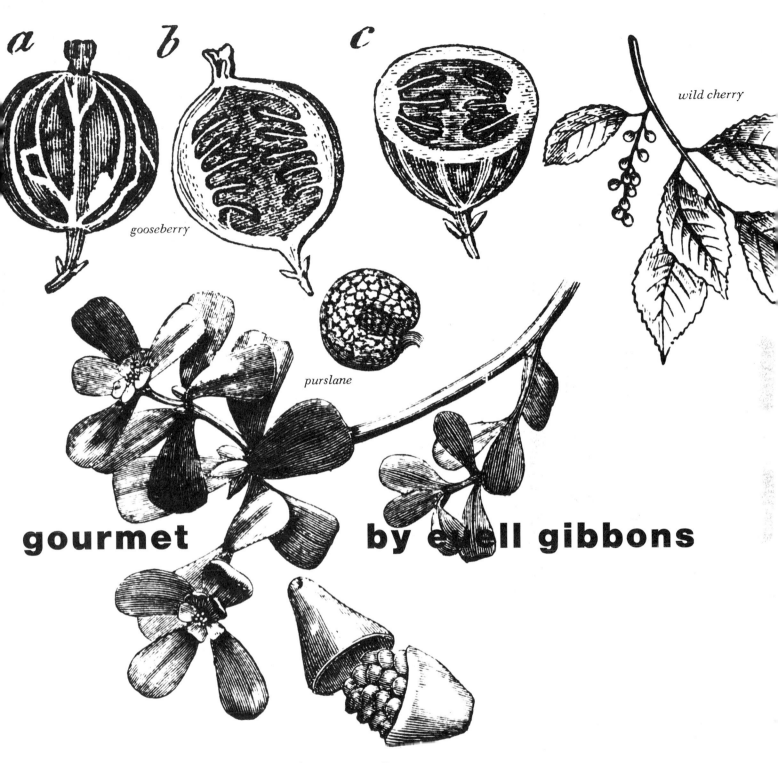

a

b

c

gooseberry

wild cherry

purslane

gourmet by euell gibbons

An expert demonstrates

how wild foods can transform survival

camping into a pleasurable dining

adventure for the outdoorsman

b

a

My wife has almost unlimited faith in my ability to conjure up food from almost anywhere. We were state-parking around Pennsylvania, and one day we went from World's End to Promised Land. From the latter state park, a trail leads to Bruce Lake Natural Area, a bit of roadless wilderness in northeastern Pennsylvania. We packed in and pitched camp by the side of Bruce Lake, a beautiful but small body of water that was left when the glaciers receded from this area thousands of years ago. As I assembled my fishing gear my wife said, "I'm depending on you to furnish enough fish for dinner, a good green salad, something wild for a vegetable, and some kind of fruit for dessert." That's a pretty tall order when one is in a strange country and the sun is already in the west.

I anticipated no trouble getting fish, for Bruce Lake is reputed to be a good hole for largemouth bass, but after an hour of trying every lure in my tackle box I began to get panicky. The bass, if there at all, simply weren't biting. Finally I was reduced to using worms to catch six-inch perch and five-inch bluegills. These were plentiful, and I soon had all I wanted.

How about the rest of the meal? The shallow end of the lake was gradually being taken over by cattails, a wonderful plant that furnishes several kinds of foods. This was June and the pencil-like buds topped about one cattail in ten. These slender, green staminate bud spikes make a very palatable vegetable when boiled in salted water and liberally dressed with butter. A few of the blooms were already showing bright yellow pollen. I rubbed the pollen into a plastic bag. Although the blooms are too old and chaffy to eat as a vegetable, the pollen is as fine as the finest cake flour, and one can use it to make golden flapjacks that are a joy to both the eye and the tongue. It would also serve as a very palatable bread-ing for the little fish fillets.

The blooming cattails were far outnumbered by the shorter, and fatter cattail plants that every cattail bog seems·to produce out of sheer exuberance, since these plants never blossom or seed, and seem to serve no purpose except to furnish me with some of the most delectable food to be found in the wild. I pulled a few dozen, cut a six-inch section from the base of each plant, and discarded the rest. Then I peeled the bases, layer by layer, until a snow-white heart was revealed, so tender I could easily pinch it in two with my thumbnail. It has a bland, cucumber-like flavor, is rather high in carbohydrates, and makes an excellent vegetable raw or boiled.

For a slightly more hearty food I took some of the ropy cattail rhizomes that were under the mud. These are about an inch in diameter and have a core of almost pure starch. Cut into six-inch pieces and roasted over the campfire, they would taste a bit like fibrous sweet potatoes.

Across the lake I could see where a small forest fire had run a few years before. I made my way around to it, for such old burns are usually rich in wild food. Sure enough, among the charred logs, low-early blueberries were just ripening to perfection. I filled a plastic bag with this excellent fruit, then looked for other offerings. In a sandy spot, purslane sprawled over the ground. This is a triple-bonus food producer, as it makes a good salad or cooked vegetable, and the stems make fine dill pickles.

I could now see a dinner of fried panfish fillets, boiled cattail bloom spikes, a salad of purslane and sliced cattail hearts, a starchy vegetable of roasted cattail rhizomes, and a dessert of fresh blueberries. I proudly carried my loot back to camp and that evening we envied no man his dinner.

I have been fascinated by wild food as early as I can remember. I was born in eastern Texas, and at five years of age I invented my first wild-food recipe. I pounded together shelled hickory nuts and sweet hackberries to make a wild candy bar, and from the first taste I was hooked. By the time I was ten I knew every wild cherry and plum tree for miles around, and knew where the finest black haws and mustang grapes were hidden. Then, when I was twelve, my parents moved to the hill country of New Mexico. I soon discovered that this semiarid land was rich in wild foods, and I reveled in prickly pears, yucca fruit, and buffalo berries. I learned to rob the nests of pack rats to get quarts of sweet piñon nuts. It was here that I acquired my first gun, a .22 rifle, and I became a great hunter, adding the tangy taste of game meat to my wild parties. I was already, at this early age, committed to wild food as a hobby.

There are three ways to have fun with wild food: the wild party, the survival trip, and the everyday repast of the wild gourmet. I practice them all. Guests who have read my books on wild food can hardly be given the beef-and-potatoes routine. They expect to find wild, exotic, and colorful dishes on my table, and I try to deliver. Such guests are invited to come early, for gathering the food is half the fun.

Anyone who will take the trouble to get acquainted with the wild foods of his own area can forage the materials for such a feast any time from early spring until snowfall in just about any section of the country. Let's see how it works in Pennsylvania in late autumn.

I had invited four nature-loving friends to come early. They took me at my word and arrived before breakfast. I served them wild strawberries (from the freezer) rolled in wild-rice pancakes and doused with maple syrup that I had tapped from wild trees last spring. This was to inoculate them against any future timidity they might have about eating wild foods.

It was a perfect Indian summer day, with the foliage so gaudy that it almost seemed in bad taste. We went up the mountain and gathered several quarts of acorns under the rock-chestnut oaks, and a pint of wintergreen berries, or teaberries as they are perhaps better known, from the tiny evergreen plants growing under the oaks. Unexpectedly, we found several pounds of oyster mushrooms growing on a dying birch tree. Nature arranges these little bonuses for those who approach her in the right spirit.

Down the mountain again, we cruised the back roads with every sense alert to the flora about us. We stopped to gather soft ripe persimmons, wild black walnuts, shagbark hickory nuts. A second bonus came when one of the men noticed wild ground cherries, or husk tomatoes, growing by a roadside fence. These low plants were covered with little straw-colored husks shaped like lanterns, and inside each lantern was a golden berry.

A few shovelfuls of earth turned up a patch of wild Jerusalem artichokes, giving us all of these tasty tubers we could use. While shaking the dirt off them, I discovered another kind of tuber, or rather three of them, about the size and shape of golf balls, connected together by string-like roots. With a glad thrill I recognized groundnuts, or Indian potatoes, the wild tubers that helped the Pilgrim fathers survive that first hard winter. Alerted, I now noticed the thin, whitish vines twining up the surrounding vegetation. A half hour's hard digging and several quarts of sweat later we had enough Indian potatoes to go with our wild meal. While our shoveling arms were limber we decided to dig under a sassafras tree for some roots to make the tea we would drink with all this wild food.

I did make my guests browse for lunch. We found black haws hanging in great blue-black clusters on haw bushes. Black haws, which are no relation to red haws, are almost as sweet as dates, and will furnish unlimited ergs of energy, but the edible pulp is thin and the seed large, making them a bit indelicate to eat in the dining room. I pointed out that a late autumn hunter who got weather-bound by an early snow could still find enough food to keep up his energy. These haws, and the persimmons, are found above the snow on trees or shrubs. Several of the viburnums, relatives of these haws, bear edible fruit that hangs on until after Christmas. And then, if the emergency becomes dire, the lost hunter can always get nourishment from the inner bark of trees—this tender cambium layer is actually flavorful on a few trees, such as black birch and slippery elm. The inner bark of all the pines, the willows, the birches, and the elms can be eaten. Just remove the outer layer of dry bark, then peel or scrape off the juicy white inner bark. It is better cooked, but eaten raw it will sustain life and supply energy, as it is rich in sugars and starches.

We still needed a green vegetable, so we walked across a fallow field gathering winter cress. This smooth-leaved member of the mustard family is at its best in late fall and very early spring, and its best is better than nearly any vegetable I know, wild or tame. Along a hedgerow at the edge of the field we found frost grapes still ripe to perfection. Our final stop was at a spring where the watercress stays green and edible all winter. We were ready to return home and make the menu for our wild party.

One of the guests furnished the main dish. He is a mighty bow-and-arrow hunter, and during the bow season he had brought down a fat buck. As his contribution to the wild banquet he had brought a prime saddle of venison. By sneaking this into the meal we came out with a pretty fancy menu:

Chilled Wild-Grape Soup
Tenderloin of Venison with
Oyster Mushrooms in Coconut Cream Sauce
Buttered Jerusalem Artichokes
Fried Indian Potatoes
Boiled Winter Cress with Crisp
Bacon and Minced Onion
Salad of Watercress and Wintergreen
Berries with Wild Garlic Dressing
Acorn Muffins with Ground-Cherry Jam
Sassafras Tea
Persimmon-Hickory Nut Chiffon Pie

The wild-grape soup is one of the family of Scandinavian fruit soups, and more American cooks should know about them. The frost grapes were covered with water and boiled until the juice began to flow. They were then put through a sieve to remove the seeds and skins, returned to the heat, thickened slightly with cornstarch, sweetened to taste, and boiled until the soup had a clear, bright color, then chilled. Cold, it has enough body to be called a soup rather than a juice, and its texture and sweet-tart flavor make it an ideal appetizer.

Coconut cream is *not* the water from inside the coconut. Rather, it is made by finely grating the meat of a fresh coconut, adding boiling water, and squeezing out the oily cream. Every hunter knows that venison cooked like butcher's meat can be dry as sawdust, but when it is cooked with coconut cream it is juicy, succulent, and utterly delicious. We stewed the oyster mushrooms in undiluted beef consommé until tender. I filleted two boneless tenderloins from the saddle of deer and cut them into dollar-size steaks. I quickly browned them in a very hot pan, then dropped them into the boiling coconut cream. Then the mushrooms and consommé were added, and the whole allowed to cook just long enough to tenderize the venison. The meat was excellent and the gravy superb.

Jerusalem artichokes are not artichokes, nor do they have anything to do with Jerusalem; otherwise they are well-named. They are tuber-bearing sunflowers furnishing one of the more palatable tubers found in the wild. They can be eaten raw, but we peeled and boiled them until barely tender, then seasoned them with butter, salt, and finely chopped fresh parsley.

The Indian potatoes were scrubbed clean, sliced (peel and all), and fried at just the right time, so they arrived at the table piping hot. This is a fine starchy tuber, but it tends to become uninteresting when cold.

The wintercress was washed, boiled in salted water until tender, then garnished with minced onion and crisp, crumbled bacon, which unfortunately wasn't from a wild pig. The watercress was not cut, but the large stems were picked out by hand, leaving the tiny sprigs and leaves whole. These were tossed with the wintergreen berries to make a salad as beautiful as a Christmas decoration and, when dressed with oil and vinegar, to which a bare hint of wild garlic from my lawn had been added, one that tasted as good as it looked.

Chestnut-oak acorns are almost edible just as they fall from the trees, but they are greatly improved by grinding and leaching the meal in boiling water to remove some of the bitter tannin. After shelling the acorns, we put the kernels in an electric blender, covered them with boiling water, and blended them at high speed until the acorns were finely ground. The resulting mush was then poured into a muslin bag and the tea-colored water strained out. More boiling water was added and squeezed out until the water began to look clear. This process removed the bitterness; the meal had a sweet, nutty flavor. We used it, still damp, to replace half the flour in a muffin recipe. To make the muffins even richer I added a cup of chopped black walnuts.

Ground-cherry jam is something special. We covered a quart of the ground cherries with water and simmered them until tender, then crushed the fruit, and stirred in one envelope of powdered, commercial pectin and the juice of one lemon. When it began to boil we added four cups of sugar and cooked it, stirring over high heat, until it came back to a boil. We then rapidly boiled it for two minutes, and it was finished.

The sassafras roots were chopped into short lengths, scrubbed, then dropped into a kettle of water and boiled until the tea turned red. We drank it with a little sugar and found its root-beer flavor delightful.

Neither the persimmons nor the hickory nuts were cooked in making the pie. The persimmons were strained through a colander to make a soft pulp, and the hickory nuts were shelled and chopped. One-half cup of brown sugar, one envelope of unflavored gelatine, and a dash of salt were mixed thoroughly in a saucepan. Three egg yolks and a half a cup of milk were beaten until foamy, then added to the mixture. It was cooked and stirred until it just came to a boil, then a cup of persimmon pulp was stirred in, and the whole mixture chilled until it mounded slightly when spooned. The whites of the three eggs were beaten until stiff, then a scant quarter of a cup of sugar added as they were beaten until smooth and satiny. The persimmon mixture was given a final stirring then folded into the egg whites along with a cup of chopped hickory nuts. This filling was generous and we heaped it into a graham-cracker crust. When chilled until firm, it was unbelievably delicious, a fit ending to a fine meal.

Such a wild party is, frankly, a stunt, a dramatic method of demonstrating the quantity and quality of wild food available everywhere to the skilled forager. Most of my scrounging is not so spectacular. While poking along on a country road I may run across a fine patch of poke salad and gather enough of the tender sprouts to make a cooked vegetable that rivals, if it doesn't actually surpass, asparagus. Or I might see a patch of common orange day lilies growing by the roadside and pick some of the green, unopened buds to cook and serve like green beans. It could be a tangle of cat brier that attracts me, for when it is producing an abundance of fat, tender sprouts it is easily gathered and is a palatable vegetable, either raw or cooked.

The most rugged and challenging way to enjoy wild food is the survival trip which requires that all food must be collected from the wild. After dozens of such excursions, I still feel a thrill of trepidation every time I set off on such an adventure. So far all my survival trips have turned into continuous feasts.

A few years ago I helped develop a course in ecology and survival for the Outward Bound School, in Maine. It was proposed that I teach students, sixteen to twenty years of age, mostly from large cities, to recognize, prepare, and eat the wild foods found in that area. As a test each boy was to be given a minimum of equipment, then marooned on an uninhabited island, and required to scrounge all his own food for three days and nights.

What better way to test the practicality of such a plan than to try it myself? As the boat inched toward the rocky shores of a tiny, unfamiliar island, I stood in the bow, tossed my duffle bag ashore, then leaped onto a jutting rock.

I had the same equipment I proposed to allow the boys: a seven-by-ten-foot sheet of plastic from which a shelter could be contrived, a sleeping bag, a knife, a fishline with one hook, a first-aid kit, some foulweather gear, ten matches, and a half-gallon of water.

As I turned to look over the island, the first thing I saw was food—huge, plum-size rose hips hung orange-ripe by the hundreds from wild rose bushes. Then I saw red raspberries hanging ripe on their canes, not many of them, but all I could eat today with others that would be ripe tomorrow. I split a rose hip, raked out the seeds, stuffed a ripe raspberry in each half, and ate it in one bite. Delicious! I could feel the apprehension flowing out of me. I could live on this island.

Everything I saw wore a new perspective. The windrow of storm-tossed debris that ringed the island at high-tide level was no longer unsightly litter, but possible treasure. The bark from that birch driftwood would furnish unfailing tinder, guaranteeing a fire from each precious match. That old number 10 can would make an ideal cooking pot. Even those inevitable beer cans would furnish cups and small cooking vessels. A flare parachute, a relic of some navigational emergency, would make a good carrying bag.

Even more important were the edible plants that grew on the upper shore. There were clusters of beach peas that would be hard to tell from the garden kind. Sea rocket contributed leaves and tender pods with the flavor of horseradish. Orach, a close relative of garden spinach, and an even better food plant, grew in profusion. Glass wort, a succulent, leafless, translucent little plant, green as emerald, offered its juicy, tangy, salt-sour flavor. Goosetongue, a tiny relative of plantain, the common lawn weed, offered crisp, linear leaves that could be nibbled raw, or cut and cooked like green beans. I literally ate my way around the island and arrived back at my duffle bag with the flare parachute loaded with assorted vegetables.

I unrolled my sleeping bag under a spruce, rigged a tent over it, and carefully arranged the edges to form gutters draining into a depression, which I lined with plastic. The island grew in size as the mighty

Maine tide receded. The motto of the seaside forager is: "When the tide is out the table is set." Great reefs of blue mussels promised more seafood than I could ever eat, but experience has taught me that when one is living on nature's manna, one should try to obtain it in fifty-seven varieties, so I had no intention of living on mussels alone, much as I like them both steamed and broiled. Fat, round periwinkle were crawling over the weeds at low water. On the rocks still barely covered with water were hundreds of green urchins, prickly globes about three inches in diameter. Mussels, periwinkles, and urchins, although largely neglected in America, are all very tasty sea foods, highly appreciated in many parts of the world. I picked up a wooden crate that had been thrown up by the tide and filled it with assorted creatures.

As I was carrying this sea-offering up the shore I stepped on a gravelly spot and tiny fountains squirted my leg. I had found a clam bed, very small in size, but so crowded that I easily dug out several dozen clams with my hands. I semidomesticated all my sea creatures in a high-tide pool, so they would be available whenever I felt hungry.

Dinner was delicious: shelled beach peas boiled in sea water, steamed clams, a salad of mixed green seaside plants, and a dessert of rose hips stuffed with raspberries.

As I was eating, the fog arrived. It didn't depress me, for I had a use for that fog. As it drifted through the spruce tree under which my tent was pitched I heard a satisfying drip, drip, drip on the plastic. Soon I was dipping beer cans full of water from the plastic-lined depression. Here was all the fresh water I needed.

I was awakened at dawn by gull cries. I leaped from my sleeping bag, fearing that those thievish gulls were at my hoard in the tide pool. Instead, they were innocently feeding on the vast quantities of food bared by an extra-low tide. I grabbed some containers and joined them. There were half a dozen slithering, fluttering little eels, three to six inches long, under the first rock I overturned. I caught at least a pound of these tiny fish which are delicious when boiled whole.

When I had all the eels I wanted, I began to notice the other inhabitants of this under-rock environment. Small green crabs either scuttled off or daringly offered to do battle. Then I noticed other crabs, moving lethargically or not bothering to run away at all. These were softshells, a gourmet's delight, so I gathered a supply of softies for future reference. As I raked through the sand under the rocks I discovered great fat bloodworms. No, I don't eat bloodworms, but they make wonderful fish bait, so I took some. From rocks still below water I gathered several pounds of dulse, a reddish, edible seaweed. As it comes from the tide it tastes like a salted rubber band, but after a few hours of drying in the sun it becomes tender and tasty, and if one happened to be really hungry, an emergency supply could be dried over the campfire.

All that exercise gave me a ravenous appetite. I built a driftwood fire and began shelling sea urchins. The edible part of an urchin is the orange-colored roe contained in five sections inside the brittle test, or shell. There is only about a half-ounce of this delicacy in each creature. Eaten raw, I find the flavor more delicate and delicious than caviar; cooked, they lose this exotic flavor and taste very much like scrambled eggs.

Survive? I could have fed a crowd three gourmet meals a day with hors d'oeuvres and snacks in between. Even the city kids who came to the school later lived like kings on these islands after a few days' training. When the boatman returned after three days I was fat, contented, and not at all eager to leave my little kingdom. ◉

Fishing the Solitude Streams

Text and photography by Charley Dickey

These trout live in brooks isolated by dense, difficult forest. They belong to men who know the science of the short rod and the impossible cast.

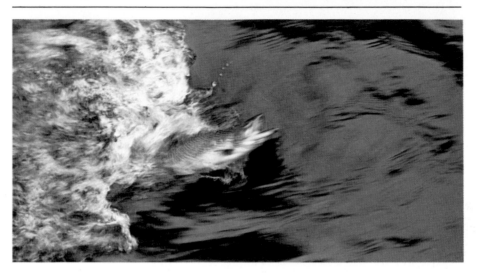

Preceding pages: Ringed by troublesome trees, Tennessee lawyer Fred Moses uses short-rod tactics to outwit wary brook trout in Great Smokies. Below: Side-arm cast for reaching hidden fish. Right: Casting from behind waterfall blind.

Some aspects of fish management are simple. If you want fishing for everyone, move fish. If you want native trout only, the people must move. In other words, you stock easily accessible streams for anglers who like to fish within casting distance of their cars; and you keep pristine and almost inaccessible the cold, clear little mountain streams where the native brookie—*Salvelinus fontinalis*—holds forth. To reach the miniature trout streams you often must climb high and hard.

Fish and game commissions know that if an area is left wild, the average fisherman will not try to penetrate it and there will be little fishing pressure. Such is the case in the Great Smoky Mountains, where close to seven hundred miles of streams are carefully managed. Generally, the water near the highways is stocked with brookies and rainbows, but there are vast wilderness areas where the brookies, native-born and bred, thrive under overhanging branches that make conventional casting impossible. Here you must crawl through the brush like a salamander. Often, to present your fly you must "dap." If dapping won't do, you may "dart." Sometimes you must kneel to cast. But you do catch fish.

Bald River Gorge, not far from the town of Tellico Plains in eastern Tennessee, is an example. There are six miles of this little river with no approach roads, no improved trails, and no way of getting in but leg power. Succeed here and you will be able to fish successfully

In Tennessee mountains, where streams tumble and meander, Moses nets a respectable brookie. Shin-barking rocks forced a merry chase, while line twanged against stones. Stiff-hackled fly (below) rode snagless over leaves and branches.

any trout stream in the world. In fact, the wide-open fishing of rainbow and brown trout streams in the West will seem absurdly easy.

Many fishermen think of the brook trout as a northern fish, but the Adirondacks and Maine have no monopoly on sizable brookies. It is also a native of the southern mountains and is found in western South Carolina, northern Georgia, and northeastward up the backbone of the Appalachians.

The area near Tellico Plains is one of the best for brookies in the South, but there are many prime brookie streams throughout the Great Smoky Mountains and Cherokee National Forest. There the brookie has the basic needs of life in cold, clear water, hiding places, and ample food. And there you may find sizable brookies in streams not over a yard wide, where no rainbow or brown would ever go.

One of my favorite fishing partners, Fred Moses, is a master brook-trout fisherman who conducts a law practice in Knoxville, an hour from the Smoky Mountain area. He is a keen and practical observer who believes there is no substitute for long hours on the streams, not simply waving a rod but studying the water, wading techniques, camouflage, and the best presentation of the fly.

Fred totes as little gear as possible, wears light hiking shoes, and carries waders during cold-water season. Otherwise he wades in quick-dry britches and wading shoes. Felt-sole shoes wear out in heavy hiking; Fred makes his own soles from carpeting. He wears drab clothing on the stream, dull browns and greens, and rubs the sheen from new clothing and shiny buttons. Because a trout's blind spot is from behind, Fred usually stalks upstream, staying as far from the bank as he can, wading in only when necessary.

The cast must be surgically precise. Sometimes it is best to work downstream. A stiff tail wind may make this mandatory, or he may wish to let the current float the fly around or under obstructions. Because trout have such acute vision, the fisherman must remain unseen, make no vibration, and cast no shadow. He must even consider the shadow of his flickering fly line. When approaching a pool, Fred uses the cover provided by rocks, fallen trees, shadows, and grassy clumps. Like some jungle infantry-man, chin deep in the lush Appalachian rhododendrons, he moves his feet as quietly as possible. He seldom casts standing erect.

The basic equipment is simple. With little chance to cast more than twenty or thirty feet, Fred uses a seven-foot, three-ounce rod, though a rod of from six-and-a-half feet to seven-and-a-half might accommodate. The action ought not to be stiff or fast. He prefers a Cortland weight-forward line (WF7F)—a "torpedo," the weight of which will let him shoot several yards of well-dressed level line gathered in the left hand. He prefers an eight-foot leader and a tippet of three-pound test.

Like fishermen the world over, Moses carries more lures than he uses. Most flies are tied on a #14 hook, and they are standards such as Adams, Royal Coachman, Light Cahill, and Pale Evening Dun. He takes his Coachman in hairwing. The spiders in stiff hackle are good for the same reason: When

Brushrodder relaxes in open pool of mountain stream where full-length flyrod can swing.

brushrodding, you want a hackle that will ride the hook up, free of rocks and foliage.

To find out what trout prefer, Fred often puts on another fly with a three-inch leader. The second fly, or dropper, will vary from the terminal fly, doubling the temptation. When Fred drops his fly he puts it where he figures a brookie should be lying. He studies the rocks, moss, bottom, current, and water depth carefully. If he has seen the fish, he quarters the target, presenting the fly slightly above and to the side.

There is a tendency to worry about distance. Most fish are hooked within fifteen or twenty-five feet of the fisherman, many less. Sometimes you face the "no cast." That's the time to dap. In dapping, the line and leader is scarcely longer than the rod. The angler has worked his way through dense foliage to the stream bank. He pokes his rod out over the stream, and, dap, his hair-and-feather insect falls naturally upon the surface. The dapped fly may be bounced, or floated a short way around boulders, under fallen trees, and into bank pockets. Dapping may not look like much, but it is filled with suspense and produces fish.

In addition, you ought to learn to execute the sidearm and the flip cast over water too overhung for a smooth overhand.

To outwit an overhang barely higher than your rod tip, you may roll cast—an easy, liquid pick-up accomplished by drawing the rod back to about eleven o'clock while the line, partially retrieved, lies on the water. Now your line will roll up and out as you cast forward, and with a neat flip, your fly will turn over and out, fifteen feet or more upstream. As a final resort you may use the dart or bow-and-arrow cast, in which the fly is held between thumb and forefinger, and shot forward on release by the bent rod.

When Fred realized he was losing a lot of fishing while resting on the trail, he started exercising his legs as he had during his football days at Tennessee. Today, at fifty-four, Moses can run three miles a day, and rides a bicycle to work when weather permits. To understand his drive, consider the fish he chases. The beauty of the brookie is universally appealing. Depending on water conditions, geography, and season, brook trout raiment varies—I have seen them as silvery as a shad in Saskatchewan, almost black in Quebec streams stained from coniferous debris. In the South, their red spots may be missing. However, whether you catch them in the brilliant mating reds of fall or not, you have the same trim fighter, fins slashed with white—not a jumper, but a hard runner that often carries you headlong down a series of step-pools.

There are obvious pools, ripples, or pockets in any stream that even a beginner will recognize as likely havens for trout. However, Fred thinks the novice wastes a lot of possibilities by rushing from obvious pool to obvious pool. "The stretches between are generally passed," he says. "It doesn't take much water to wet a brookie, and a small pocket may hold a really large fish. Get the fly back under the bushes, in those shadows. The fish are where they want to be."

The only time I've known Fred to get skunked was once when he insisted on going into the Smokies after a week of torrential rains. High in the hills, on the most slow-moving water, his most gentle dapping technique was to no avail. Finally he quit in desperation when the rangers warned him about a landslide alert.

Moses' record fish may not compare with the brook trout of the Canadian wilderness, but it is a respectable sixteen-and-a-half-inch fish that weighed two-and-one-half pounds. As I recall, the fish struck on a cast of little more than thirty feet—which figures to a yield of approximately one-half inch of trout per foot of enameled line — which must be a record in someone's book. ◉

PHOTOGRAPH BY BILL BROWNING

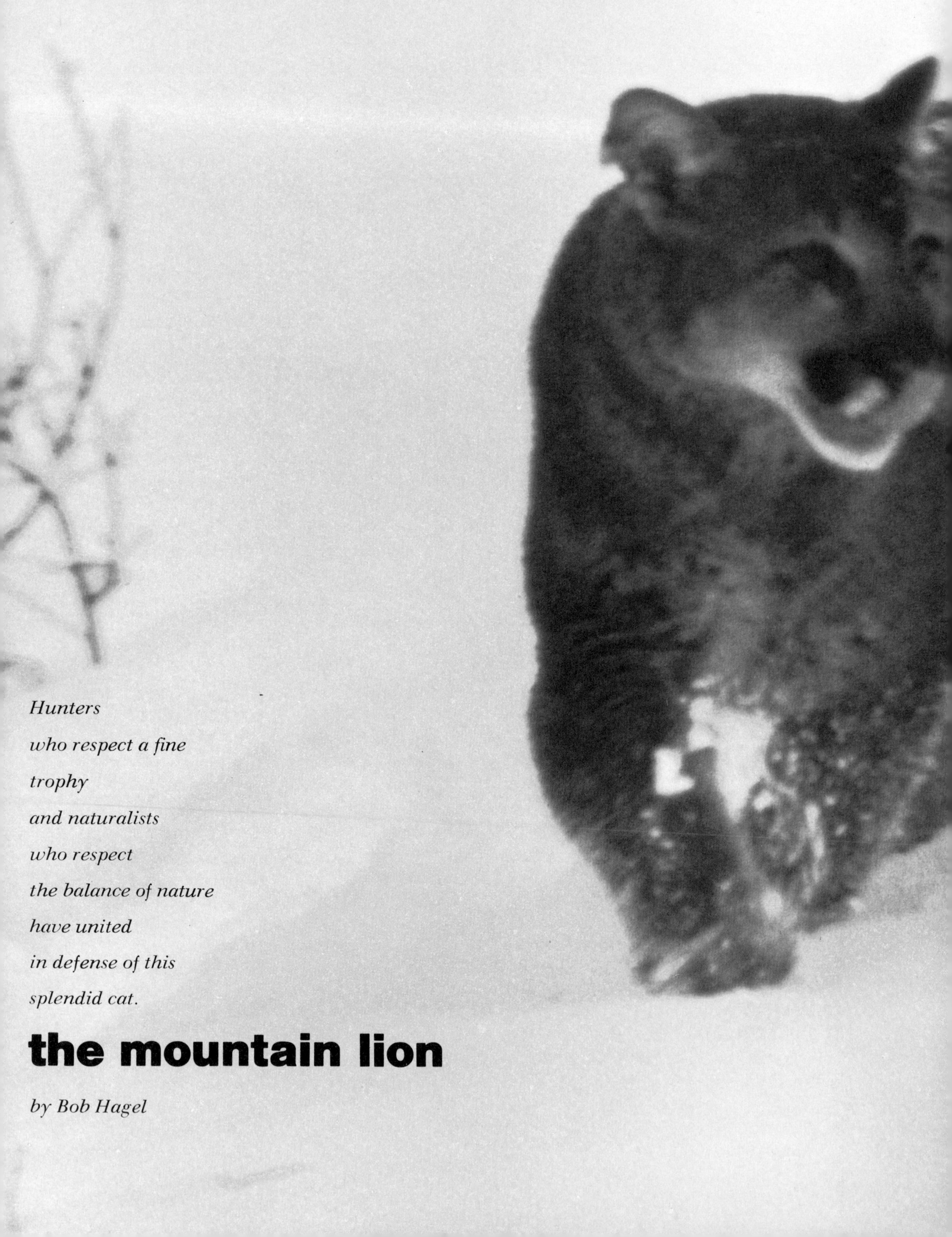

Hunters
who respect a fine
trophy
and naturalists
who respect
the balance of nature
have united
in defense of this
splendid cat.

the mountain lion

by Bob Hagel

Often nocturnal, stealthy, and swift, the mountain lion is but a shadow in its forest or canyon. Men live years in lion country without seeing one.

The noses of well-trained cougar hounds let you unravel his trail. Bounding tracks in the snow tell the story of this fugitive— how he hunts, where he sleeps, how far he ranges. For thirty years I have followed such trails. At the end of many I shot the big American cat. I seldom do today.

Let me tell you about one of the last big males I killed before my turn of heart, reconstructing events first as the cat saw them, using my notes for those few days in December, 1954, in Idaho's Salmon River country. The animal weighed 160 pounds; its size was apparent in its prints.

The big mountain lion had moved slowly through the last fringes of brush at the head of a draw, each step slow and measured, big feet sinking into the snow. At the edge of the brush he paused, and he must have sat there for a minute scanning the timber on the ridge before gliding toward it.

Traversing the slope, he approached the ridge under cover of low-hanging Douglas fir limbs clotted with mistletoe. Here he gained an unobstructed view of the far slope and canyon below. Crouching on his haunches, he waited, his long tail curving around him.

The heavy fir timber of the north face dropped steeply into the canyon below, where it ended in the rocky, brush-choked bottom. On the south-facing slope there were scattered small cliffs and rock out-croppings. Mountain mahogany grew among the rocks, and bunchgrass showed seed heads above the snow. A lone stringer of aspen ran up the bottom of a small draw near the edge of the cliffs.

There was movement in the mahogany at the edge of the cliff nearest the aspen, and a little band of mule deer fed from behind the cliff into the open. The only reaction the big cat probably made was a slight tensing, the ears coming forward, the black tip of his tail twitching. Later I saw the path his tail had left in the soft snow.

For a few minutes he sat. Perhaps he lifted his nose and sniffed the breeze drifting up the canyon. Then he was on his feet in a smooth, flowing motion. He crossed the canyon bottom about level with the deer, then angled up toward the spur ridge overlooking the aspen patch in the side draw. As he approached the crest he moved behind a small bunch of chokecherry brush, his belly moving closer to the ground and his steps becoming shorter as he neared the ridge. Then he lay flattened on the ridge, only the top of his head showing beside the brush. The mule deer were still browsing on the mahogany.

The big cougar eased forward into a scattering of sage and, with belly dragging on the snow, almost seeming not to move, he at last gained the cover of the aspen grove. Without breaking a single twig, he wormed his way through the undergrowth to the very edge of the aspens. He traversed seventy-five feet of sagebrush. A buck was feeding about twenty-five yards away.

The cat hit the snow just behind the buck and, in the next half-leap, caught him in mid-air. One huge front paw, armed with five two-inch, sharply curved claws, reached over the buck's shoulders, the other grasped his nose, while the big jaws closed over the buck's neck near the base of the skull. For an instant cougar and deer were enveloped in a white cloud as loose snow boiled up around them.

The rest of the small band of deer dashed down a depression among the boulders, and up to a rocky point on the far slope. Here they stopped, long ears cupped, noses twitching, wide eyes searching for signs of pursuit. Then, as if knowing the danger was past, they moved over the ridge and started nervously feeding around the slope.

The cougar shook himself, sat down beside the buck and licked the blood from the back of one forepaw. Then he took the buck's neck in his jaws and dragged him down and around the sidehill into the aspens. After eating his fill, he began to cover his kill. When he had finished, there was nothing to be seen of the deer except part of one antler. The carcass would remain covered, safe from the ravages of magpies and ravens, until the cougar uncovered it again when hungry.

Heavy with fresh venison, the old tom leisurely made his way up the slope to the base of a cliff near the place where he had killed the buck. There, under the shelter of an overhang, he stretched out. He looked down toward his kill once, lay the great head on his paws and dozed.

I thought I knew where the cougar was headed, so I started back toward the pickup. Tomorrow we'd hit the track from the other side of the mountain. Sooner or later that big cat would get hungry and make a kill. It might be another day or two, but when he did, and if it didn't snow enough to wipe out the tracks, we'd catch up with him.

Cougars usually went down into the next canyon and out through a low pass on the far side, but this one didn't. Coming up a canyon into the pass from the far side, I found the snow unmarked by cougar tracks, and was forced to pick up the trail only a few hundred yards from where I had left it the day before. It was almost noon of the second day when we again took the trail.

After going nearly into the canyon bottom, the trail led back up the slope to the top of a high mountain that stood far out from the main range and was circled by several drainages. No sooner had the cat reached the top than down he went again—way back to the bottom of the canyon he had just vacated. He meandered down the canyon bottom for a quarter mile, then headed for the top of the same peak again. The mountain reared at least 1,500 feet above the canyon and climbing it was getting monotonous, but that was where the cougar was headed and we had to follow his tracks to find him. The track was older now than when we had picked it up the day before; it would be foolish to turn the dogs loose.

This time the big cat crossed a spur ridge and dropped into a rocky brush-choked canyon, pulled out of the cliffs on the far side, and again headed for the top.

As I topped the rim of cliffs and saw the trail headed again for the top of the high point, I almost gave up. I had been traveling since long before daylight and it was now within two short hours of darkness. Worst of all, I knew I was losing ground. If I started now, it would be dark long before I reached wheeled transportation. Even the hounds looked sadder than usual, perhaps wondering why I didn't let them go find that cat. It looked like a storm, and I knew that if it snowed too much I'd lose my track. The trail went up and up; my legs would scarcely push my weight from one short step to the other. Then the cat dropped over a sharp ridge into the next canyon, and I was suddenly aware that he was hunting. I found where he had sat beneath the fir on the ridge before beginning the long stalk. Then, as we pushed through the aspen, the hounds told me the long quest was near an end and the chase about to begin.

The big red hound whined, whirled, and put his front feet on my chest asking me to unsnap the leash. The black-and-tan pup pulled forward hard, choking himself down, and bawled his frustration. Fifty feet farther and the mound of snow over the kill came into sight. There was less than thirty minutes of shooting light left.

The young dog opened up with a fit of bawling that fairly shook the needles from the trees, took an old track where the cougar had snooped off into the brush, then came back on the same track to the kill. The old hound, a "closed trailer," silently circled the kill, then lined out up toward the cliff. The black-and-tan pup was soon yelling close behind.

I stood catching my wind, and listening with little chills chasing up and down my sweat-soaked back. Suddenly, as the hounds reached the base of the cliff, a long eager bay from the old red dog drifted back down into the fading light where I stood. This was his way of telling me the cat was going and the chase was on. Then there was only the deep bellow of the black-and-tan heading for the bottom of the canyon.

Fifteen minutes later I stood beneath the Douglas fir trying to silhouette the cat against the dying light; the sights of the big pistol stood out against the reddish body in fair relief. The gun bucked in my hand and the lion leaped into the air. He was dead by the time the dogs got to him.

When the dogs had finished worrying the prize tom, I stood looking down at this mysterious American cat, and there in the deepening gloom of the winter night, I was aware of a new respect, born of admiration of one hunter for another, and of a new conviction—to me the cougar was no longer the wanton killer of defenseless animals I had once believed him to be. He was a competitor that took heavy toll of the game I hunted. His instinct to hunt and kill was stronger than mine, and he hunted not for the joy of playing the game, but to stay alive. Here was one of the truly great trophies: the American lion, maligned by many, admired by few.

Growing up in Idaho, Montana, Washington, and Nevada, I knew hunters, trappers, and stockmen, and I listened to what they said about mountain lions with open mouth and shining eyes. Some of these old-timers had hunted buffalo from the Great Plains to the Rockies. They had hunted cougar for state and federal agencies, as well as stock associations. These men were my idols. And, to the man, they believed the cougar was strictly vermin, and should not only be controlled, but exterminated. If man was to have game for himself, they believed, the mountain lion had to go.

Today, opinions on cougar control vary drastically. Some feel that the various states with cougar populations should pay bounties, that professional cougar hunters should be employed by the Predator Control Division of the Fish and Wildlife Service, and that the big cats should be exterminated.

Others firmly believe that the big feline has a definite place in the modern hunting scene as a game and trophy animal, and that there should be seasons and limits as there are with other big game species. They feel that sport hunting would be sufficient to keep the cougar population from increasing to the point where it would be a menace to other big game animals. They have a strong argument when one considers that not so many years ago only a few men made a business of guiding cougar hunters. Today there are dozens of outfitters specializing in cougar hunts, operating from Mexico to British Columbia. In fact, several western states have not only revoked the bounty system, but have put the cougar on the game animal list, with one cat a year per hunter allowed.

There is yet a small third group that advocates hunting the cougar without dogs, that is, still-hunting it—man pitting his wits against cougar with no outside help. This may sound good to those who do not know the big animal. And, in fact, a few cougars are killed every year by hunters who are after other game, but these come as a bonus and are strictly coincidental. Try to hunt a cougar without dogs and he'll make seven kinds of a fool out of you. To establish this as law would be to invite disaster for both the hunter and the cougar. They would soon increase to the point where they would be a menace to other game animals and stock.

For many years I relentlessly pursued the big cats over some of the roughest cougar country in the western United States: the Salmon River country of Idaho, a land of rushing streams, rocks, and trees, where there are only two directions: up and down. I began hunting cougar for bounty with the firm belief that if they were not killed, down to the last cat, there would not be enough game for man. (When one considers the size of the cougar—a mature female will weigh as much as 120 pounds, a male from 150 to 200 pounds, occasionally even 225 pounds—it adds up to a lot of game killed

201

over a lifetime.) Perhaps my belief was first shaken during the many wonderful trips with my friend, Stewart Brandborg. Brandy, who today is Executive Director of the Wilderness Society, was making a mountain goat study for the Idaho Fish and Game Department. Although we were studying goats and not cougar, I usually took a hound along, and we hunted cougar a little and talked cougar a lot around the fire. A professional wildlifer, Brandy thought that even though the cougar did take a lot of game, there was game enough for both man and cat. Further, he believed that in certain cases the cougar was actually beneficial to game herds, and could be balanced by sport hunting alone. I wasn't entirely convinced then, but today I am.

I have spent endless days tracking cats and examining clues I found in the snow to see exactly what cougars do and why. I hunted for bounty—that was part of my living—but after hearing Stewart Brandborg's ideas, I looked more closely before I shot, proved or disproved many theories, blew holes in myths.

One thing I soon knew: Cats do not kill the "deer-a-week" they are credited with, neither do they kill for the pure pleasure of killing, as many would have us believe.

Let's look at the facts: First, a cougar does not kill every deer he stalks. He is lucky to kill one out of four. I have followed several cats for as long as three days—the cat's travel time, not mine—between kills. They also kill and eat many rabbits, squirrels, porcupines, and even mice. They love beaver, and catch an occasional grouse.

While they are rumored to eat half a deer at one meal, this is far from the truth. Actually, a big male's stomach will hold only some ten pounds of fresh meat. Brandborg and I weighed the contents of the stomach of a big male that had just gorged on a cow elk. It went right on the ten-

pound mark; later kills ran even less.

In the first twenty-four hours or so after making a kill, a cougar may eat two or three times, then he may wander away and sleep off the feast for a day or so before another meal. Figure it out. A cougar kills few small deer, but he does kill a lot of lone bucks which are easier to stalk, so most of his deer kills will give him one hundred pounds or more of meat. How many will he eat in a week?

I have yet to see where a cougar has killed an animal, eaten only one meal, and then left it never to return (unless he was thoroughly spooked). I have seen where a cougar, usually a female with young, has killed two or three deer or elk apparently within a period of two or three days, but they eventually cleaned them up.

A wildlife researcher making a study of cougar in Idaho said that the deer-a-week figure is far too high and that a young deer's weight every ten days to two weeks would be more accurate.

Also, remember that cougar populations, like those of other predatory animals, depend upon the population of their prey in any given area. If game becomes scarce in one area, the big cats move to another. If man takes a heavy harvest of game, the cougar moves to greener pastures, and, in the back country where man exerts light hunting pressure, the cougar lives and thrives and helps hold the game within the limits of available forage.

Actually, it does not take a great deal of control to hold cougar populations in check. A litter usually contains three kittens. Yet, by the time they are a year old, usually only one or two remain. Males, on occasion, kill the young, but apparently not all males do this. There are, of course, other causes of death of the young.

It seems that the female does not breed until she is at least two years old, and, unless something happens to the young, will not breed again for two or three years. The kittens will stay with the female until they are about two years old, and I know of no one who has observed a female accompanied by both very young kittens and nearly grown young. All of which adds up to a very slow increase in population.

Another influence on cougar populations is family life. Many young males change range, perhaps chased off by their own sires. If food is scarce, young cats are more likely to look for new range when they sever ties with their mother.

Actually, except for these small groups of mother and young, there is little family or social life in the cougar community. Males do a lot of brawling for no reason apparently, except that they do not like each other. Some, of course, is done when more than one male finds a female in a receptive mood, which may happen at any time of the year.

I know of two cases in which cougar hunters found where two big males had fought in fresh snow, and the torn-up snow and brush, the cat hair, and the blood were something to behold. In both cases, one of the cats was killed after a chase by the dogs, and they were so badly slashed and chewed that one wondered how they had survived. I have killed several old toms that had their ears chewed down to stubs, noses split, and head, neck, and shoulders so badly clawed that they looked as though they had been run through a slicer. Females must be more amicable, because I do not recall ever seeing one that was scarred to any extent.

Another story that has given the cougar a bad name is that they are prodigious killers of livestock. All of my life I have heard tales of how the early ranchers in this section of Idaho were unable to raise horses because of the cougar's love of colt meat. Yet in this same area today it is rare for one of the big cats to kill either cattle or horses. Many times I have followed the tracks of hunting cougar in the snow, where the cougars meandered through wintering cattle and horses, but never was there any indication that they had tried to kill one. Over most of the cougar's current range in the United States, there is no evidence that they are even a minor factor in livestock losses.

Many of the tallest tales about mountain lions are woven around the belief that they spend a great deal of time following unsuspecting humans in deep woods with an eye to an easy meal. There is evidence to substantiate some of these tales, but most of it is so well embellished with imagination that it is very difficult to separate fact from fiction.

People generally believe that when a cougar follows a human, he is trying to work up nerve to attack. Actually, the cougar is a very curious animal, and in most cases simply follows a man to see what he is up to. I've had cats follow me—one even stalked me—but everything indicated they were curious, not hungry.

One morning a couple of years ago I was hunting elk during a heavy snowstorm. I was working up a ridge with the snow slanting into my face; as the snow began to thin a little, I stopped under a big pine to wait for it to lift so I could check an opening that I knew was across a narrow draw. I stood there for perhaps fifteen minutes until the snow thinned enough for me to see there were no elk in the opening, then I turned and started up the ridge again. Beyond the pine was a small thicket of fir, and as I turned and started around it, there was a sudden movement and a gray shape crashed through the underbrush. I saw flashes of it, but thinking it was a deer, did not even raise the rifle. Then it dashed into an opening and I could see that it was a good-sized cougar.

The story was there in the fresh snow. The cougar had come over the ridge in long strides and headed for the pine. One hundred feet before he reached it he became aware that something was already behind the tree. The big tracks showed the cat had come to a sudden halt, then advanced in short steps, belly close to the ground. Then, when no more than sixty feet from the tree, he had crouched and waited to see what was on the far side. Suddenly, I turned, came around the thicket straight at him, and he took off like he had a bee under his tail.

Stalking me for the kill? Certainly not, he was only curious. Perhaps if it had been a deer instead of a man behind the tree, the story would have ended differently.

This leads to a long look at the reports of cougars attacking humans. The mature cougar is certainly capable of it, but authenticated cases of one actually killing a human are rare. There have been widely scattered cases, from the early settlements of New England to relatively recent cases in the Northwest, especially on Vancouver Island, British Columbia.

One of the few authenticated cases was cited by Stanley Young in his book, *The Puma*. A thirteen-year-old boy was attacked and killed by a cougar near Malott, Washington, in December, 1924. Tracks in the light snow showed that the cougar had followed the boy as he walked along a trail in a draw bottom. When the boy became aware of the cougar he apparently ran for a tree and, as he attempted to climb it, the cat leaped, pulled him down and killed him. About a month later a female cougar was killed near the vicinity; her stomach contained fragments of the boy's clothing and an empty cartridge case he was known to have had in his pocket. The cougar had apparently been in good physical condition, and it is to be wondered if she would have attacked had the boy not fled.

One point that is generally overlooked when a cougar does attack or kill a human is that there is always a possibility that the cat is rabid. Even small animals like fox and skunks have attacked people when infected by rabies. In any event, attacks by cougars on humans are rare.

To add drama, there is the controversial story that cougars scream like women in distress. Do they really scream? I've put in most of my life in cougar country; I've hunted them for more than thirty years; I've spent hundreds of nights in some of the best cougar country in the United States at all times of the year, but I have never heard one scream. I've heard them make the usual cat sounds, growling, hissing, spitting, and yowling, and the young cats give shrill whistles and chirps, but never anything that could be called a scream. I've heard some weird and unearthly noises in the back country—the screech of certain owls in the night; the terrible, piercing cry of a fawn pursued by a coyote—but I was always able to be certain it was not a cougar that did the so-called screaming.

While *Felis concolor* is by no means near extinction today, neither is he found in much of his former range. In fact, one subspecies, *F. concolor couguar*, that inhabited the country from the western tip of Lake Superior to Maine, and from the Canadian border to northern Florida, may be entirely extinct. There are a few cats left in parts of Florida, possibly a few in Louisiana, but it is doubtful if any remain north of there, east of the Mississippi. As to north-and-south distribution, they are still found from the southern tip of South America to northern British Columbia. There are thirty-one recognized subspecies.

Much of their range, however, is sparsely populated, and chunks of it contain no cougar at all. Part of this is due to over-control and, to some extent, the fact that game populations are not large enough to support the big cats. Here in the western mountains they are holding their own, but pressure from sport hunting is increasing.

There is a vast difference in hunting the great cats in the mountain country of Idaho, Montana, and the Northwest, and the dry country of the Southwest. From southern Utah and Colorado to the desert country of southern Arizona and northern Mexico, the mountain lion is hunted mostly on bare ground from the top side of a pony because the chase is often long on a cold, sun-beaten trail. Packs of hounds are used, anything from three to a dozen, with, perhaps, an average of six. A big pack will have strike dogs, cold trailers, tree dogs, and usually a few just along for the trip, yelling their long-eared heads off, adding to the music and excitement but doing little real good. When the dry air and hot sun bakes the scent from a fresh track in an hour or so, you need dogs specialized in certain phases of cougar trailing to unravel the tracks.

In the northern end of the cougar's range most of the hunting is done during the winter months with snow on the ground. Here horses are next to useless, and hunting is done on foot, often on snowshoes. Most of these hunts are made with one to three dogs. Any pooch with a reasonably good nose can trail a cougar that passed in snow several hours before. But only a well-trained specialist will ignore the cross trails of other animals. While I have used as many as three or four hounds when I was with other hunters, I never used more than two when alone, and I have done most of my hunting with only one good hound.

How you travel, by horse or afoot, determines the kind of gun you carry. In the horse country of the Southwest nearly all hunters carry a short rifle of some kind, usually the Winchester Model 94 carbine in caliber .30-30. Any short rifle that fits close to the horse in a saddle boot will do the trick—a scope is unnecessary, ranges usually run in feet instead of yards—and any cartridge from the .22 Hornet up will do.

When you trail the cats on foot in snow country you must pack the rifle in your hand or in a sling on your back, and for that reason many hunters use a pistol. The rifle is not only in the way when you need both hands to hang on to a branch on a canyon wall, it may get tangled in brush when you're crawling through a thicket, and then when you need it, it is apt to be full of snow, which is dangerous.

A pistol firing anything from the .38 Special with heavy loads on up will do the job well. Some hunters even swear by the .22 long rifle cartridge, but I prefer the .38's and .44's.

In snow a hunter can always tell if the track is of a trophy-size cat before he turns the dogs loose; on dry ground you find out after the cat is treed. I've passed up small tracks that were obviously not made by trophy cougars, to go on and look for a bigger cat. Of course, a big track does not necessarily mean that the cat will have a skull large enough to make the record book, but it is almost certain that a small cat will not have a skull of that size.

If there is a greater sport than hunting the big cats with good hounds, I'd like to try it. And if there is any sound sweeter than the baying of hounds on a hot track, drifting up from some rocky, brush-choked canyon bottom, I have yet to hear it. And added to all of this, a big male cougar is one of the finest trophies that can be taken on the North American continent, a trophy you can hang with pride beside the best in any trophy room. (I have four cats in the Boone and Crockett record book; of several dozen top entries, one of mine was tied for eighth place for many years.) When I hunt today, I follow the big track or none at all. ◉

Diary
of a
Voyageur

*by Robert Frisch
Photography
by Paul Baich*

*Beginning his northward
journey where the early trappers
and traders ended theirs,
a modern naturalist travels by canoe
through one of Canada's
wildest, most isolated regions.*

The Canadian fur trade of the eighteenth and nineteenth centuries depended on *voyageurs* who traveled, during the short five months of the warm season when the ice was not impenetrable, beyond the Great Lakes to the lands whose waters drain into the Athabasca basin. Loaded with trade goods, they set out from Montreal every spring when the waterways were barely free from ice, paddling and portaging to the country *"d'en Haut."* With their great piles of furs they returned before freeze-up; sometimes they covered a total of six thousand miles in a season.

In June and early July of 1968, naturalist Robert Frisch and photographer Paul Baich made a three-hundred-mile canoe trip through the same kind of North Country wilderness traversed by the voyageurs. Although the distance traveled was not comparable, the experience was very much so, for little has changed along the most remote stretches of Canada's wilderness. And, in one way, they surpassed the feats of the early voyageurs. They began their northward journey where the early trappers and traders had ended theirs. Loading their canoe at Great Slave Lake in the Northwest Territories, about two hundred miles above Lake Athabasca, they made their way still farther north via the Marian and Camsell rivers to Great Bear Lake.

Mr. Frisch holds degrees in virology and bac-

teriology, but his deepest interest is in the total ecology of the remote wilderness. Mr. Baich is on frequent assignment for the National Film Board of Canada. For both men, the purpose of this journey was to gain a deeper understanding of the northern wilds.

At times, squalls forced them to shore, where they waited for favorable weather and then proceeded even if night had come, for this was the season of the long sun. Although they carried staples, much of their food consisted of what the wilderness had to offer—fish, ducks, spruce grouse, muskrats. They camped wherever the terrain presented advantages such as a rocky point for easy landing, or an elevation high enough so that breezes discouraged the clouds of mosquitoes.

Often the portages or the effort of paddling against the current became backstraining labor, but work was interspersed with the joys of fishing for abundant northern pike, pickerel, and lake trout. The country offered innumerable glimpses of wildlife—moose, black bears, wolves, beavers, otters, eagles, owls, swans, and many more.

Along the way, photographer Baich recorded the majestic scenery pictorially, while naturalist Frisch kept notes on his impressions of the North Country. Accompanied by a selection of the photographs, here is Mr. Frisch's "Diary of a Voyageur."

*Preceding pages: Author sets out from Great
Slave Lake immediately after spring break-up of ice. Left: This region of
Northwest Territories has vast forests laced with waterways.*

Summer is brief in the North. The country is big, the canoe slow. So I like to set out in good time. And the best time to set out is as early in the season as possible: with the ice at break-up. There is water again to travel on, but not yet enough of it for waves to swamp the canoe. It is light round the clock. The mosquitoes are still innocent water creatures dancing harmlessly in the teapail—though they will mature before the journey ends. All these are good reasons for starting in early June, but for me the most compelling reason is quite simply the great event of break-up, the opening of the new season.

Break-up in the North—no one who has experienced it can misread its meaning. It is the signal for arrival and departure, for stirring from holes and dens, for travel, on wings and legs, in flocks and singly, by air, by water, by floe. Even the vast unmoving land itself seems caught up in the tide, as the first green sweeps north, passing the message from branch to branch till the very blue of the horizon catches the new tint. Sky and water carry those travelers for whom North is still not north enough: the geese, the loons, the ducks, the tiny waders, and the great white swans. Then is the time to dip the paddle and follow that first lead where the ice parts from the shore.

The yearning will be understood by anyone who has ever craned his neck after a chevron of northbound geese, or tried to project in the mind's eye the white swirl of snowbirds from the hurtling highway to the barrens of northern Canada where they will nest. That should be reason enough to follow them. To find a chance to do so is another matter. Having found it, or taken it, I want to give those less fortunate a glimpse of what I have seen. And then, if someone should ask where to journey in that enormous country, I'd say it doesn't much matter. You study a map for places that look empty except for the thin blue veins, the rivers that will carry you. I picked the stretch from Great Slave Lake to Great Bear Lake because of how it looked on the map— great and empty save for a string of waterways linking two enormous lakes.

That something should be better because it is bigger is, I suppose, generally held to make sense. But perhaps the unconverted will ask, as the Mackenzie river pilot did, What if it happens to be big but empty,

just more and more miles and miles of bloody miles and miles? The answer is that it is empty only on the map. In reality it is crammed with life. And although there isn't much you can "do" with that life, it is important to some men to come into close contact with those other inhabitants of our planet that were here long before us, be they lichens or spruce or moose or mosquitoes. The land can seem very big and silent, but there is always a presence, or a vast summation of presences, never an emptiness.

The Great Slave-Great Bear country bore this out as much as any I have traveled. Even by northern standards it is remote. No canoe brigades shipping pelts for the Hudson's Bay or North West Company ever reached it. In fact, it is not known to have been seen by a white man until well into the second half of the nineteenth century when a redoubtable Oblate missionary, Father Emile Petitot, traversed it by dogsled. The water route remained unknown until the fall of 1900, when two similarly indomitable travelers, the explorer-geologists Bell and Camsell, lost their way grop-

ing through its maze of waterways. They probably would have died but for a chance encounter with a band of Dogrib Indians. In the Thirties and Forties, a flurry of prospecting and mining followed the discovery of pitchblende and gold. An occasional rusted can, a massive pulley chain, the tilting mine tower at Hottah Lake are all that now bear witness to these activities, although mining—now for silver—has started up again near Great Bear.

In winter, the Dogribs hunt the caribou that have come down to their winter feeding grounds from the Barrens, and tractor trains roar through the white darkness on their way to the mines. In summer, the land is quiet. The caribou have departed, and even the splashing of a moose or the grunt of a curious bear is a rare sound. Most of the sounds you hear are provided by wind and waves and the voices of birds. As to people, I met no one except a few Dogrib Indians.

At that time, in early June, Great Slave is still a frozen waste, but on shallow Marian Lake, its thinly jointed northern

*It is no mean trick
to keep one's footing while guiding
canoe through rocky shallows.*

arm, break-up is well under way. In places, the shore lead expands into miles of open water; the canoe slides from wave to wave; the water skims past to the swing and dip of the paddle; the shorelines, even the lagging distant hills, seem to be on the move. Between the blues of lake and sky, the ice is a mere white line, a far streak of dazzling unreal mirages. But I know better than to believe that the retreat of the ice has been completed. It isn't long before the white line comes creeping back. Way out as yet, just below the edge of the horizon, I see it closing in across the breadth of the lake. Slowly the proportions of blue and white are reversed; and in another hour all that remains of the lake is another narrow lead, the melted margin of an expanse now white and solid, edging uncertainly towards the next point of land. It looks as if the ice is grounded there—I stand up for a better view—and there seems to be no way through.

But spring has done its work. As I paddle up, I find the white barrier blotched and veined with green. My canoe noses into tinkling ice candles, crystals, lance points, dumbbells, floating chandeliers, wrought by water and sunlight from winter's crumbling armor. They swirl about my paddle, splinter before the slow push of the bow. Barely making headway through their marvelous profusion, I inch the canoe around the spit. And there, three boat lengths ahead, water laps and rocks the ice margin. I break free, the jingle of ice candles fades astern, the chill breath diminishes, ahead spreads the rippled blue of another stretch of lake. Old-squaw ducks in white and chocolate plumage circle their plump mates, calling *a-han-lac, a-han-lac* in a frenzy of absurd ardor. Loons surface to stare at my canoe, skunk-ducks rise in a succession of skittering take-offs till the whole wide lead rings to wingbeats. And so I make my way through the long days and brief twilights

of early June on this first lap toward Great Bear, amid the vast yet subdued clamor of break-up, the noises of birds and water and ice music, all contained in the silence of this immense land.

Into Marian Lake, out of the North, flows Marian River. Paddling up its mouth, I find myself in another world, or at least in another season. I have been heading north, but I seem to have come south, for spring here is no longer just the stir and release of break-up, the passage of migrants across conquered winter, but the new season established and quietly at work. Warblers sing from a filigree of early green, thrushes from bristling, bright-tipped spruce, and the river, the pulsing artery watering and feeding this outpost of spring, seems to have washed away the memory of winter. At sunrise, shortly after midnight, I peer from my tent and watch a party of Indians vanish into the milky mist. Later I follow them upstream but I never again catch up with them.

As the slow bends and varied prospects of the river pass to the steady thrust of the paddle, the shoots of horsetail and water lily poke ever higher toward my keelstrip, and the weft of green thickens on willow, alder, and birch.

There are, of course, days when a cold wind blows from the north, snatching bird song from bent branches and driving even the hardy mergansers to shelter. Spring lies low then, even when the sun is brilliant, and travel is hard, the spate of the river racing in wind-driven flurries against the bow, elbowing it to shore, slewing it out into the brunt of the current. But crouched well forward, knees braced against the ribbing, one pushes on; the sun makes its round and dips northwest; the sky grows calm, the light golden; and before long the lengthened shadow of some outcrop signals the end of another day's journey. Soon the lonely outcrop has sprouted the orange triangle of a tent. A fire crackles under a black kettle, and a thin plume of smoke streaks down-river on the dying wind. Sometimes fluffs of duck down accompany it, and once the yet softer down of two young and tender owls, for great appetites rule the ways of the bush. Most often, though, the victim is a fish. A tug, the line criss-crossing the current, a silvery splutter— and a pike or pickerel flaps on the weathered rock.

A new day spreads radiant under a light breeze. On the fissured gneiss, arnica copies the sun's motif; even the bare ridges on the skyline have caught a faint bloom. Spring reoccupies the land.

The La Martre confluence passes; the river slackens; rapids appear, churning and tossing beside a portage trail where I trot, bent under boat and pack. Around noon, the river threads into a maze of oxbows, ponds, backwaters, fringed by marshes and sheltered by groves of birch. The marshes have not yet come to life, but the green of the birch seems to darken the very radiance of the sky, so intense is its light. White and mottled limbs spread canopies of feathery foliage, soft earth is heaped into strange mounds clothed in lime-green growths. I paddle closer to examine them. They are roses, entire beds of them, their leaves just beginning to unfold. A sense of unreality makes me wonder where I am, for this is a fairy-tale landscape in the grim Northland. But no fairies haunt it. Instead, a mosquito jabs into my neck, and another—and I feel at home again, reassured that I am still on the right river, in the right country.

Soon black spruce once more loom into view, the river constricts between outcrops and gateways of rock, the land darkens. I am moving into the uplands. The mosquitoes that so suddenly appeared are out in force. No longer can I paddle bare-backed on warm days. I wear a headnet to shield my face from them, and my hat stays on my head. The insects ride atop, until I scoop them off and make room for more. The summer season is open—but, I ruefully reflect, one must be prepared to pay for it.

Through wide, cool lakes, over sweaty, stinging portages, around bend upon bend of the river, I make my way upstream. Gradually, the river loses its thrust and volume, rushes fitfully through riffles and shallow rapids, falters in rocky pools, branches to vanish into the forest. But I keep pulling up along its tortuous thread. And late one night, I float out into Mazenod Lake. I have reached the height of land between Great Slave and Great Bear, the backbone of the interlake country. Here the Shield piles up against the western Paleozoics in great ridges and heights of naked rock rooted in cool, deep lakes. Countless islands lie about as though splintered off their massive bulk. But so broad is the layout of these hills that they merely extend the range of sight: As its profiles steepen, the face of the land expands to yet vaster proportions. Even from the low perspective of the canoe, these are prodigious horizons. The canoe is a strange, tiny object by the water's edge as I watch from a bald hilltop and see two eagles wheeling in the void. Those horizons—it seems impossible to cross them, to escape them. But somehow I have come over that edge of the beyond, over there in the dim southeast, and somehow I will no doubt cross the opposite horizon.

The first step is the portage over the divide. I soon find myself hoping that it will turn out to have been the worst. For hours I plod and pole and paddle through floating bogs and shallow ponds, muskeg, and black peat, in ever-thickening clouds of mosquitoes, only to end up in a fiendish, putrid-pink-and-mustard-colored mire which seems spewed up from the very bowels of the country. I find there is a floor of ice a few feet down that supports me in most places;

Small inset map of Canada shows area of Northwest Territories where author made long wilderness canoe trip. On large, detailed map, route is traced from Great Slave Lake through Marian Lake, along Marian River, Faber and Hottah lake systems, and Camsell River, 300 miles north to Great Bear Lake.

but where it doesn't, I start vanishing very fast. Soaked to my beard, and covered with a crawling pelt of insects, I finally drop my pack at Sarah Lake. It is June 21, summer solstice, and I am over the hump. Sarah Lake is the source of the Camsell River, which, with a little luck, will bring me to Great Bear, downriver all the way.

Here, fed by the current of the Camsell, are the great lakes of the upland: Sarah itself, Faber, Rae, Hardisty, Hottah, Grouard. Most have their bodies embedded in the western sediments, their arms in the Precambrian. Like huge squids, they straddle the physiographic boundary between the two regions that themselves span nearly a continent. They are still largely encased in ice, with only the arms and the eastern margins open. Chill air blows off these last emplacements of winter. The trout are sluggish from the cold and dark that has imprisoned them for so long. But though winter may still make a last stand above these cold depths, on land the battle has long been won. In sight of the ice, batteries of bright flowers blaze from the rock. Swallowtails patrol the shores, and just inshore the green is deployed in dense, unbroken ranks from mossy floor to tallest fir tip.

I travel mostly by night, when the wind is down. Sunset sets fire to sunrise, all stars are extinguished in the flaming skies, and I can see as far as at noon. During the day I sleep, hunt, sit by the surf with my pipe, waiting for the wind to drop.

At Rae Lakes Indian Village, I am windbound. I buy provisions, mend the canoe amid a swarm of children, attend service at the chief's house, squat in a tent eating moose meat, bannock, and boiled loon. We converse as best we can.

"Moose meat good?"

"Good, good." I chew.

"You get whitefish this morning, Paul?"

Paul Drybone nods. "Big, some." He spreads his hands. "Plenty fat, too. You got medicine?"

"Just rum."

Much laughter and wagging of heads. They always want medicine, the white man's magic.

A plane arrives. The Oblate father steps ashore, shakes hands all around, shepherds his flock up the path to the village. The pilot lounges by the plane and smokes a cigarette, looking a little out of his element. In half an hour, the plane roars away. I leave in the evening. For a while, I can still hear the dogs. Then only my paddle.

Again a change comes over the land. Enormous knuckles and shoulders of rock squeeze the forest into cracks and hollows, broken rock lines the shores, islands of gigantic rubble and scoured stone jut from the depths. In places, Hardisty Lake looks like a vast flooded quarry, abandoned long ago but not yet wholly reclaimed by life. Thin subarctic voices are beginning to be heard: graycheeks, longspurs, winter chippies. The limpid notes of whitethroat and hermit no longer can be detected. Yet the plant life supported by this stony land is curiously bright, delicate in texture, at times almost Arcadian. Birch lightly cloak the ancient rock; lichen intricately patterns it in lightest shades of jade; wherever I step ashore, saxifrage and cinquefoil cluster; and the birds all seem to sing in a major key.

Vast moorlands now lie before me as I embark on a short cut to Hottah Lake, windswept and mosquito-ridden muskegs, their knee-deep pile starry with flowers and rutted with the trails of caribou. Again I plod and backpack, pole through sluggish runnels, cross lakes toward strange, treeless, featureless shores. Then one night I enter a river. Lush, leafy thickets slide past, a moose stops feeding to turn its head, domed outcrops loom black above the spruce. As the mist lifts through the rays of morning, a new landscape lies revealed. It reminds me of the country before the Indian village, but is yet grander, superbly harmonious, imbued with a severe beauty that slows the paddle.

Dark rock ascends above dark forest, settles along high skylines where no trees grow, steps back into valleys and plains. Far vistas end in other ranges equally tall and bare, though to the eye they look gentle in the dove-blue distances. The sky is a flawless azure, the lake immaculate. A superb and noble land, but somber even on this brilliant summer day.

Hottah Lake—sprawling preamble to Great Bear. For three days I travel along its islands and shores, sleep in the moss of barren skerries, boil the kettle on huge ice-scoured ramps of volcanic rock, keep the pitching bow headed into the wind that blows off the lake's icy mantle. It is July now, but climbing a high hill at sunset, I see ice stretch away across the open reaches of the lake toward the western lowlands. A hundred square miles of ice, or more. From under my raised headnet I peer out upon a vast and savage scene. Westward beyond violet islands, where a mound of grounded shore ice gleams, the frozen lake extends in remote lavender pallor. To the north, framed by shaggy spruce, the sun's red afterglow darkens the horizon. And away in the northwest, dim ranges rear, fold upon fold, like a surf of the earth's crust—the inshore uplands of Great Bear. Beyond the whining cloud of mosquitoes, silence reigns.

Two days later I skim down a riffle through a towering portal of rockslides and russet cliffs, while an eagle drops from its aerie to circle above. This is the first gate into Great Bear country. The waterway digs deeper. The land tightens and contracts. Dense forest fills all the hollows, bristling far up the dark slopes. At midnight on Grouard, the lake gleams like a bowl of molten metal. Under the southern night shadow, a view unfolds that seems to reveal a last stronghold of the spirits that once ruled these domains. There are domed hills over violet-black gulches. There is lichened rock, pale as bone exposed at twilight, a streaked sky, utter silence. It is midsummer now in this North Country, and the birds are silent at night.

Eagle Falls is a fifty-foot cascade shattering the river into writhing whiteness and spume. More rapids, too risky to run. An afternoon on a river now wide and deep, branching into rockbound bays, arms, channels, but still hemmed in by high ground, confining the view to the groping course of the valley. Then, by degrees, the banks grow bolder, rock gains ground, cliffs loom. And, at evening, suddenly Conjuror Bay, the forecourt to Great Bear—calm, deep, glacially cold, spreading in silence between the waterbound bastions of its islands. They seem as empty as the bay. No birds are seen or heard, no boat appears, though people live not far away. The presence of Great Bear, hidden still behind the heights of Richardson Island, lies like a spell over the scene. The dark islands brood over their reflections, the gray trout pass in the depths. Trawling, I travel slowly towards the narrows of Hloo Channel.

And, at last, Great Bear. Or rather, the immense yet minute segment of it that I can see on this clear and sunlit morning. It ends in a thin, white rim, out along the edge of the sky. I stand up and, leaning on my paddle, look north. The horizon, pushed farther now, shimmers with ice mirages. Below it, whiteness blazes, the length of the lake. It is July 11, but Great Bear is still icebound. A field of rotting cakes clinks and crunches past, dappling the green depth with highlights and glassy shadows. Ice music, ice lights, ice blinks, welding blue to blue. At my last camp, roses had been in full bloom. Nevertheless, I began this journey in ice, and amid ice it ends. ◉

WILD REALM:
The most
splendid routes
to sport are the high,
windswept trails
of the
pack tripper.
Text
and photography
by
Erwin A. Bauer

Preceding pages: Packing in Glacier National Park. Typical pack-trip camp life includes snug tents and hearty food. Guide tends horses while cook wrestles chow. Far right: Author lands trout in Montana's Beartooth Primitive Area, where hundreds of alpine lakes await the horseman.

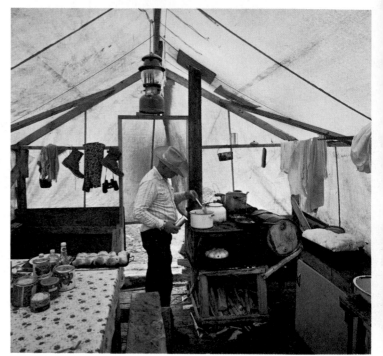

■ I have devoted a lifetime to adventure—to hunting and fishing around the world—but can recall nothing to match this place and this fishing. To begin, Mummy Lake is as remote and lonely as any alpine lake. Surrounded by ice fields and awesome peaks, it reminded me of all the world's wildernesses. The lake was full of fat and willing cutthroat trout; it wasn't easy to keep from catching them.

After an hour we took our fish up. I gathered dead dry brush and soon we were warming by the fire while the trout cooked. It was time, as the flames played across the flanks of the boulder backing the fire, to relax and consider the scene around us.

The fishing in this lofty country, I decided, could compare with the best in North America. And on this particular day, perhaps it *was* the best. In either case I reflected that it wasn't available to fishermen unless they were willing to pack in for it. I also reflected how we had done exactly that a few days earlier.

All through the night before, a soft rain had fallen and by morning the forests around Sunrise, Alberta, and the road's end were saturated. To make it worse, the rain persisted while Mac Mackenzie, Doug Wilson, my son Bob, and I saddled a string of reluc-

tant riding and pack horses. Launching a pack trip in a rain is never a cheerful chore. Spirits become as damp as the foliage. Horses do not like soggy blankets tossed onto their backs and diamond hitches are tough to tie with cold, wet hands. Mac swore; one sorrel mare had shied and tried to bite him.

Somehow we secured our gear onto the horses and Mac led the way along a thin trail which follows Healy Creek. Nobody whistled or sang as is normal on departure. It seemed a poor beginning.

Only a handful of the million or so visitors each season to Banff National Park in Alberta ever see the Healy Creek trail; it is too

far from the pavement. Two hours and seven or eight miles later, we rode out into another, brighter world. The trail had climbed steeply and by noon we cleared both timberline and the curtain of rain clouds. All at once Healy Pass and the surrounding snowy peaks loomed ahead of us. Behind was a gray rain-filled void which might have been bottomless. In an hour the summer sun had dried us out and soon after that we reached the grassy alpine meadow which flanks the pass. There we dismounted.

The view in all four directions from Healy is magnificent. To the north and south stretches the main range of the Rockies which begins in Mexico, and which reaches a peak in Colorado and finally dwindles away toward Alaska and the Yukon. All of it is pack-trip country and we were in the center of it. To the west towered our trip destination—the Pharaoh Peaks—an awesome jumble of formidable icy lakes and mountains, all unaccountably with such Egyptian names as Scarab, Haiduk, and Mummy. Just below us several mountain goats strolled across a sheer rock face.

After the horses were unpacked and hobbled, we pitched two light sleeping tents and a cooking tent. Firewood was gathered to last through dinner and breakfast, then Bob and Doug assembled fly rods. Thirty minutes' fishing brought enough twelve-inch cutthroats for dinner. White goats watched from high above as the trout crisped in a skillet over the open fire. Just at dusk a blond grizzly bear passed a few hundred yards away without giving us a glance; there were pikas and marmots to be dug from the rock piles around us.

Then the night fell, and the warm sleeping bags....

We would fish a dozen lonely lakes in the Pharaoh range; it is hard to say when the last fishermen had visited them. We shivered around evening campfires and suffered the bittersweet saddle soreness most trail riders know. While dinner trout cooked, somebody usually passed a bottle of bonded. We drank from tin cups, mixing it with cold mountain water. Bourbon never tasted better.

We rode through some of the most spectacular real estate on top of North America.

It wasn't always easy riding and there were many times when footprints left behind were our own as well as our horses'. Still we lived at least fourteen days apiece during one wonderful, memorable week of riding and camping on wilderness trails. During that time we saw no other humans. Little of this could have been accomplished except by pack train and pack trip.

In America, the heritage of horse power is as old as the westward expansion across our Great Plains and through the Rocky Mountains. The first explorers, soldiers, surveyors, trappers, prospectors, merchants, and even preachers to go west were pack trippers of sorts. But there is far more of it today than when the West was being won, although virtually all of it is now for pleasure and adventure rather than necessity. That makes it a purely American pastime today.

A pack trip can be of any duration: a couple of days, a weekend, a week, or a month. The longer the better. Previous riding experience is helpful. Mountain goat, grizzly bear, caribou, bighorn sheep, and other big game don't thrive near cities and highways. For these a sportsman has to explore remote places far from civilization. The hunting pack trip has long been the ultimate experience for the hunter.

A good many outdoorsmen have become hopelessly hooked, as I was, on the first trip. The time of my addiction began just after World War II on what was to be a reunion of hunting buddies returning from scattered battlefields. Our destination was the Bob Marshall Wilderness in Montana. We had

made contact with our outfitter, Howard Copenhaver, an Ovando rancher. The general object of our trip was to collect an elk and a mule deer apiece, something Copenhaver predicted would not be too difficult. All of us had had considerable hunting experience in the East for whitetail deer.

Some may not consider our trip a success because during two weeks of hunting we bagged enough game to keep the camp well supplied with meat—and not much more. But the last night under canvas all of us agreed that it had been the trip of a lifetime. I suppose that still would be the consensus if the same companions had not made many other pack trips together.

Our camp there in the Bob Marshall country was typical of pack trip camps. It was really a tidy tent village beside Danaher Creek in a lush meadow turned golden by the onset of autumn. The creek meandered aimlessly and each bend undercut the bank to form a shadowy trout pool. Cutthroats ran to three and a half pounds. In the background towered Scapegoat Mountain and a massive chunk of granite called the Chinese Wall. One morning we stepped out of our tent to film the Wall in the strange post-dawn light and found the whole valley covered with a thick hoarfrost. A herd of elk had recently crossed the meadow, leaving telltale tracks in the white grass. We decided to follow the tracks after breakfast, but they soon dissolved under a warm morning sun.

I recall many other remarkable events of that pioneer trip. One afternoon Frank Sayers and I rode toward the crest of a thin, cool ridge, dismounted and continued to the top on foot. There on rimrock we stretched prone to glass the dizzying slopes below. Immediately Frank spotted a huge grizzly excavating shale to capture a marmot for dinner. But the bruin couldn't quite dig its quarry out of a deep den, and while the rock flew, he growled and batted at the air with his forepaws. I thought of a small boy having a tantrum.

On a later pack trip to British Columbia's Mt. Assiniboine with my sons, a friendly young moose strolled right into camp. There it stood watching us chop firewood, and stayed while we reshoed a pack mule and broiled steaks. Pack-tripping, penetrating remote areas, leads to this elemental contact with big game. It is likewise unique in that, in this century, absolutely no progress has been made. All the gear—the pack saddles, blankets, pack covers, even the methods of lashing—is the same as it was in great-grandfather's day. In fact, not much has altered since Marco Polo made his trek.

On a typical pack trip, an outfitter furnishes stock, both riding and pack saddles, camping equipment, food, all necessary tools from axe and crosscut saw to baling wire and horseshoe nails. It is the exceptional packer who does not ply his riders with robust and, occasionally, gourmet food.

As a rule of thumb, outfitters figure one saddle horse and one pack animal per person, but there may be need for an extra pack horse or so for the group. If the group is small, the packer may choose to handle the chores, wrangle the stock, and do the cooking; a good many trail riders prefer to do these things themselves.

Hunting or cold-weather pack trips cost slightly more than summertime rides. A typical trip in Montana or Wyoming will run $35 to $50 per person per day. The farther north, the higher the tab. In the Yukon, where it is necessary to pack hay for the horses, hunting trips may run as high as $150 per day, including the services of a guide, as the law requires.

One of my best pack trips took me into the Gila and Pecos wildernesses of New Mexico. On brisk, bright days we browsed in picturesque box canyons seldom seen. Behind beaver dams we caught brown trout. We explored little-known cliff dwellings where fresh tracks were etched everywhere in the earth. In a lonely draw, one rider found a decaying log cabin with a grave and crude headstone nearby. The headstone read: "William Grudgings—waylayed and murdered by Tom Webb—October 8, 1893—age 37 yrs 8 months."

The pack tripper, like the prospector, lives for that next trip. One wonders, "If I had one final pack trip, where would I go?" The temptation to ride out into Montana's Beartooth Wilderness for a bighorn ram would be great. So would a trip into the headwaters of Oyster Creek in the southern Alberta Rockies for a ram and a bull elk. I couldn't help but consider a white sheep and grizzly hunt in the little-known Nahanni Buttes country of the Northwest Territories, or one onto Toad River, British Columbia, after Stone sheep. And, of course, there is Healy Creek trail leading to the remote and incomparable Mummy Lake high in Alberta.

What does a person need to make a pack trip? Great physical stamina or riding skill isn't necessary, but obviously it is helpful. If your companions ride well and you do not—trail-ride locally in advance of your big pack trip.

Many outfitters realize their clients may be city-soft, and plan a short first day's ride, going a little farther the second, and so on, until a long rough ride becomes, surprisingly, a pleasure.

There are few dull moments on the normal pack trip. The route may lead over a pass on top of the world via a ribbon trail barely clinging to the mountainside. Then suddenly in the eternity below is a chain of blue-green lakes where overnight camp will be pitched.

Trout are rising to an evening hatch.

This is your kingdom. It may be had, for the price of a horse. ◉

While hunter glasses Highwood Range of Alberta Rockies for game, saddle horse that made hunt possible stands at ease, waiting the next move. Pack string has been hobbled in alpine pasture near camp.

The Eternal Everglades
by Wyatt Blassingame / Photography by Patricia Caulfield

A magnificent Floridian river of grass beckons sportsmen and naturalists alike. Sweeping south and east from Big Cypress Swamp and Lake Okeechobee, the Everglades is part of a wildlife environment where man is overwhelmed by opportunity. Black bass, snook, tarpon, and many other species of fish await his tackle. Whitetail deer, turkey, ducks, and geese await his gun. But caution on the wanderer's enthusiasm: Too lost in sport, he may spend a prolonged vacation in a treacherous vastness where occasionally fishermen, bird-watchers, and fugitives have vanished forever from the face of the earth.

Within rich depths of the Everglades, reeds sway unbroken; coots court noisily (far left); orchids bloom among pond cypress; and raccoon searches for birds' eggs. Preceding pages: White ibis come in to roost on mangrove island under last rays of sun.

Last year I fished a part of the Everglades with John Wilhelm and a Canadian sportsman on his first trip south. Fishing out of the little village of Goodland with John Stephens for guide, we worked on an incoming tide along the edge of mangrove islands, casting up yellow jigs under the limbs for snook and redfish. Most of these ran two to four pounds; any that were bigger than that would run around a mangrove root and cut the line.

This fishing usually hits its peak with a flood tide. So when the tide turned, Wilhelm asked his guest if he would like to try for some big snook. The Canadian looked puzzled. "Will that be in the Everglades?"

"Sure," Wilhelm said.

We ran a couple of miles west. Here the passes were wider, the open Gulf visible occasionally between the islands. The water was shallow, but dropped now and then into deep potholes where the big snook lay. We trolled, using bullhead jigs that John Stephens had wired to needlefish, and letting them bounce along the bottom. The fishing was much slower than among the mangrove roots, but the snook ran twenty to thirty pounds.

The Canadian was both delighted and puzzled. "I thought you said we were going to fish the Everglades."

"We are," Wilhelm said. "We have been in them all morning."

The guest shook his head. "I thought the Everglades were, you know, fresh water, bass, jungles. That sort of thing."

He was right. The Everglades are fresh

Top: Whitetail deer move from island to island; rare roseate spoonbills, snowy egrets (right) feed in pond. Wild turkey (far right), most difficult hunter's game, captured by telephoto lens.

Casting for largemouth black bass. Ten-pounders are not uncommon, share upper tidal reaches with snook and tarpon. Hooked and jumping, bass (below) makes pretty picture above water.

*Opposite: Alligator
lounges amid reflections in
sawgrass sanctuary.
Above: Bull about to make
lateral swipe at fish.
Huge red-bellied turtle
(at left) shares
log with alligator in
Great Cypress Swamp.*

water, bass, and hardwood jungles. They are also a lot of other things.

The Glades cover approximately 2,700 square miles. At least this is a commonly used figure. There can be no exact measurements since precisely where the Glades start and stop is often a matter of opinion.

Whatever their precise limits, Lake Okeechobee is the mother of the Everglades. From the lake the Glades run southward to the Gulf, a distance of slightly more than one hundred miles. The shape is a blunted crescent moon, with its horns pointing westward. On the east the Everglades end where a low ridge bars them from the Atlantic, some ten to twenty miles inland. A good part of the western border merges into the Big Cypress Swamp. Cape Sable at the tip of the Glades is the southernmost point on the U. S. mainland. Of this vast area, the Everglades National Park makes up less than ten percent.

Okeechobee means "big water." Much of the 730 square miles it covers is only a few feet deep. These grass-grown shallows furnish excellent duck hunting in the winter, and some of the best bass fishing in the world year-round.

The streams that flow into Okeechobee from the north and northwest are chiefly fed by heavy rains that occur mostly during the summer months. In winter these streams become a series of small, self-contained ponds. But in the summer they pour vast quantities of water into the great, shallow basin of the lake.

In years long past, there was no ordinary,

Opposite: Panther
snarls at photographer.
Above: Everglades kite,
a very rare species, is attacked by
red-winged blackbird.
Young cottonmouth (at left) stalks
frog; less poisonous
than Everglades rattlers, it
seldom bites humans.

free-flowing stream that led from the lake to the sea. But the earth beneath the lake, and indeed all south Florida, tilts very gently to the south and southwest, like a table with two short legs. With the summer rains the water overflowed in little streams along the entire lower rim of Okeechobee. Ahead of it the country lay flat as sunlight. And the trickling streams spread out across this incredibly flat country in a shallow river fifty, even sixty miles wide in places. Slowly, gently, it moved toward the Gulf a hundred miles away.

It was this vast, scarcely flowing river that created the Everglades.

Some of the first white men ever to set foot on the North American continent sailed along the edges of the Glades. But when they went ashore, it was well to the north. The Glades themselves were unknown to the Spanish except by hearsay. Indeed, there is doubt that even the pre-Columbian Indians actually inhabited the interior of the Glades. It was the Seminole War of the 1830's and 40's that forced the Indians to seek safety in the interior. And it was because of the war that Colonel William S. Harney on December 4, 1840, left the Atlantic Coast near where Miami is today and headed west with ninety men and sixteen canoes. He captured a few Indians and killed a few. He also crossed the heart of the Everglades from Atlantic to Gulf, and one of his soldiers wrote the first eyewitness account of what lay between.

What lay there, as the writer reported, was not one strange, mysterious world, but several.

To the north where the water spilled from Lake Okeechobee and crept over the flat land in a vast, shallow stream, grew the sawgrass. A foot high in places, six feet and higher in others, brown in winter, green in summer with water flowing through it, the grass spread in every direction until the sky dipped down to meet it. This is the country the Seminoles called Pa-hay-okee, meaning "grassy water." In her book on the Everglades Marjory Stoneman Douglas called it the "River of Grass." It truly is, and the name has become common usage.

This sawgrass, according to botanists, is not a grass but a sedge. The blades are serrated, the points sloping downward; pull your hand upward along a blade of sawgrass and it can slash you like a knife. In fact, there is no need to pull your hand along it. Sawgrass has the living quality of an enraged hornet. It can jump at you. Or make you believe it did anyway.

In the flatness of this country a variation of a few inches in elevation makes a tremendous difference; on higher ground trees replace the sawgrass. These "tree islands" can be seen as far as the eye can reach across the ocean of sawgrass. Some are of pine or cabbage palm, others a mixture of hardwoods: moss-hung oaks, mahogany with dark, glossy leaves, lignum vitae with small blue flowers, and something called gumbo limbo with a reddish brown bark on which multicolored tree snails love to cluster.

In contrast to the tree islands there are scattered sloughs through the sawgrass where the water deepens, and where the bass fishing can be superb. The only way to reach them is by airboat. Several years ago George Slater, who guides out of Andytown, took me to have a go at these bass.

It was night. George wore a frog-hunter's light on his cap and the beam leaped ahead against a solid wall of sawgrass that flattened as the airboat raced into and over it. A mile of this and suddenly there was open water and the boat slowed and stopped. A cypress loomed against the sky.

"Use a weedless spoon and pork rind," George told me. "The bass feed out of the edge of the grass into the open. Cast a foot or two back into the grass, then pull it out."

There had been a brief period of total quiet after the airboat engine quit. But now the night sounds were beginning again. Frogs by the millions: peepers, tree frogs, bull frogs, a gigantic chorus as surrounding as the darkness. In the beam of George's light eyes glittered. An alligator bellowed.

On the third cast I got a strike I will never forget. In the beam of the spotlight it seemed to be taking place on some fantastic stage: the dark water, the lily pads flat upon it, then the grass rising past the circle of light into darkness—and, suddenly, the explosion at the edge of the grass, the water shattering like a broken mirror, and the bass coming clear of it, head shaking, mouth open.

I got two bass here and George said, "We'd better move. The mosquitoes are closing in."

South of where we fished that night, about two-thirds of the way from Okeechobee to the Gulf, and inside the National Park, the fresh water of the lake meets the salt water of high tides. Where the salt water begins to dominate, the sawgrass disappears, and gradually the mangroves take over.

The world of the mangroves has little in common with the world of the sawgrass. In places it is a mass of fantastically twisted and tangled limbs, trunks, and roots. The roots of the red mangrove do not grow from other underground roots; instead, they grow from the upper tree downward until they reach the earth and burrow into it. The black mangrove (the waxy, dark green leaves of the red and black are almost identical) does not have these down-growing roots. Instead, it puts up a multitude of aerial roots, soft spikes that thrust up from the muck beneath. Raccoons, snakes, alligators, and bobcats move among the mangroves with ease. To man they would be impenetrable if it were not for shallow waterways that wind and twist among them.

The mangroves begin, roughly speaking, anywhere from seven to twenty miles inland from the Gulf. Near the Gulf the twisting waterways become more frequent, sometimes wider. And here is the world of the mangrove islands.

Along the Gulf at the northern edge of the Glades is the area known as the Ten Thousand Islands. This is an understatement. The good Lord may know the number of islands; no one else does. And even the Lord may have trouble keeping up with them. Every hurricane will obliterate a few, while creating new ones.

This coastal region from the Ten Thousand Islands south past Lostman's River, past the Broad, the Shark, past Whitewater Bay and into Florida Bay, offers some of the best redfish, tarpon, and snook fishing to be had in America. You may catch more tarpon at Boca Grande, maybe; but there the fish are hooked fifty feet or more below the surface and fighting one is sometimes like fighting the wreck of a sunken ship. In the shallow waters of the Ten Thousand Islands or of Florida Bay a tarpon does not sound. He jumps, because there is no way for him to go but up.

Besides the tarpon, snook, and redfish, there are great schools of mullet and speckled trout. Cuban fishermen after this bounty were known to work along the coast as early as the eighteenth century. By the time Colonel Harney made his journey across the Glades there were occasional American fishermen in the area. But just who the first white settlers were and exactly why they came, no one can say. In fact, through archeological studies, more is known about the pre-Columbian Indians than about the first white settlers.

In recent years drainage programs have made changes in the Everglades. Such programs have been under way since the 1880's. About 1905 the State of Florida got in on the act. The trouble was that even then nobody bothered to make a full, scientific study of what effects drainage might have. One engineer sent to survey the Everglades in order to drain them, reported that it was impossible to make a survey until after the drainage. That was pretty much the extent of early scientific study.

Except for brief pauses due largely to wars and economic depressions, drainage has been going on ever since. In 1928 the Tamiami Trail from Miami west across the state was completed. This created an almost solid dam between the lower Glades and the mother Okeechobee. After a 1928 hurricane drowned more than 1,000 persons in the Okeechobee area, a tremendous levee was built around much of the lake. New canals were dug.

With the levee and canals, water no longer seeped over the rim of the lake to flow in a wide river toward the Gulf. Over great areas the sawgrass died and was cleared away. In its place came lush fields of beans, celery, and sugarcane.

Nature resents being diddled with. The sawgrass had been growing here for many thousands of years, taking most of its substance from the water and air. It grew tall, and died, and fell back to rot, forming a black muck ten to twelve feet deep in places. Lightning-set fires had always swept the sawgrass. But in the past, even in dry seasons, there had always been water close beneath the surface. The fires had burned the sawgrass, but the roots had been protected by wet muck. Now, where water had been drained away, the earth itself began to dry and shrink. When a fire swept the sawgrass, it did not stop on reaching the earth. The muck itself burned, deeper and deeper. Great oily clouds of smoke hung over the Everglades for weeks on end.

Such fires drove the wildlife ahead of them. Even where there were no fires, the lack of water brought death. In many places alligator holes held the last water. Around them the deer, the bobcat, the birds, all the life of the Glades had to gather. And the alligator holes dried. The wildlife departed or died. Skeletons ringed the dried holes. Great flocks of egrets, ibis, herons, spoonbills abandoned their nests.

South of the Tamiami Trail, where lies the Everglades National Park, conditions were particularly bad. The highway tended to block off most of what little water there was.

The Everglades National Park did not come into formal existence until 1947, but for more than fifty years conservationists had worked for its establishment. Bit by bit almost one and a half million acres were gathered. Yet the park had scarcely been dedicated before much of its life was threatened by further drainage.

Conservationists objected, and all the stronger as conditions grew worse, year after year. Soon they were not concerned with wildlife alone, for as a result of drainage the water supply of Miami and other East Coast cities was threatened by salt intrusion from the Atlantic.

The Army Corps of Engineers was put in charge of what is now the South Florida Flood Control District. Army engineers have never been famous for their devotion to esthetics, but they are susceptible to political pressures. Also, given time and money enough, they can accomplish almost anything. In recent years large Water Conservation Areas have been established along the northern part of the Glades. Here water may be impounded or released at will. Huge canals lace the flat earth with dikes that sometimes loom like mountains in the distance. And an agreement has, at long last, been worked out with the park whereby a sufficient amount of water will be released to keep the River of Grass alive.

Today the canals offer excellent bass fishing and are easy to reach. Much of the land inside the water conservation areas is privately owned, but it is leased to the State and

Rich growth marks alligator pond's edge. Everglades' muck bottom rides on layer of limestone.

large parts are operated as Game Management Areas. Here deer populate the bayheads, and deer trails often lead through the sawgrass. In winter there is some of the best duck hunting in Florida.

Below the conservation areas is the National Park. You may enter it by boat at Everglades City on the north. From Homestead, just south of Miami, a road runs through the park to Flamingo at its southern tip, where, under park management, there is a large marina, a good motel, and wide campgrounds. There is no hunting in the park—except with camera—but there is excellent fishing, both fresh- and saltwater.

Inside the park, nature is sometimes more destructive than man. Fires still sweep the sawgrass. Great storms have devastated the wildlife from time to time. Hurricane Donna stripped not only the leaves but the very bark from millions of mangrove trees. When the storm was over entire mangrove forests were dead. Herons and egrets had been killed by the thousands. That was in September, 1960. Today where the edge of the roadway rises a few inches above the swamp, wherever there is a slight elevation, mangrove seedlings are already growing tall. The weird roots of the red mangrove are pushing out into the swamp. The black mangroves are spreading their stubby spikes into the water.

The Everglades have endured, constantly changing but unchanged. For the sportsman their bounty is unlimited. ◉

DENIZEN OF THE CRAGS

The shaggy, high-spirited mountain goat is a marvel of adaptation to a hard environment—and he makes a magnificent trophy.

Text and photography by Bob Hagel

The canyon split the mountain as if some giant cleaver had sliced it down the center. Down in the shadowy bottom, nearly four thousand feet below the rim, a clear, cold creek dashed among huge slabs of rock that had toppled from the cliffs above. The canyon floor was choked with brush—red willow, chokecherry, serviceberry, red birch, and alder. Here and there, where a bend in the canyon afforded a small area flat enough for a little soil, an occasional Douglas fir or spruce thrust toward the jagged skyline.

The lower slopes were composed of sharp ridges, ledges, and sheer-sided chutes widening toward the toe of the slope into talus fans. A little over halfway between water and peak, there was a somewhat less precipitous section of the slope, where fine shale and soil mixed to form a bed that supported a lush cover of grass, forbs, and low shrubs. Above this bench an unbelievably rugged cliff reared its scarred face to the very crest, broken here and there by huge vertical cracks, jutting bulges, and tiny ledges. Along the bench near the foot of this cliff, a small band of mountain goats fed in the first rays of the morning sun. They stood out white against the bright green of the early summer grass and the dark gray of the loose rock: three nannies, two fluffy kids less than a month old, and a yearling.

The kids, making short excursions to hop up onto a boulder, peered inquisitively down into the canyon, then scampered back to the nannies. Each time a kid returned to its mother, she sniffed it as if to make sure this was indeed the right kid, rubbed it with her nose, then resumed grazing. The yearling fed a few yards away, part of the group, yet outside of it. If the yearling ventured too near one of the kids, its mother would make a short, fast dash at the intruder with lowered head and shaking horns, and it would quickly retreat. The nanny without a kid paid scant attention to the other goats, but fed along with them.

A game trail led from the bench where the goats fed through a saddle into the next canyon. Along this trail a big male coyote trotted, and as he came to the edge of the saddle he stopped beside a bush, gazing toward the goats, his ears pricked forward. After a moment, he started walking slowly toward them, head low, never taking his eyes from them.

Suddenly one of the nannies stopped feeding, seemed to squat slightly, stood perfectly still for perhaps fifteen seconds, then turned, sniffing the air in the direction from which the coyote was approaching. She walked slowly to a large boulder, hopped upon it, and peered intently down at the coyote. The latter, having stopped so suddenly that one foot was still uplifted, stared up at her. Then, as her kid came up to the base of the boulder, she stamped her feet, lowered her head, shook her black horns menacingly, whirled, and started up the slope toward the base of the cliff, with the kid crowding her flank. The other goats fell in behind her, with a speed that was startling after their previous leisurely movements.

In single file they passed onto the face of a ledge so narrow that it was almost invisible. They somehow crossed a vertical chute, then stopped on a point of broken rock. One after another they bedded on the flat tops of the rocks, some of them with their front feet hanging out over nearly a thousand feet of thin mountain air. Here they felt secure from even the most persistent enemy.

Oreamnos montanus—the Rocky Mountain

244

Above: Hunter glasses distant peaks, hoping to sight goats in area where a close stalk may be possible. Far left: Goat exhibits climbing agility that is chief defense of species. Left: Nanny and kid amble toward grazing meadow on mountainside.

goat, or simply mountain goat, or white goat as it is sometimes called—is such a superb climber that it rarely has anything to fear from predators. A strictly American animal and the only member of its subfamily to be found in North America, it has long been regarded as a magnificent trophy, at least by those sportsmen who are willing to withstand the rigors of rugged mountain hunting and sometimes inclement weather. Though its sharp, relatively short black horns cannot compare with the sweeping curl of a sheep, its bearded head and shaggy white body give it a majestic appearance equal to the sheep's. And it fascinates sportsmen not only as a trophy, but as a unique denizen of the mountainous wilds. There are aspects of its physique and behavior which exemplify perfectly the survival of the fittest.

A calm, methodical, nearly disdainful climb to a pinnacle of inaccessibility is typical of mountain goats when danger is detected, whether the enemy is coyote, bobcat, cougar, or man. The only exception is when they are harrassed by eagles and cannot escape the aerial attack by climbing. If a mature goat is forced to battle an enemy, its needle-pointed horns are effective weapons, but its chief protection lies in its astounding climbing ability.

For this reason goats have few enemies. At rare times, particularly in the northern reaches of the cougar's range, the big cats manage to kill goats when other game is scarce. Bobcats also occasionally kill goats, mostly kids, but this predation is negligible; in the North, wolves may kill a goat when they find one away from the cliffs, but that isn't often either.

Many sportsmen believe that eagles, both bald and golden, kill large numbers of kids, as well as

some older goats, thus reducing goat populations in sections that seem capable of supporting much larger numbers. True, eagles have been known to swoop in and carry off a very young kid that has been left momentarily unprotected by its mother, but this is rare. The birds may attack repeatedly, but they seldom succeed. On more than one occasion I have seen an eagle dive again and again at a mature goat, but I have never seen one actually grab the goat with its talons. Once in a great while a goat may lose its footing while being harrassed by an eagle, and plunge to its death. But predation by eagles has no great influence on goat populations.

Probably a lot more goats die from natural causes than from predation. The young are usually born in the roughest part of the craggy terrain, high atop the canyons that lie between the summer range and the lower winter range. They start trailing their mothers when only a few hours old, and it is inevitable that some of them will make a misstep. Even mature goats are occasionally found where they have fallen from cliffs. Perhaps snowslides and rockslides account for the most deaths. I have found many skulls and carcasses among the debris left by slides in goat country. The goats themselves sometimes start snowslides by feeding across a steep slope on a warm or rainy day.

But occasional accidents do not indicate that goats are poorly adapted to their environment. On the contrary, they are so incredibly well suited to their mountainous homes that they sometimes seem to become overconfident. Perhaps because they have so few really dangerous enemies, mountain goats exhibit a peculiar lack of concern for danger.

There are few places goats cannot go, and they make very few mistakes. Many times I have seen mountain sheep spook and dash into a chute or onto a ledge only to face a dead end that forced them to seek another avenue of escape, but it is indeed rare for goats to be panicked into making such an error. I've watched them move up a cliff that seemed as slick as a tin roof, but there were always tiny projections and cracks that gave them something to hang onto. They can stand on their hind feet and hook their front feet over a projection, or stick a hoof into a crack, then pull themselves up. Though it is apparently much easier for a goat to go up than down, they can go down cliffs that would be impossible to climb. They will at times descend a slick rock face that is too steep for any traction, dashing down it so fast they do not have time to slip—and there always seems to be some ledge or projection below for them to stop upon.

Among their most spectacular stunts is a more or less horizontal movement along the face of a seemingly perpendicular cliff. They calmly walk out where the ledges and projections are too small to be seen by human eyes, even with powerful binoculars. Occasionally they make a short leap or a few quick hops where footholds are few and far between.

Yet mountain goats are not long-distance leapers, and they never show the spectacular acrobatics of sheep. In fact, almost everything a goat does is methodical and seemingly effortless. A sheep will go up or down a narrow chute bouncing from side to side, or sail out into space without the slightest hesitation, landing on the far side of an abyss to continue running with hardly a break in stride. A goat would make a detour or climb instead of jump, but at threading a ledge high on the side of a vertical wall, the goat is supreme. This shaggy mountaineer can pick his way along stretches that would be too narrow for a wide-horned sheep.

The contrast in climbing techniques is partly due to differences in the construction of the hoofs of the two species. Sheep have a ridge around the outside of the hoof, where a hard shell projects below the concave sole. This affords good traction on any small projection, but may slip on smooth surfaces. The goat's hoof has a soft, rubbery sole that is somewhat convex and projects below the hard outer shell. The hoof's rim will grasp rough spots on the rock, while the spongy inner sole acts much as crepe rubber does in gripping smooth surfaces. Where a sheep must jump a goat can walk, cling to a smooth surface, or make a sudden stop without sliding off into space.

When not eating, a goat spends most of its time lying in a bed it has dug out of the shale or dirt among the ledges, usually where there is quick access to a high, rough cliff. A favorite spot is some prominent point where the animal can look off into space. A goat may stand for hours on such a point, often leaning into a wind that whips his long beard straight back under his chin and flattens the mane on his humped withers. Or he may lie down on a point or overhanging ledge, with his front feet draped over the edge. Sprawled there or ambling across the ledge, a trophy may look like a big, white, shaggy dog.

Built much like the American bison, a goat is deep in the chest, but slab-sided and thin. This provides a heavy, deeply muscular front end for better balance and strong climbing ability. It also allows for a large lung capacity without having a wide, blocky body that would interfere with walking narrow cliff ledges.

It is doubtful if any other animal except the polar bear can withstand colder, windier, more miserable weather than goats experience every winter. They are equipped with a coat of fine, wool-like hair next to the hide, and an outside layer of long, coarse hair to serve as a windbreak and to shed snow and water. During a hard rain, goats will shake the water from their coats the way dogs do. Under the hide lies still another layer of insulation, this one of soft, rather blubbery fat. Unless a goat is sick, it will always be fat when winter comes. The billies lose much of the fat accumulated in the summer during the rut, but they retain enough of it to serve as insulation.

Even though the Rocky Mountain goat is little affected by weather or predation, there hasn't been any great increase in the species' range or numbers since the first white explorers laid eyes on what some mountainmen described as "little white buffalo." Mountain goats were originally native to the area now encompassed by Montana, Idaho, and Washington, and extending in a broken, spotted pattern up through western Canada into southeastern Alaska. All herds found in other states have been transplanted. Below the Canadian border there are probably as many goats today as there ever were.

They are quite prolific; nearly all females over two years old give birth to one kid each year, with an occasional set of twins. However, mortality is high during the first year, and from studies conducted on various goat ranges it appears that less than a third of the kids usually survive beyond the first year. Hunting can affect goat populations if the herds are readily accessible and if the kill is not controlled, but limited hunting does not seem to decrease herd size.

Where goats have been transplanted to new ranges, they seem to increase rapidly for a few years, then level off. Very few herds south of the Canadian border number more than a hundred. Large herds usually split up into groups of less than ten, with an average being three to four.

Diseases may have some limiting effect, and the size of a herd is, of course, influenced by the winter forage available. The migration between high summer ranges and lower winter ranges is restricted to the terrain that goats will call home. They are occasionally seen in fairly flat country, but only when moving from one area to another. In some regions, especially the Salmon River country of Idaho, they winter in the lower river breaks where the southern exposures are usually free of snow, and where mountain mahogany and other browse is abundant. In many goat ranges of the high-timberline country, the broken, rocky areas are formed wholly in the subalpine belt. Below that there are no cliffs, only heavy timber

and deep snow, so the goats winter mostly on subalpine scrub conifers, or cling to the high ridges where the wind keeps the snow swept away and where only scanty grass, lichens, and a few small shrubs are available. Infant mortality is high here, and nannies become so emaciated that they undoubtedly abort many kids, and are unable to nourish some that are born.

It has been suggested that, inasmuch as mountain goats are polygamous, only billies should be killed by hunters, but a males-only season will not work. It is true that if a female with a kid is killed, the kid is almost certain to die before spring, but very few hunters can tell the females from the males. If there were a males-only law, many females would be killed by mistake, then left where they fell when the sex was discovered.

Both sexes have horns, females are often quite large, and even many guides are not always sure which are the billies and which are the nannies. If the goat is alone, it may or may not be a male. Dry nannies are often alone, and even yearlings occasionally wander away from a group.

Neither body size nor the length of horns, whiskers, or chaps is at all reliable in indicating sex. If the goat is alone there is nothing by which the untrained eye can judge size, and all goats, mostly because their color contrasts with the surroundings, look bigger than they really are. The length of beard or chaps varies with the size of the animal, male or female. As for horns, some of the longest on record were taken from females. The contour and thickness of the horns are the only reasonably sure sex indicators, except at very close range or during the rut.

It takes a very experienced eye to differentiate between male and female headgear. The horns of the female are never as heavy at the base, and there is usually a difference in curve. A billy's horns are inclined to have a quite even curve from base to tip, while those on a nanny are normally straighter for the lower two-thirds of their length, then have a rather quick backward curve. The best way to judge is by the base diameter, but it takes a lot of experience to be

*In typical meadow below timberline, goats
graze contentedly, but remain alert and will head
for high pinnacles if alarmed by intruder.*

certain, especially at long range.

Several years ago I spent a good deal of time with my friend Stewart Brandborg, who was making a goat study for the Idaho Fish and Game Department. Much of this work was done at long range with binoculars and spotting scopes. All goats observed were recorded by sex, if at all possible. In most cases we later approached close enough to make certain. It is surprising how easy it is to make a mistake even after continued observation.

A few of the old billies provide an exception to the rule, being so much larger than the average that there is little doubt of their sex, even when alone—which they normally are. Why some of them grow to such abnormal size is hard to say.

The average female will stand about three feet high at the shoulder, and a mature male may be four to six inches taller. In the fall, when goats are normally quite fat, a mature female will weigh a hundred and twenty-five to a hundred and fifty pounds, and a mature billy will weigh around two hundred and twenty-five. They are certainly not so big as they appear.

To the hunter, the size of a track is important in telling if there is a big billy in a band of goats. The print is nearly square, the toes being very blunt and usually slightly spread. The track of a mature nanny will measure about two-and-a-half inches across, or from front to rear, while that of a large billy will measure three inches or a little more. I have measured tracks of abnormally large billies, and they were just under four inches.

I remember a hunt a few years ago when a novice killed a kid that couldn't have weighed fifty pounds. It was late in November, and with their long winter coats the goats looked larger than normal. My hunting partner and I had spotted a small nanny and her kid on a cliff. While we were glassing for larger goats, we saw another hunter working up the ridge on the far side of the canyon. We took our time climbing the ridge, hoping the goats would move so that we would not have to push them out and maybe spook something better. Suddenly there was a shot and the nanny nearly ran over us as she fled.

The hunter on the far ridge poked his head over the top and yelled down to ask if we had seen that big goat come by. On being informed that only a small nanny had run past, he said he had shot at a big billy, missed, and killed the kid. The snow showed only the tracks of the female and her spring kid. The hunter had been tense after a long stalk and the kid was the first animal he saw. It looked to him as big as a horse and so he shot it.

Goat seasons are usually held at the worst time of year for taking a trophy. In most states the season opens in early September and often closes in early October; in most of Canada and Alaska it opens in August. Many goats have not fully shed until late July or early August, and in September their coats are still short. Of course, some goat habitat is inaccessible in November and December, when goat hides are really good, so a harvest must be made early if at all.

Even the best goat horns are relatively small. A very good length is only about ten inches on the outside curve, while anything much over that, if the base circumference is six inches or more, is one for the book. One way to judge horn length is to remember that an average mature billy will measure about eight-and-a-half or nine inches from the corner of the eye to the end of the nose, or about ten inches from the forward edges of the horns to the end of the nose. The measurements for a really big billy would be at least an

inch longer, and for a big nanny they'd be an inch less.

In addition to the problem of judging very small dimensions, there is also the problem of deceptive curve. Some horns stick up at a forward angle to the front of the head while others lie at about the same angle as the front of the skull from nose to eye. Those that stand up appear longest, while those that lie back are sometimes partially covered by the mane and appear short. Some horns have more curve than others and appear shorter than they actually are. However, with practice an observer can become pretty accurate.

While it always pays to look over any goats you see, it is not often you find a really good billy mixed in with the nannies except during the rut, between mid-November and mid-December in most areas. Prior to that time, you'll usually find the trophy billies by themselves.

Early in the season you may hunt in excellent goat country, yet never see a billy. While the nannies, kids, and younger goats usually stay on the more open southern exposures during the late summer and early fall, the old billies like the shaded north faces. If their range is below timberline, they'll pick an extremely rough slope with plenty of timber—a place with shade, feed, and a few small springs. Some of the old, really big billies will remain in an area of only a few acres all summer. They'll dig beds out of the shale and dirt around their favorite cliff, beat a trail to some nearby spring, and pick a small, secluded feed area. You'll probably have to go in and find them, because the timber will usually be so thick you can't spot them from a distance, as is the normal procedure in goat hunting. When you do find a billy he is nearly always a fine trophy.

Most people think of goat hunting as being mostly long-range shooting, and it often is, not necessarily because goats are especially spooky, but because there's no way to approach the crag where the target is perched. Usually, if you try to stalk along the same route the goat used, you will be exposed much of the time. Worse still, the animal will probably get your scent. So a hunter must often shoot from long range, and then reach the kill by the easiest route.

I remember guiding a goat hunter many years ago on a boat trip through Idaho's Salmon River canyon. The canyon walls were unbelievably rough and broken, with great gashes cut into the slopes by small streams. The ridges bristled with crumbling spires, and between the spires, narrow chutes of slivered rock, sliding shale, old stumps, and logs dropped steeply to the canyon floor.

We had climbed up one of those hostile chutes, dodging loose rock that came crashing down, clawing upward, sliding in the loose shale. A couple of goat skulls on ledges along the walls didn't make us feel any more secure.

When we at last poked our heads over the backbone of the ridge, we found ourselves between two massive spires that made it impossible to continue in either direction along the ridge. In front, another chute fell away for five or six hundred feet to a slope composed of broken ledges and grassy benches, an ideal goat pasture. There were several animals there, but the nearest was at least four hundred and fifty yards away.

There was no chance for a stalk, but if the hunter could kill his goat at that range we planned to work our way to the bottom and take the trophy down the canyon to the river. From a solid rest over a flat rock padded by a coat, he made a one-shot kill. That should have been the end of the story, but within two hundred feet of the bottom we came to a ledge that was too high to drop over. We had already slid down over one slick ledge and could not get back up, nor could we get out of the chute on either side. Fortunately, we both had shooting slings on our rifles. By hooking them together we were able to lower ourselves far enough to drop the rest of the way safely. Since then, I've always carried at least fifty feet of light rope when hunting goats.

Some goats tend to ignore people, especially if they have not been hunted. This leads many hunters to conclude that the animals are stupid, or that their senses of hearing, sight, and smell are less finely developed than in some other animals. A goat on a high point can see for miles and it can see a man passing far below, or on some distant ridge, but the goat *seems* not to see him. Actually, the goat is well aware of the man's presence, and is also aware that there is no way an enemy can approach. If goats spooked every time they saw a coyote, bobcat, or cougar wandering around they would never stop running. Goats that have been hunted enough to recognize the sound of a rifle shot quickly demonstrate that their vision is excellent and that they are sufficiently intelligent to flee hunters.

Their hearing is also keen, but they are accustomed to hearing rolling rocks and debris sliding down the shale, so they are not usually alarmed by these noises. On the other hand, a hunter stalking one at the edge of timber may snap a dead limb and lose his chance for a trophy.

They can also catch man's scent just as far away as a deer, elk, or most other animals can, and when they do they will usually get out of the area fast. A goat's sense of smell sometimes seems poor because of the very erratic air currents in goat country, where the breeze whips every which way around the cliffs. If you find a goat lying or feeding where you can approach with the wind in your face and with a deep draw or chute between you and the goat—preferably a very rough draw, because the animal considers such terrain a natural barrier that will slow up an enemy—you can often get to within a few yards of your target. This is especially true of lone goats that are not part of a herd.

A big problem is to bring down a trophy without having it fall off a cliff or roll down a mountain and break its brittle horns. This most often happens when a hunter shoots a goat standing on a small, high point from which it will obviously topple when hit. But it can also happen when a hunter fails to make a swift, clean kill and the animal runs to such a point before dropping. To prevent trophy damage and try for a clean kill, perhaps the best place to aim is halfway up the

shoulder. Care must be taken not to aim too high, for a goat has several inches of mane above the vertebrae at the shoulder.

Once the trophy has been shot and caped, the remaining question is what to do with the meat. Many novices believe the myth that wild goats have a bad odor and that the meat is all but inedible. Domestic goats are certainly not sweet-smelling; however, the mountain goat, biologically speaking, is not really a goat at all but a type of antelope, and has very little odor. As for edibility, a billy that is not too old or a nanny of almost any age will provide fine eating. The biggest trophies—in other words, the very old, large billies—are too tough even for a long-simmered stew, but meat taken from average animals is excellent.

In some states, the law requires that the meat must be packed out, even though the edibility of some billies is questionable. Moreover, this law encourages many a hunter to kill a nanny or small billy if he finds one where it will be easy to pack out. Since a young goat is valuable breeding stock, killing young animals cannot be desirable from the standpoint of maintaining the population. And killing a nanny that has a kid will probably doom the kid. The law, then, does not solve the problem, nor can I furnish an answer.

Those of us who have lived in the wild goat country and gained a vast admiration for the species can only hope that the majority of sportsmen will hunt in a manner worthy of a splendid trophy. The very sight of these sovereigns of the peaks should make a man pause before he shoots.◉

253

ACKNOWLEDGEMENTS

Cover: Photograph by Erwin A. Bauer

Pages 100-101, 109: Collection of the Adirondack Museum,
Blue Mountain Lake, NY.

Pages 102-103: "Howl of the Weather," Remington Art
Museum, Ogdensburg, NY, all rights reserved.

Page 103 (bottom left): "Alexander Mackenzie,"
from *The Frederic Remington Book*, edited by Harold McCracken,
Doubleday; photo by Jack Richard.

Page 112 (top & bottom left): Seneca Ray Stoddard. Collection
of Maitland DeSormo, Saranac Lake, NY.

Page 112 (bottom right): Seneca Ray Stoddard.
Collection of Atwood Manley, Canton, NY.

Page 149: Map from *A Tour on the Prairies,*
by Washington Irving, edited with an introductory essay
by John Francis McDermott. New edition copyright
1956 by the University of Oklahoma Press.

Pages 170-179: Collection of The Thomas Gilcrease
Institute of American History and Art, Tulsa, OK.

Page 199: Photograph of cougar by Rod Allen from
National Audubon Society.